ANGELS UNAWARES

ANGELS UNAWARES

TWENTIETH-CENTURY PORTRAITS

T. S. MATTHEWS

TICKNOR & FIELDS • NEW YORK • 1985

Library of Congress Cataloging in Publication Data

Matthews, T. S. (Thomas Stanley), date
  Angels unawares.

   1. United States—Biography.   2. Biography—
20th century. I. Title.
CT220.M37   1985   920′.009′04   85-4779
ISBN 0-89919-378-1

Printed in the United States of America

s   10 9 8 7 6 5 4 3 2 1

And all about the courtly stable
Bright-harnessed Angels sit in order serviceable.

— JOHN MILTON

Be not forgetful to entertain strangers: for
thereby some have entertained angels unawares.

— EPISTLE OF PAUL TO THE HEBREWS

◁ CONTENTS

⁛ PREFACE

⌇ A Word About Angels

There was once a man who believed that everyone in the
world has two guardian angels — not one but two. He said
they are likely to be favorite aunts (deceased), and that
their permanent station is about two feet behind your right
shoulder and a foot above it. I think this belief too cheerful
to be altogether convincing. Nevertheless, I do believe in
angels.

They may or may not be guardians; I think they are certainly messengers. Who sends them, and what sort of message do they carry — and to whom? Do they themselves
always know who they are and what they're up to?

I can only raise these questions, not answer them. (Do
seeds in the wind know what they're doing? Or birds? Yet
such "lesser" orders of creation act as if they know what
they're about, though with a perception quite alien to
ours.) Perhaps we can't always recognize an angel when
we meet one. For Calvinists, at any rate, the dark angels
may be easier to spot. Anthony Burgess, the English nov-

elist, has been reported as saying, "Don't let the rationalists kid you about there being nothing after life. There's plenty and it's bad."

One of our great problems has always been calling things by their right names. Adam made a modest start on this endless inquiry (Where am I? Who am I? What am I doing? Where am I going? Who is my father?) by naming the animals. Ever since Adam's day we have been revising his list or adding to it. The trouble is, the names haven't always stuck. The more we look at the world around us and within us, the less certain we are that we have found the right name for anything. Our modern word for "angels," to take one example, is "communication." A pin-headed word!

All the people who appear in this book are dead. Although the word is used sparingly in the following pages, I believe that some of them were or may have been angels.

And the messages they brought? That too is impossible for me to tell. As some professor has almost said, the message is the mystery. Whatever the message was, and whether we understand it or not, it must have been, to someone's mind, worth sending.

ON FROM CINCINNATI

॰⟦ ON FROM CINCINNATI

⟅⟆ IT IS 1901; the century has turned. A hundred years, all the 1800s, have gone over the edge with the setting sun. The survivors feel a little breathless but up-to-date. It is impossible to say what I feel, since I have only just been born. My birthplace is Cincinnati, a grimy little city (it was grimy then) where my clergyman-father is dean of the Protestant Episcopal cathedral. This small and hideous nineteenth-century edifice, which will soon be demolished to make room for office buildings of greater sincerity, squats on West Seventh Street, eyed equivocally by our narrow town house just across the way.

Dickens visited Cincinnati briefly and rather liked it. Mrs. Trollope lived here for two years and hated it. When Lafcadio Hearn was a reporter on the Cincinnati *Commercial*, he described West Seventh Street, particularly "Nos. 206, 208 and 210 . . . a locality of such picturesque wretchedness as, perhaps, may not be found elsewhere within the city limits, — not even in the labyrinthine hollows of the famous negro quarter in the East End." The house we lived in, forty years after Lafcadio Hearn, was No. 226.

⟦3

The time and place reek with smoke from domestic fire-
places and the stink of factories. Paved streets are cobble-
stoned more often than not; the smelly, noisy traffic — including the smoke-belching, clanging fire engines — is
drawn by horses. Automobiles have only just been invented; in the next few years a few flimsy and sputtering
specimens will venture out amid jeering skeptics, frightened horses, and billowing dust. No radio yet, no airplanes,
and of course no television.

Most of my relations, of whom there seem to be a great
many, live in Glendale, a self-conscious village fifteen
miles north of the city. "The other Matthewses" and the
Clevelands, who are also my father's kin, live there; but
the predominant tribe is my mother's family, the Procters.

My sisters and I are still small, pale, and puny children
when we are transplanted to Glendale. Our life there
seems an eon; in fact, it amounts to less than six years, interrupted by a memorable twelvemonth in England. Brief
as our stay there was, Glendale will be with me for the rest
of my days; and when I think of "home," Glendale (alas
but what the hell) is the place that claims me.

Our childhood is shaded — yes, it is like being sheltered
under the spread of a great tree — by a power whose two
initials, P and G, seem to us as omnipotent as the SPQR of
ancient Rome. Just as, in Roman days, everyone in the civilized world knew that those letters stood for SENATUS POPU-
LUSQUE ROMANUS, so everyone in our world knows that
P & G stands for Procter & Gamble, our family business,
which — ever faithful, ever sure — takes good care of us.
P & G is a constant satisfaction and pride to us all, though
we never say so. Later I discover that outside the family
circle the view is widely held that there is something up-
start if not inherently shameful about making soap —
which in 1910 is still Procter & Gamble's chief stock-in-
trade.

The Matthewses, who love to do people down, especially their close relations, let it be known in a backhanded way that they are aware of this contemptuous view and partly share it. They pride themselves on never having been "in trade." My grandfather Stanley Matthews was in turn a lawyer, a U.S. senator, and a Justice of the Supreme Court of the United States. His oldest son, Mortimer, also a lawyer, is able to indulge his expensive taste for dairy farming because his wife, Marianna, is a Procter heiress. So is my mother, whose fortune enables my father to live in comfort without touching a penny of his salary.

My mother's youngest sister, Bessie, is married to Ralph Rogan, an officer of P & G and head of the advertising department. They live in ostentatious style in the grandest house in Glendale, The Oaks, which had been Grandfather Procter's house. Bessie had been a spoiled child and became an equally spoiled wife, cosseted by her adoring husband and in turn knuckling under to her two brattish daughters.

All my immediate family are directly connected with P & G, either by marriage or paycheck. Cousin Alec is a kindly, white-haired old gentleman with a hoarse voice; his head and hands are always a-tremble. He often attributes his longevity to two lifelong habits: voting the straight Democratic ticket (an amazing heresy in a family that takes the Republican Party as one of the primary articles of the Christian faith) and drinking his Bourbon neat.

Uncle Cooper, grandson of the founder, is president and principal shareholder of P & G. He and Aunt Jean are childless, and Uncle Cooper's principal heirs are Cousin Alec's two daughters, Mary and Martha. Martha died young and Mary never married, so most of the Procter fortune goes to Mary and eventually to Martha's children, though quite a bit of it is spread among the rest of us.

With Uncle Cooper's death, the Procter management of

P & G comes to an end; it has lasted for three generations, more than a hundred years. Sam Benedict, a nephew of Cooper Procter and my first cousin, is Secretary of the Company, and his brother Cooper works in the advertising department; another cousin, Bill Matthews, serves an unhappy term as a buyer but quits as soon as his father's death makes him independent. When Cooper Benedict dies and Sam retires, no one in the family is left in P & G. Now the Company is run by strangers with strange names. But the family still draw their quarterly dividends, which continue to keep us safe and sound.

⁰⁰⫿ HARRIET PROCTER

⌣⌐ SHE WAS A GREAT TRAVELER: a spinster, with little to do and plenty of money to do it with. She was never idle, and traveled as if it were her business. A tall, gaunt woman — if she had been less rich, she might have been described as rawboned — she dressed any old how in mussy, old-fashioned clothes: black silk with white ruffles, black hats that looked like a mixture of cobweb and honeycomb. She was our great-aunt, and seemed to us as old as the earth.

We liked her in an impersonal kind of way, as if she were a comet or an eclipse of the moon, which was the way she used to appear and disappear, wherever we happened to be. She always came from some distant part of the world, bringing strange information and lots of photographs.

Once, she visited us in our summer cottage in Michigan, at Harbor Point. She had just come back from China and Japan, full of information about Oriental food. One Japanese delicacy she told us about was some sort of cooked fern, and she even persuaded Mother to try it. We searched the woods for the right kind of fern and came back with armfuls of bracken — not the fern the Japanese ate, but Aunt Harriet thought it might do.

The bracken was boiled or stewed according to her specifications, and we all sat around the dining room table, chewing and chewing and trying to get it down. I think it was Mother who was brave enough to say finally that it simply turned to piano wires in your mouth and was quite inedible. As Aunt Harriet pointed out, it was the wrong kind of fern.

Our incumbent governess (we didn't like *her* much) was so fired by Aunt Harriet's report of Oriental root-eating that she grubbed about in the underbrush till she found what she thought was ginseng. After biting into this root to see if it had the right taste, she took to her room and didn't emerge for a week. It was poison ivy.

✸⟦ JANE GRAY

⤙ My father's sister jane was the family butterfly. She was usually an absentee aunt, who appeared only on visits; but she sent the most exciting Christmas presents of anybody, all the way from Paris. And for a year or two she tried to settle down in our Ohio village.

Aunt Jane always smelt remarkably clean, and of some sort of faint scent as well, but her Sunday smell was special: it was like beeswax. In itself, the smell was not disagreeable, but it meant that if you smelt it, you were sitting next to her. None of us liked to sit with Aunt Jane in church, but one of us always had to. We took turns. The reason we didn't like to was that we had to be on our very best behavior. Aunt Jane had a tremendous sense of propriety, for herself as well as for other people, and in church her sense of proper behavior was at its height. She was always straightening us up about something. As her favorite nephew, a title and position I was never allowed to forget, I came in for special attention.

It never occurred to us that an invitation to spend the night at her house could be declined. We went whenever we were asked, always one at a time. In a way, spending the night with Aunt Jane was even more of a chore than sitting next to her in church, because it lasted longer; but there were perquisites. The things you got to eat in her house were simply delicious and were served with a special air in a special way. Everything in her house was "just so"; the maids' starched uniforms and dour, shut faces, the shining parquet floors and dustless bric-a-brac, the tinkly-chiming French clocks, the grand piano whose keyboard was cleaned every day with eau de cologne, the beds with mounds of pillows, the top ones fringed with lace.

Aunt Jane was of course a great believer in frequent baths. She believed in beginning the day with what she called "a cold tosh" — a bathtub half full of icy water in which you were supposed to immerse yourself, totally if briefly. I was a little boy who had been brought up to be reverent of all authority, and it didn't occur to me to cheat. When I went to say good morning to her, which was also a command performance, she always asked me if I had enjoyed my tosh, and I always said I had, very much. Years later, my sister Charlotte told me that when *she* stayed with Aunt Jane, she simply put one hand in the icy tub and made splashing noises, with gasps and little-girlish screams, and when Aunt Jane put the inevitable question, her lie was straightforward. This revelation shocked me; my sister had been bold where I had been timid.

One of Aunt Jane's civilizing experiments was the Monday night family dinner party. These dinners caused a good deal of talk: there was considerable grumbling about unnecessary "dressing up," and it was not the custom in those parts to have candles on the table. Uncle Mortimer pretended not to be able to see properly in such a dim light, and went peering around the room, bumping into people and apologizing with exaggerated politeness, saying that it was so dark in here he couldn't see what was what.

Aunt Jane did not consider herself a member of the Midwest, though she had been born there. She had spent her girlhood in Washington, her married life there and in Boston, and after her husband's death lived mostly in France. In Washington as a girl she had acted as hostess for her widowed father, and to the men who came to his dinners she must have been pleasantly diverting. She was pretty, and her primnesses were all worldly. She had been brought up in the days when young ladies were expected to have a "good carriage": she held herself always very straight, and in spite of a rather waddling walk, she carried her short body with dignity. Her smile, which nobody could quite believe in nor quite disprove, had been cultivated with equal discipline and care.

It was in Washington, at her father's house, that she met her future husband. Like her father, he was a Justice of the Supreme Court. He came from Boston, in a day when no Bostonian was designated "proper": all the ones who counted were either proper or better. He had side whiskers, a commanding presence, and a name that fitted him like a hand-made glove: Horace Gray. He was thirty-five years older than Aunt Jane. For breakfast he invariably ate porridge and fish, this diet of phosphates being necessary, she told us, to his voracious brain.

What her married life was like can only be conjectured. It didn't last very long, at any rate; the child bride was soon a widow. She "traveled"; if she lived anywhere, it was in France, with occasional visitations to her house in Boston, on Mount Vernon Street. The family opinion was that Aunt Jane's spiritual home was France, and that all her peculiarities were expatriate. It was also taken for granted that she spoke French "like a native." It was a surprise to me to discover, years later, that she could hardly speak French at all, and in fact depended completely on the bad offices of a reprobate French maid, who, after her

fashion and for obvious financial reasons, remained faithful to her over many years and long absences.

At the time of the First World War, Aunt Jane was living in France. She somehow managed to finance and then
preside over a military hospital in Brittany. Her chief interest seems to have been designing attractive uniforms for
the nurses, and she must have had an efficient deputy to
run the place, for it functioned. After the war, in her vague
but impressive way she set about rebuilding a French village that had been destroyed by the Germans. For these
services she was awarded the Légion d'Honneur by the
French government. This rather pleased some members of
the family, but the general feeling was that Jane had been
throwing her money about again and had probably been
cheated.

We were not actually afraid of Aunt Jane; though we
treated her with deference, we took our cue from her
grown-up contemporaries and didn't, at bottom, respect
her. And yet there was something about her we rather admired and almost liked: she was silly but she had spirit; at
her best she showed the attractive quality of a foolish but
plucky girl; she could make us laugh, and our laughter
was sometimes at least partly applause. We liked the almost childlike way in which she could confound and exas-
perate the other grownups.

Aunt Jane was certainly a lady. She thought of herself
as a great lady — which I think is not so certain, unless a
great lady can also be a bitch; I know that combination is
said to exist. Although she could be insufferably rude, she
was never rude without meaning to be. She was always
showing people their place, even though they did not always oblige her by stepping down into it as quickly and as
humbly as she seemed to expect them to.

She had been brought up to revere certain established
authorities — the head of the family, the Church, the

State — and to these representatives of the Supreme Power she gave what she considered unquestioning obedience and unwavering loyalty. But there were some heads of families she wouldn't even nod to, some priests (who weren't, she considered, gentlemen) she openly despised, and some officials she had no hesitation in flouting. Family loyalty was her guiding principle, an unswerving conviction that some people were superior to others and that the Matthewses were superior to all others.

When I first saw her after her return from Vichy France her spirits were high, but her appearance was shocking. Months of wartime rations had reduced her to a bony caricature of the plump Aunt Jane I had known. My father clapped her into a New York hotel (a suite, of course) and ordered her into bed until she got her strength back. Aunt Jane, who didn't at all mind being coddled, for once obeyed him meekly. My father pursued his advantage, sold her white elephant of a Boston house, put her on a strict allowance, and consigned her to the comparatively inexpensive New York hotel for an indeterminate sentence. By the time Aunt Jane had recovered sufficient strength to resist, her wings had been clipped. Although nobody realized it, least of all herself, she had got away for the last time.

Meanwhile, as a person who always put the best face on her situation — since it was, after all, hers — she settled down to prove that life in New York could be quite as civilized as life in Boston or Paris. In her own little hotel suite she managed to keep the flag flying. There, among the crowded knickknacks of her past, all the old just-so-ness prevailed, and the flowers and the faint, expensive scent. Of course it was not quite the same; the hotel servants, although terrified, were not terrified into the perfection she demanded.

She had always gone to concerts and the opera and to church, and she continued to go. In France she had been

accustomed to having her own chauffeur (who was in ca-
hoots with her French maid), and I'm sure she never pene-
trated the Paris Métro, certainly never fought her way on
to a bus. When she settled to the new regime of austerity
in New York, she gave up having her own car and took a
taxi whenever she went out. And the manners of the
hackies, particularly their regrettable tendency to smoke
while driving, got Aunt Jane's dander up. She never let
such behavior pass unchallenged. No sooner had the driver
lighted cigar or cigarette than Aunt Jane addressed him:
"Boy!"

When it dawned on him that she was indeed talking to
him, he would reply, "Yes, lady?"

"Are you an American?"

"Who, me? Sure I'm an American, whaddya think?"

"Don't you know that nice American boys don't smoke
on the box?"

Whether or not the taxi driver exactly understood this
form of words, he got the drift eventually. Then one of two
things happened. Either he threw away the stinking of-
fense, or he drew in to the curb and she got out of the taxi.
Without, of course, paying her fare.

Until she came to New York, Aunt Jane had never seen
a movie in her life: she dismissed the movies unhesitat-
ingly as one of the American vulgarities that were beneath
her notice. One day she discovered that there were sacred
movies as well as profane, and that changed her point of
view completely.

The first one she went to must have been a terrible risk;
nevertheless, she took it. Perhaps she was bored; perhaps
there was no concert that day; perhaps she had heard that
The Song of Bernadette was the story of a miracle, and she
loved miracles. At any rate, she went — and her eyes were
opened. She went back to see *The Song of Bernadette* thir-
teen times. And gradually she evolved her doctrine of

sacred movies. Since Bernadette was a saint, and Jennifer Jones played the part of Bernadette, any movie in which Jennifer Jones acted could be considered sacred. Although this was obviously an extension of Aunt Jane's principle of family loyalty, I thought even she was a little uneasy about its extent. The beatification of Jennifer Jones helped a great deal, but it still left the list of permissible movies quite limited.

The older she grew, the more hopeful Aunt Jane seemed of various imminent miracles that would save her favorite situations or straighten up her favorite people. Though by this time I was a middle-aged man, far gone in journalism, whenever I saw Aunt Jane her parting words to me were (in a whisper, if someone else was there, but always with an arch smile) "I'm still praying!"

She herself lived, not so much in the constant expectation of a miracle as in the constant knowledge of one. This sounds mysterious, and it was — to me, at any rate. It was years before I made any sense of Aunt Jane's shy smiles and veiled allusions, or fitted them to the equally veiled remarks of my parents, with their sighing references to "poor Jane." It finally dawned on me that Aunt Jane had a lover, and that he was imaginary.

Aunt Jane loved secrets, but when she had one you always knew it. Not that she would let it out — only the delighted mischievous twinkle and one or two *very* tiny hints, not enough to give it away — unless, as was often the case, you already knew it yourself. But this was such a great secret, and so entirely her own, that for a long time she must have kept it strictly to herself. I was certainly not her first confidant: she must have explored — tentatively, cautiously — in several directions for what she hoped would be a sympathetic ear before she recklessly turned to me. For by that time, although I still didn't take it seriously, I had been "briefed."

I even knew his name: Sir Cedric Something. (If he had a last name, I have forgotten it.) He was an Englishman, very well-to-do and of course of good family. He followed her everywhere and sent her flowers nearly every day, but they had never exchanged a word. Whenever she went to a concert or to the opera, he was there too, several respectful rows behind her. When she left the theater or the concert hall, he stood aside for her, his eyes downcast. Sometimes he wrote to her; naturally she would not show anybody his letters.

Learning these details as a matter of rather eerie gossip was a very different thing, however, from being told them, in bigger and bigger hints, by Aunt Jane herself. I was not sympathetic; I was repelled. But I made the mistake of pretending not to be, and as, with her face flushed and eyes shining, she gave hints that began to turn into statements she labeled fact, my revulsion and fear of the abnormal came out in anger. I told her that if Sir Cedric was an honorable man, it was high time he showed it; if he was indeed staying at the hotel just around the corner, I would go now, this minute, to confront him and ask him what his intentions were. (I think now it was a brutal thing to have said, but I said it.) Aunt Jane collapsed like a little girl caught in a fib, but the next moment collected herself and attacked me with spirit: What did I know of the matter after all, and what concern was it of mine? This justified rebuke petered out into vague and guarded suggestions of further undisclosed secrets of great import that would be trusted only to a really understanding person. I left her in her sitting room, surrounded by Sir Cedric's flowers. She never mentioned him to me again.

It was the movies that finished Aunt Jane, and in a literal sense. By that time her permissible list had grown sufficiently to include Olivier's film *Henry V*, and she had hardly begun on it; in fact, she was seeing it for only the fifth time. Just before the final fade-out she got up to leave, for she hated to be caught in crowds. As she turned into the aisle, she slipped, fell, and broke her hip.

She was an old lady, well over eighty. Nevertheless, Aunt Jane was determined to walk again and was perfectly certain that she would. They operated. They put a silver pin in her hip; the pin came out. They said there was nothing more they could do; they tried to break the news gently to her and urged her to rest quietly in bed — they meant for the remainder of her days. Aunt Jane refused to listen, demanded further treatment, terrorized the nurses, antagonized the doctors. She was moved to a nursing home in New Jersey, a home that specialized in taking care of broken and dying old women, whether they were ladies or not. The place was run by German nuns, devoted, hard-working, and kindly. In a few weeks Aunt Jane's demands for special and undivided attention, and her really unparalleled rudeness to attendants, whom she regarded as her social inferiors, had made her so unpopular with the nuns that the mother superior told my father he would have to take Aunt Jane away. He managed to patch up a kind of armistice, on condition that Aunt Jane have her own private nurse, whom my father engaged. This woman was treated by Aunt Jane as a dog-hater treats a cur, but she was patient and professional, and she stuck it out.

There had been an interval of some weeks between the hospital and the nursing home when she stayed at my father's house, where of course she was in bed and had to have a trained nurse. This unfortunate woman was soon at the end of her tether. Besides expecting her bell to be answered instantly at any hour of the twenty-four, Aunt Jane demanded of her nurse all the services and servility of a ladies' maid. Having grown more formally religious with age, she now required the sacrament to be brought to her every morning at seven o'clock. This meant that the nurse had to be on hand long before that hour to make Aunt Jane presentable; one of the least of her chores was changing the silk ribbon threaded through the old lady's boudoir cap to match the color of the church season.

One day the nurse waylaid the Reverend Victor Stanley, the young curate who brought Aunt Jane her daily Communion, and told him that she simply could not go on, that he must tell Aunt Jane not to be so demanding and brutal to her. Victor listened sympathetically but pointed out that if he said anything to Aunt Jane, he might only make matters worse, as she would be sure to guess who had put him up to it. That morning he found that Aunt Jane had dropped off to sleep, and he was just leaving the house when the nurse caught him, to say that Mrs. Gray was awake now and wanted her Communion. As Victor came in again, Aunt Jane told him that an angel had appeared to her in a dream, saying that she must wake up, because Mr. Stanley was coming with a message for her. Victor saw his chance. "I *have* a message for you, Mrs. Gray," he said. "I'm going to stop bringing you Communion unless you behave more kindly to your nurse."

"Who told you I behaved unkindly?"

"An angel," said Victor.

Aunt Jane never gave up in her determination to walk again. She ordered a stroller, a seat suspended from a circular contraption on castors — the kind of thing babies used to be put in before they could walk — and practiced on it daily. And her progress was really amazing; even the doctors admitted it. She was villainous and indomitable. After months of effort, she actually managed to take a few steps unaided. She was delighted and very proud of herself. But that was as far as she got. One day I had a summons from my father: Aunt Jane had taken a turn for the worse and had been removed to a hospital.

It was there I saw her for the last time. She was in a

ward, curtained off from the other beds; she had insisted
on that. She was disgusted that she was not in a private
room, but there had been none available at such short notice. She looked pathetically little and old, but her spirit
was unquenched. She apologized for receiving me in such
surroundings — unworthy of both of us, she intimated. I
knew she was to go to the operating room in half an hour,
and so did she, but she never mentioned it. She conducted
our last interview, however, as if she knew it was the last.
She went over the list of my sons, reassuring herself about
the splendid character and talents of each one and congratulating me and herself, as if in the name of the family,
that not one of them would "go into trade." I kissed her
goodbye and left her.

The operation, they said, was successful, and she died a
few days later without recovering consciousness. My father
and I interviewed a local undertaker about funeral arrangements; she was to be buried in Boston, but we had to
pick out a coffin. My father, who considered undertakers
(he refused to recognize them by their own fancy name of
morticians) a pack of grave robbers, wanted a perfectly
plain, inexpensive coffin. There weren't any, of course; the
"casket" we finally got was the simplest of the lot, but it
had the usual silvered handles and plush lining, and cost
several hundred dollars. I knew my father was thinking
that even in death Aunt Jane was being extravagant, and
at his expense.

One of my sisters told me that when they were going
through Aunt Jane's possessions at the nursing home, they
came upon a nearly complete outfit of baby clothes, beau-
tifully embroidered. It must have taken her many weeks of
surreptitious work; no one had ever caught her at it. At her
funeral in Boston, which my father and I attended, there
were a decent number of flowers, but this time, none from
Sir Cedric.

BESSIE ROGAN

AUNT BESSIE was the youngest of the Procter sisters; like my mother she was born at The Oaks, and she continued to live there all her life. She must have inherited the house from her father, or at any rate got it with the consent of her sisters and brother, all of whom by that time had houses of their own. And yet for some reason I resented Aunt Bessie's presence at The Oaks, almost as if she were a kind of interloper. Perhaps it was because I also resented her presence among the Procters. In her way, she was as spoiled as my father and seemed as eccentric to the Procter pattern as Aunt Jane was to the Matthews.

In younger days she must have been a nicer shape, and may even have qualified as a fine figure of a woman. But when I knew her, Aunt Bessie was fat — much too fat. Though she was not tall, she must have weighed at least two hundred pounds and looked like a very large paperweight, or — if you gave her the marks she deserved for her imperiously handsome face — like a sawed-off Juno. She had frizzy red hair and hard blue eyes, a large, shelf-like expanse of snowy bosom, a freckled, brazen face. She

carried herself arrogantly. Her voice was harsh and stri-
dent, and gritted up to a cockatoolike screech when she
laughed or when she screamed an order. Unlike the other
Procters, Aunt Bessie was ostentatiously rich. She liked the
expensive things of this world and bought them, and
boasted of it. With her fortune and Uncle Ralph's salary
as Secretary of the Company, she may well have had more
to spend than her sisters.

Uncle Ralph Rogan, who was known as a model husband, bought her everything she thought she wanted. I
considered him more attractive as a man than she was as a
woman and potentially, at least, more of a person. But
apart from her he seemed to have no life of his own. You
couldn't have called him henpecked, for no pecking was
required: he was always at her feet, looking up devotedly
to see what she wanted next. And yet everyone liked Uncle
Ralph, and I don't know that anyone was sorry for him. He
was known to be Aunt Bessie's slave, but everyone accepted
that fact, as he did. They liked him for himself. He was
one of those naturally lean men, like my Uncle Cooper,
who never put on weight as they get older. His dark face
was long and solemn, with a broad Irish upper lip — the
tragic face of a muted humorist. I think he was the only
man in the family connection whose college was Cornell.
This was not exactly held against him, but it was remembered. Cornell was different from Princeton and Yale and
was said to have a cheer that sounded a little extreme, compared with the frog choruses of Yale and the locomotives
of Princeton: "Cornell I yell. I yell Cornell!"

Even as a child I thought Aunt Bessie a disagreeable
contrast to her sisters, but in two ways she was just like
them: when something struck her as funny, she couldn't
help laughing, and then she collapsed into the likable,
even lovable person all Procters were meant to be. And
though she would have to be classed as a monumentally

selfish woman, on occasion she was capable of extreme generosity. Sam Davies, a young cousin of hers, lived for years at The Oaks and seemed to me the epitome of the worldly young man about town. Many years later, he told me that Aunt Bessie had often made him feel like a poor relation, and that at those times he hated her; but when he made her laugh, or when, for no reason that he could see and completely out of the blue, she gave him something he very much wanted, he knew that he loved her after all. She could laugh, and she could be generous. As human beings go, not a bad epitaph.

There were two Rogan children, both daughters. The younger one, Mary, was too young for us to bother with: she was a fat child with a placid expression and long, carefully curled ringlets; the older one, Elizabeth, had a pointed face, a look of permanent discontent, and her mother's freckles and harsh voice, several notes shriller. Elizabeth was always "telling on us," complaining about us, getting us into some kind of trouble. Aunt Bessie was in a state of constant anxiety about her children, especially Elizabeth: her whereabouts, party behavior, state of mind, and dress. I can still hear that searching cry, penetrating the dusk of a Fourth of July family party, cutting through the flurries of conversation and the *zizz-zizzz* of the pinwheels: "Eliza*bith!* Eliza*bith!*" Years and years later, when with the daily thousands of other commuters I heard the hoarse chant of the train announcer at Manhattan Transfer ("Newahk, Eliza*bith*, Prince*tin* Junc-*shin*, Trennun, Phila*dul*phiay!"), it reminded me of Aunt Bessie, calling to her strayed lamb.

My last remembered sight of Elizabeth was when she was in her teens and I was on a visit to The Oaks. I thought her prettier but shriller, and not a bit more trustworthy — in short, much the same. She grew up and married the boy next door, as everyone in Glendale did in those days. I sup-

pose she must have had children, but I didn't hear about
them. What I did hear about were her fox terriers. She and
her husband, Tom Carruthers, bred these dogs; it was apparently their principal interest in life. The last word I
ever had from Elizabeth was a telegram announcing that
one of her terriers had been placed first in the Westminster
Dog Show and demanding that *Time* (of which I was then
managing editor) report the fact. I replied, congratulating
Elizabeth on her victory but denying that the news was of
sufficient national interest to warrant *Time*'s mentioning
it. We never corresponded nor saw one another after that.

My family left Glendale for good in 1913, and I saw
Uncle Ralph only at rare intervals, but whenever we met
he would ask me if I had taken up track or done any running, and would shake his head regretfully when I said
that I hadn't. (He had seen me win a fifty-yard dash for
boys under twelve and said I had a natural stride and
should take up running in earnest.)

My father used to say — and I hope it was an original
remark — that the martyrs were the wives of the saints.
This always seemed to me more like a Procter observation
than a Matthews. The saying didn't apply, in his ironic
sense, to Aunt Bessie and Uncle Ralph. Aunt Bessie may
have considered herself a martyr to the long series of ill-
nesses that turned her into an invalid and Uncle Ralph
into the most devoted of her nurses, but I am sure he never
thought of himself as a saint — though, as far as his relation to her was concerned, I think he must have very
nearly qualified.

Even in good health Aunt Bessie was imperious, queru-
lous, and exacting. What she must have been like, and
what it must have been like for Uncle Ralph, in those long-
drawn-out, gradually descending years of her invalidism, I
hate to think. He got her every palliative, comfort, and
"cure" that money could buy; he did everything for her

that a patiently adoring husband could do. He spent less
and less time at the office, more and more at her bedside.
She was accustomed to going south in the winter, to a
house Uncle Ralph had built for her on the Gulf coast of
Florida, at Clearwater. When the train journey, even in a
Pullman drawing room, became too arduous, he set the future style for the rest of the family by buying a plane,
which was fitted out like a flying ambulance. I'm not sure
he didn't buy two planes, one as a spare.

Before Aunt Bessie had taken even intermittently to her
bed, she had set her lasting mark on The Oaks. By the mere
addition of one hideous room she changed and lowered the
whole character of the house. This new room had been
jammed into an angle of the house between the library and
the conservatory, which the addition partly swallowed up.
In this one room she succeeded in concentrating all the
family bad taste: the walls and ceiling were of clawed
stucco, the furniture was wicker, curtains and coverings
kitchen chintz; and the whole space was so stuffed with expensive radios, phonographs, and later a television set, that
it looked like a small-town dealer's showroom.

This became the favorite room in the house; in fact,
apart from the dining room at mealtimes, I don't remember
seeing the family in any other. It was here I last saw
Uncle Ralph, after Aunt Bessie had finally lingered to her
death. His daughter Mary was with him, no longer a fat
little girl in ringlets but a tall, calm young woman with
her father's Indianlike cheekbones and the high-arched
nose of the Procters. Now that Uncle Cooper was dead, she
was the handsomest member of the family. Her husband
was with her, my old chum and second cousin (hers also)
Billy Burchenal.

For the first time Uncle Ralph seemed an old man. He
had retired from the Company to give his whole time to his
invalid wife, and now that long job was finished too. He

was pleased to see me, but he was no longer interested in my future, nor in anyone's except his grandchildren's. He got up to show me a framed photograph of a house next to his own in Clearwater that he had just built for Bill and Mary. The photograph had been taken from the air and was as clear as a map. Soon, he said, they would all be flying down there for the winter.

⸬ GRACE CLEVELAND

⤙ ANOTHER SISTER OF MY FATHER'S, Aunt Grace, was tiny, fragile-looking, and as lively as a grig. Her husband, Uncle Harlan, who died too soon for us to remember him, must have been a big man, for their six children were all large and heavy. They were also bright, though not necessarily sensible, and two of them — who both died young, like their father — were brilliant, in the ponderous Cleveland way.

Aunt Grace managed her widow's household with apparent ease and great spirit. She couldn't have been as delicate as she looked. There is a portrait of her — was it by de Laszlo? — that does her more than the usual injustice of portraits, and shows her looking not only fragile but silly.

Aunt Grace's main concern was her children's education, and it was a family assumption that no proper education could be had in the Midwest. She took a house in New York. It was at Aunt Grace's house on Lexington Avenue that I remember her at her best. I liked going to see her. It was when I was a schoolboy that I first became aware of her as a hostess who seemed to attract interesting people and fire them to exciting intellectual talk. Except for old Mr. Yeats, the father of the poet, who the people were and what the talk was about I can't recall, but I remember the impression like a taste on the tongue. Perhaps it was because I was beginning to understand grown-up conversation, which had once sounded as meaningless as monkey chatter; but it couldn't have been only that.

People often take odd turns as they grow old. Is it because they have outlived their natural term, and the force of growth is still alive in them but too feeble to do more than push out a few eccentric knobs? Lively herself, Aunt Grace had something in her that made others lively too, but she was neither intellectual nor scholarly. In her old age she came to imagine herself both, and in a field that always seemed to me narrower and more sterile than theorizing about the authorship of Shakespeare's plays: the fulfillment of prophecies. The Old Testament and the Book of Revelation were her principal divining rods, with which she could strike a freshet out of the stoniest headline in the day's paper.

JOHN AND OTIE BURCHENAL

⌒◁ COUSIN JOHN BURCHENAL was the man we were most afraid of as children. It was partly his grating voice, which could erupt without warning into a bull-like bellow, and his temper, which was hair-trigger. His face was long-nosed, long-jawed, and pugnacious. He was usually simply aloof from us, but could on occasion be jolly; he wasn't one of those grownups children instinctively dislike, but in his neighborhood we went warily. I was astonished to discover, later, that among his own contemporaries he was regarded as one of the kindest and certainly the funniest man in town.

His wife, Cousin Otie, looked as if she had just stopped crying and might be getting ready to laugh.

LEN AND ALEC JOHNSTON

Cousin len and cousin alec were brothers, tall, good-looking, smiling men well liked by everyone, and especially by the ladies. Their hair and moustaches were silver-gray. Cousin Len was a bachelor and what was known in those days as a dude: he was always very well groomed and dressed with care and elegance. He had a long, sternly melancholic face and rather watery blue eyes. I was sorry for him, because he had no family of his own, and perhaps he was sorry about that too. He loved children and they liked him.

There was an aura of glamour about Cousin Len because of his reputation. He was said to have been "rather wild" in his youth: among other things, he "drank." The other things were never spoken about in our presence, and we never knew exactly what they were. Had he liked ladies who were too lively? Had he had a tragic affair with a *married woman?* The truth may have been even milder; we never knew. All we did know was Cousin Len in the present: a handsome, benevolent old gentleman who told us entertaining stories and patted our heads in a way we liked. (Aunt Eva, my father's oldest sister, who was a nun — in fact, a mother superior — patted us in a way we didn't like.)

Most of my family were "comfortably off," as they would have put it, but they conformed to the twin customs of living well within their income and of earning, or appearing to earn, their daily bread. The men of the family took the C.H. & D. (Cincinnati, Hamilton & Dayton Railroad) to town every day. Cousin Alec was one of these commuters. Cousin Len never worked at anything much: I remember him as a Glendale fixture, like our sole policeman, the marshal.

Cousin Len's constant companion was Dr. Will Shepherd. Theirs was one of those friendships which starts in boyhood and lasts a lifetime. They were both essentially simple men; perhaps that was why they remained so devoted and never seemed to bore each other. They had an occasional falling-out, of course. One of their arguments became famous. Will Shepherd, nettled by something Cousin Len had said that seemed to imply that he knew as much about Will Shepherd as Will Shepherd did himself, burst out: "You think you know me so well. Why, you don't even know my first name!" Astonished, then annoyed, Cousin Len replied that he knew it as well as he knew his own. What on earth was Will talking about? Will Shepherd offered to bet him; Cousin Len hotly accepted; the stake rose rapidly to fifty dollars. When the chips were down, it turned out that Will Shepherd was right: Cousin Len had always thought his name was William, but it was not; it was Willard. Goaded into inspiration, Cousin Len then bet Will Shepherd the same amount that he didn't know *his* name. Sure enough, he didn't; he thought it was Leonard. It was Lendrum.

It would not be true to say that so evidently sweet-natured a man as Cousin Len was held up to us as a horrible example. No, but we were certainly given to understand that he was a warning of some sort — an example of a man whose past was catching up with him. It was never said in words and was too vague to be put into words, perhaps. What was it, then? Were the wages of drink, old bachelorhood? Not that, exactly. The not-quite-sayable thing about Cousin Len was that he had had more than his share of irresponsible fun when he was young, and now he was paying for it. How? Well, just look at him.

We did look at him. We observed how his watery eyes would often get waterier, for no reason that we could see. His kindly attentions, which we had always responded to like delighted puppies, began to embarrass us. Finally, we couldn't help seeing that the mere sight of us would make Cousin Len's eyes fill with tears. That made us uneasy and him somehow less likable.

Children do not notice when grownups fade away. We saw the beginnings of Cousin Len's fading; then we forgot him. I suppose his kindly melancholia, or whatever it was, grew worse. At any rate, he disappeared. I remember hearing, a few years later, with a tinge of sadness but not much real concern, that Cousin Len had died of softening of the brain. Nobody had to tell us that that was the penalty for getting too sentimental.

o   o   o

Cousin Alec was a widower most of his life, for he lived to be nearly ninety. Besides his premature white hair, like Cousin Len's, he had Parkinson's disease, which made both his head and his voice shake. But in all the years I knew him, the shaking never seemed perceptibly worse nor Cousin Alec much older.

Cousin Alec's house was a cheerful place, but I suppose he had not had a very happy life. His wife had died at a comparatively early age, and he had never had a son. His two daughters were both good-looking, but only one of them married, and she died young, as her mother had. Cousin Alec and Mary, the other daughter, who was as energetic and as busy as two ordinary men, had settled down to share their singleness. Cousin Alec was a sweet rather than a strong character, and his daughter bossed him.

As he slowly inched his way into old age, he developed little habits and fretfulnesses. One thing that particularly bothered him was damp. He felt its lurking threat everywhere and waged an unremitting war against it. When his daughter discovered that he was putting his hat in the oven, she used to look in the oven every morning and take the hat out.

The last time I saw him he was armored, cap-à-pie, against his enemy. I was in Glendale on a brief visit and was driving past his house when I saw Mary directing some gardening work. She had recently broken her leg in a motor accident and was stumping about in a cast. I hailed her, and she said, "Come in and say hello to Father." Cousin Alec was lying on a daybed, wrapped in shawls and wearing his hat. His eyes were closed. Mary leaned over and shouted in his ear: "Here's Tom Matthews, Father. You remember him?"

Cousin Alec opened his eyes, recognized me, and said in his hoarse, earnest whisper: "Hello, Tom. What's the temperature outside?"

HORSES AND
BUGGIES

⅗ HORSES AND BUGGIES

〜✦(THE TWO-THOUSAND-YEAR-OLD MAN (discovered by Mel Brooks), asked to describe the transport available in his day, replied "Fear." In the horse-and-buggy Glendale of my childhood, our means of getting about were almost as primitive, by present standards. In 1909 one of the most pernicious Sorcerer's Apprentices who ever lived, Henry Ford, began to turn out an insectoid motor car he called the Model T. Like the lucid madman he was, he took his products seriously (his consuming notion was that everyone should have one), but most people then regarded automobiles as playthings.

We never dreamed that these stuttering toys would transform our habitual way of life, dominate our national economy, change the face of war, and alter the very landscape of our world. Henry Ford's invention was treated as a joke, a "tin Lizzie," until it began to overspread our sky like a genie released from a bottle, whose ever more demanding and domineering presence would one day raise the uncomfortable question of which was master and which slave.

〚35

It was not the Model T itself but its offshoots and after-effects that spawned the hard-top road, the millions of miles of highways that now cross-belt and garter (and constrict) every oil-burning country in the world. That still-proliferating result came fast, but it didn't come overnight. In 1909, when I was an eight-year-old, the serious work of transport — by hackney cab, dray, fire engine, delivery van, carriage — was done entirely with horses.

I can still remember what it was like to ride behind a horse: the grinding sound, the gritty feel of iron-tired wheels crunching on gravel or turning jerkily on cobblestones. I remember particularly rides in rainy weather: sitting alongside the driver (hard hat and droopy moustaches), peering over the black rubber sheet, which had a letter-slot opening through which the reins were threaded. I liked it better when the weather was fine and I had an unimpeded view of the horse's constantly flexing and unflexing rump. This was just about at my eye level.

How could the horse go to the bathroom (that was the only term I knew for it) while it was trotting? For go it certainly did. First its tail would lift, exposing a symmetrical rubbery ring set in a smooth stretch of skin between its haunches. This ring, opening slightly, would emit a dual stutter, like a quick pair of belches; then the ring stretched, swelled, pouted to an O, and pushed out in rapid succession a series of brown spheroids, smoking and perfectly formed. This amazing feat accomplished, the rubber ring would give a self-satisfied wink and shrink back into its normal state, and the tail would come down like a curtain. This performance fascinated me.

I don't remember ever driving in a carriage for *pleasure*. But when we rode in an automobile, it was an outing — "going for a spin." Ladies put on special dust veils over their hats and donned linen dusters; men wore goggles and motoring caps and huge driving gloves. Everyone piled in and hung on to something while the chauffeur cranked the engine — always a tense moment, for when the engine caught he had to dart from the front of the machine to the steering wheel and reverse the positions of the two levers there — the accelerator and the spark. In those days no one ever started a car smoothly; you always went off with a jerk. And if you were small and forgot to hold on, you fell over.

Fords were a joke in those early days, a joke so popular that it helped to sell Fords, but not to people like us. My uncles and cousins had all kinds of different motor cars, but not one was a Ford. Our attitude toward cars varied: we respected Uncle Cooper's Pierce-Arrow and, to a lesser degree, Uncle Ralph's Franklin, which was air-cooled and therefore regarded as slightly eccentric: but we smiled at Aunt Jean's Baker Electric, a glassed-in two-seater with a top speed of fifteen miles an hour, and roared with laughter whenever we saw Mr. Probasco's "horseless carriage," which was steered by a handlebar and made erratic popping sounds; we called it "the sewing machine." Cousin John Burchenal owned a Packard. My father had a Stevens-Duryea, a very fine car for its time but, like all these others, now dead as the dodo. There were swarms of automobile manufacturers, all of them (except Henry Ford) turning out small numbers of hand-made cars for a handful of customers.

In the early days headlights were mostly for show; driving any distance after dark was too hazardous. I remember the ceremony of lighting up: the chauffeur opening the glass front of the headlights and turning on the container of Prest-O-Lite that stood on the running board, the hissing of the V-shaped burners, and the pop as his lighted match ignited them. As long as the car was standing still the headlights gave out a steady beam, but when it was in motion the slightest bump in the road would make the landscape jump and shimmer.

In the days when the Lincoln Highway consisted of

stretches of cement, petering out into eighteenth-century post roads and patched with country lanes, maps were a necessity. The handiest and most inclusive were contained in the Blue Book, which tried to make up for the dearth of signposts by giving the motorist landmarks to go by — a barn, a white house, a spreading chestnut tree — any kind of recognizable object that would show the faint and devious trail. As late as the 1920s, a drive of fifty miles, with or without the Blue Book, was an adventure for even a qualified pilot.

o   o   o

In those early days of the twentieth century, everyone who could afford them had servants and almost everyone we knew could afford them. The larger houses had a cook, two or three housemaids, and a chauffeur, who sometimes doubled as a butler. Those with greenhouses or sizable gardens also had a gardener, sometimes with one or two helpers; the rest of us made do with a "hired man."

The dominant strain in the domestics of Glendale was Irish: my Procter grandmother was born in Ireland, and her cook, Mary Jane, and her parlormaid, Biddy, were born there too. Our coachman, who was really a hired man, Willy McGuigan, may have been a cousin of Biddy's. Except for the maids, none of these servants wore anything that could have been mistaken for livery. I remember Willy McGuigan as always wearing a bowler hat, at an aggressively forward tilt, shirtsleeves and sleeve garters, and clenching a cigar stump between his teeth.

Our first chauffeur, name of Ross, was a red-cheeked young fellow who had been to a driving school. He didn't last long. Walter Rodefeld, who took his place, was an autodidact who never understood autos — but as my father didn't either, and as Walter never got excited while driving, as my father did, he lasted a lifetime.

When servants "gave satisfaction," they were expected to stay with the family for the rest of their lives, and they became an integral part of the household. On the rare occasions when they left or were discharged, it was almost as dreadful as a son or daughter being cast off.

But when my generation grew up and had houses of our own, only the lucky or the very rich among us could afford the kind of servants our parents had had — or indeed lived in a house large enough to hold them. Some of us had a cook, who came in by the day, and an occasional odd-job man; that was the extent of our domestic staff.

WAR — BUT WAY OVER THERE

⌇ NOW IT IS 1915. There is war in Europe — but not here. Our President Wilson says we are "too proud to fight." It never occurs to us, who are children still or nowhere near grown up, that there can be an actual collision between war and us.

We have left Glendale and have gone to Minnesota to live. Why there? No one explains these matters honestly to children, but later from overheard scraps we piece together the beginnings of an answer: my father and his bishop in southern Ohio "did not get on." In Faribault (pronounced *Faribo*, in a Frenchy sort of way), a countrified small town, he is to be dean of the cathedral and also professor of pastoral theology at Seabury, a theological seminary. There is a girls' school for my sisters, a military school for me.

At Shattuck (the military school) I make a bet with Harold Hildebrand, son of the German consul at Belize (British Honduras), that the Allies will win the war. By the time they do, Hildebrand and I are lost to one another, and he never pays me the fifty cents he owes me.

My parents like Faribault and determine to settle there

for life; they buy land, plan a house, and are ready to sign the builder's contract. Then my father is elected Bishop of New Jersey. He decides to accept, and off we go again, this time more than a thousand miles east, to Trenton. The "episcopal palace" there is a smallish gloomy house overlooking the Pennsylvania Railroad Station. Not at all the ticket. Soon my father buys a large gloomy house in Princeton, with about ten acres of land, and there we really do settle down.

To our Midwestern eyes, Princeton in 1916 seems ancient, hallowed by history, tinged with an almost English foreignness. And compared with the dry Midwest, it is almost tropically damp. Trees and shrubbery grow so lushly there that, as Edmund Wilson once said, in Princeton you feel that you are below the level of the grass.

In 1916 Princeton is a sleepy small town, hardly more than a village. Nassau Street is still unpaved, and the old Nassau Inn, dating from Revolutionary days, has not yet been pulled down to make way for the greater glory of Edgar Palmer, the zinc tycoon, and his pseudohistoric square. The red-brick Commons, looking like a sleazy hotel, stands on the corner of University Place, and the steam locomotives of the P.J.&B. (Princeton Junction & Back) pant up the grade from Lake Carnegie to a station that nestles under the trees of the university itself. This is reputed to be the steepest grade in the whole Pennsylvania Railroad system. When some foreign dignitary visited Princeton in the early 1900s, a party of undergraduate Mohawks greased the rails to such effect that the train failed to make the grade, though it tried again and again.

Almost everyone who lives in Princeton in those teenage days of the century has some connection with the college. (It calls itself a university but continues to act and feel like a rumbustious college for at least two more generations.)

There were giants in those days. They were larger than

life; their bank accounts contained multitudes of dollars; they lived in big houses well staffed with servants and were driven in big cars. On those rare occasions when they were encountered on the street, actually walking, they would nod graciously to the citizenry, who tipped their hats and bowed.

The biggest of these giants was Moses Taylor Pyne. If not the richest man in Princeton, he was certainly the most grand-ducal, and his porticoed mansion, Drumthwacket — as grand as The Oaks or grander — matched him, pillar for pillar. A man who seemed to have been born in a frock coat, and whose top hat did not so much add to his height as fulfill it, he bore in his forefront a commanding but not obtrusive paunch; his most noticeable features were his stature and his confident countenance, with its quietly grizzled moustache and well-fleshed nose.

Besides Mr. Pyne (and ranked a trifle below him) were other grandees: his brother-in-law Archibald Russell, a strikingly handsome man whose exceedingly plain wife bore him four children, stupid to the verge of lunacy. Mrs. Russell herself was none too bright. Their swimming pool was the only one in Princeton in its day. One of her son's undergraduate friends, while drunk, had dived into the pool when it was empty and cracked his skull. Mrs. Russell thereupon came to the conclusion that diving is dangerous and had the diving board removed.

Filled, the pool was an impressive sight when it was garnished and plumed by ladies of Mrs. Russell's generation, billowing in the heavy silk-and-serge bathing costumes — including hats! — of their day. The majestic and mysterious progress of one of these women-of-war through the unrippled water, with no more visible means of propulsion than Hiawatha on his canoe ride into the sunset, was a spectacle not easily forgotten.

The third member of Princeton's triumvirate, and also

a fine figure of a man, was George Allison Armour, who did not like to be mistaken for one of the meat-packing Armours of Chicago. He was a steady pillar of Trinity Church (Episcopalian, of course), where he was Senior Warden. When young Sammy Carnochan, the doctor's son, was first taken to church by his mother, she gave him a nickel.

"What for?"

"To give to God."

As Mr. Armour loomed splendidly and benignly down the aisle with the collection plate, Sammy cried to his mother: "Here comes God. Shall I give it to him now?"

The triumvirate were all directors of the Pennsylvania Railroad; on most weekdays they went to their offices in New York for a few hours, and expected the journey to be both comfortable and expeditious. They therefore arranged to be fetched and brought back in a special train consisting of a steam-engine and one Pullman chair-car, with steward and bar, which carried them from the station at Princeton through Princeton Junction to Manhattan Transfer, where even they had to change for the ferry to New York.

The Cuyler family, whose only daughter, Juliana, I will (amazingly) marry nine years from now, are impoverished but well connected: their cousins are all over Princeton — Conovers, Bakers, Potters, Stocktons, Stevenses. Mrs. Moses Taylor Pyne herself is one: Cousin Etta (or "Yawnetta," as she was known, for her habit of yawning her way through a tea party). Of these interrelated families the Stocktons are the most ancestral, the Stevenses the most brilliant (and eccentric), and the Potters the most influential. Any of their kin or anyone who marries a Potter relation has the right to be buried in the private Potter graveyard (known as Potter's Field) at Trinity Church. Thanks to my alliance with the Cuylers, there is room there for me.

A grade below these grandees were the celebrities: men like Grover Cleveland, former President of the United States, and Henry Van Dyke, the strutting little Presbyterian parson who had ridden to fame on Tennyson's coat-tails. John Cuyler, my father-in-law-to-be, was neither a grandee nor a celebrity, but he was definitely a Princeton character.

⸜⸝ JULIANA BAKER CUYLER

⌇ Mrs. cuyler was trying to fix a sewing machine in the parish house of Trinity Church. I was a boy of fourteen and a newcomer to Princeton, being "shown around" by the rector. Mrs. Cuyler asked me if I could help her with the sewing machine. I said I couldn't — which was not only the truth but a considerable understatement. She then said she had a boy at home just my age. For some reason this filled me with alarm, and I couldn't get away fast enough.

But when, a week or so later, I saw the Cuylers at home, I immediately took to that free-and-easy household like a duckling to its first pond. It was as different from our strictly regulated house as a Gypsy encampment is to the Guards' barracks. I soon saw that the broken-down sewing machine in the parish house was merely an extension of Mrs. Cuyler's home life. At the Cuylers' farm nothing worked: the screens didn't fit, table legs wobbled, the house and everything in it was dilapidated. Instead of an icebox there was a well (*inside* the kitchen), where meat, butter, and such things were hung and often fell in. In short, the Cuyler children led a life full of glorious incident. It amazed me to discover that some of them envied *me* and my regimented household.

Over the loosely federated arrangements of their daily life Mrs. Cuyler vaguely and benignly presided — or brooded. Yet the word *presided* has too much government in it to fit her, and *brooded* gives a wrong impression of her placid nature. She was there to be appealed to; put it like that. But quite often she wasn't there; she was at the parish house or Bamman's grocery store or visiting the sick. And she did in her way get things done. But meals were never on time and never turned out quite as they had been intended; the whole of domestic life proceeded by a series of makeshifts.

In those days even people with very little money, like the Cuylers, could afford at least one servant. Mrs. Cuyler had a succession of black cooks who came in by the day, and also an occasional cleaning woman. One of these was Bessie, who was the embodiment of good nature. You couldn't look at her round, dimpled black face without smiling or at least feeling more cheerful. Bessie usually brought one or two of her children with her, beautiful little creatures with great eyes and grave looks that could be changed in an instant by a smile like their mother's, shyer but brimming with the same deep happiness. They all had rather solemn names like Thomas and William and Elizabeth, never shortened. There seemed to be a new baby every year.

Mrs. Cuyler was bothered by the fact that Bessie wasn't married; she also learned that all Bessie's children had the same father. She didn't believe in interfering with people, but one day she plucked up her courage and asked Bessie why she didn't marry the man.

"I'd like to, Miz Cuyler, but his wife won't let me."

Crissie, who was the Cuylers' cook for quite a long time,

didn't have Bessie's earthy charm, but she was beautiful —
delicate, tall, and willowy. She often got tired, and no
wonder. Crissie had tuberculosis. When she died, Mrs.
Cuyler and her daughter went to her funeral at the Bright
Hope Baptist Church. They returned in tears, not only because they loved Crissie but because they had been much
moved by the funeral sermon. The preacher had been im-
ported for the occasion, and apologized for the brevity of
his remarks, explaining that he had to catch a train. Short
as his sermon was, it had been effective. The peroration
went something like this:

"The Lawd look round heaven and He see one of his
saints is missin'. An' the Lawd say to the Angel Gabr'el,
'Gabr'el! Go down to Seventeen and a Half Hulfish Street
and fetch Sis Rice!' An' the Angel Gabr'el get on his great
white horse an' he fly down to Seventeen and a Half Hulfish Street an' he dismount graceful. An' the Angel Gabr'el
say to Sis Rice, 'Sis Rice, Jesus wants you! Come up higher!'
An' Sis Rice look round and she say, 'Goodbye, folks on
earth! Hello, Jesus! Goodbye, time! Hello, eternity!' "

Mrs. Cuyler's vagueness had more serenity than uncer-
tainty in it. She never fussed, and she took things as they
came. When her children fell off things and hurt themselves, or got burned or broke their legs (the youngest particularly was prone to accidents, and some major injury
befell him every year), no doubt her heart contracted with
fear and perhaps tears came into her eyes, but outwardly
she was always calm and unhurried. When her children
went away to school she missed them, wrote to them regu-
larly, and visited them when she could.

Mrs. Cuyler could not resist free samples and always
tried them. Once she and her daughter, Julie, planned to
go on an all-day shopping expedition to Philadelphia. The
day before, Julie's mail contained an advertisement for
chocolate-flavored Ex-Lax, a laxative, with two free sam-

ples. As she tossed the ad and the samples into the waste-basket, she thought to herself, "Now, if I were Mother . . ."

Next day, shortly before they were to start for Phila-delphia, her mother telephoned. She said in a weak voice, "Darling, I don't *feel* very well this morning."

"Don't say another word," said Julie. "I know exactly what's happened."

Mrs. Cuyler's domestic life was one long rescue opera-tion, and she was always having to devise impromptu de-fenses against hopeless odds. She would tackle anything, although she wasn't very good with her hands and never achieved more than a partial and temporary success. Though she knew I was quite unable to fix or repair any-thing whatever, no matter how simple, she sometimes ap-pealed to me to help her, just because I was there.

I remember particularly one repair job on a piano leg. The leg had lost a good deal of the veneer that originally covered it. Mrs. Cuyler had collected some of the pieces that had been knocked off or fallen off; they should have been flat, but many of them were warped into a shal-low curve. She proposed to glue these pieces to the bare parts of the piano leg, holding them in place with rubber bands till the glue hardened. I did what she told me, as far as I could, but I could see it wasn't going to work. It didn't.

⚬‖ JOHN POTTER CUYLER

⌐ᴀ THE FIRST FEW TIMES I met Mr. Cuyler, I didn't like him at all. To my adolescent view he seemed a cantankerous elderly man, one to be avoided. And from snatches of grown-up gossip, I gathered that he was a largely absentee husband, a neglectful father, and a failure. I never dreamed that in a few years he would be my father-in-law and that we would become fast friends.

He was born in Savannah, into a family that in the brave antebellum days had owned two prosperous plantations. Some wealth must have survived the wreckage of the Civil War, for young John was given a gentleman's education: he was sent to school at St. Paul's, in New Hampshire. My father and he must have been there at the same time, but they had no recollection of each other. My father was a good boy and applied himself to his books. John Cuyler was definitely a bad boy and was always in hot water.

The big schoolroom where the boys studied their lessons, supervised by a master, was a drafty, barnlike hall, a dismal place on a winter evening. Insufficient heat came in gusts of hot air from grilles set in the floor and the walls.

John Cuyler discovered that the back of one of these grilles had an opening halfway up the stairs in the hallway outside. A boy who had to go to the lavatory was allowed a reasonable time — long enough to tiptoe up the stairs, put his mouth to the opening in the hot-air grille, and imitate the moaning howl of the winter wind. Some of the boys would hug themselves, shivering, and once even the master frowned and turned up his coat collar.

The penalty for most schoolboy crimes at St. Paul's was writing lines of Latin verse: a hundred lines was the minimum. John Cuyler amassed so many hundreds of lines that he figured they would fill all his spare time for several years, so he decided that he might as well go skating. The rector, out for a morning stroll around the pond, discovered him there. Presumably (though the story always ended at this point), he was chained to his desk for the rest of his schoolboy life. Or perhaps he was sent away, for part of his schooldays were spent in Germany, at Munich. He was no linguist, and by the time I knew him he had forgotten most of his German. But one of his favorite sayings may have come from those Munich days: "He was an artist, and she had also nothing." The things he remembered from his schooldays! He never forgot that a master at St. Paul's had explained the origin of the editorial "we" as a man with a tapeworm.

He did go to college, though not for long: to the University of the South, at Sewanee, Tennessee. Regular work always bored him, and the only thing he cared to remember from his college days was a laborious joke that enlivened some risky night hours for him and his friends. On the front lawn of Sewanee's campus stood a tall flagpole, surmounted by a gilt ball. Every night, until they were discovered, Mr. Cuyler's crew somehow managed to haul one of their number to the top of the pole, where he sawed off a foot and a half, being careful to replace the gilt ball. After a few days it became evident that the flagpole was mysteriously but steadily sinking into the ground.

How and when did Mr. Cuyler decide to be a painter? And was it a painter he really wanted to be, or an art student? At any rate, his family staked him, and off he went to Paris. Those were happy years. Paris at the turn of the century just suited him, as did the hand-to-mouth life of the Left Bank. He had a small talent but great zest.

A story he used to tell about another of his friends from those days showed what he thought of money. This friend, who was on a quarterly allowance, always cashed the check immediately, getting the whole amount in gold coins. Then he would stand in the middle of his studio and throw handfuls of coins in all directions. Whenever he was hard up, he would search the chinks and crannies and with any luck would find a gold piece. This story always delighted Mr. Cuyler.

His student days over, John Cuyler returned to America to practice his profession, marry, and settle down. The only part of this program that could be regarded as a complete success was his marriage. Julie Baker was a Philadelphia belle, a distant cousin of the Cuylers, and even prettier than the pictures he painted of her. Her father was a clergyman, and her face was most of her fortune. Toward the end of his life Mr. Cuyler once said to me, "You know, if I had to do it all over again I'd marry someone as much like Mrs. Cuyler as possible, but with a lot more money."

They set up house in Princeton; it was to be the first of a long series. "We've moved eighteen times in this town," Mr. Cuyler used to say, "and never once out of the sound of Trinity Church bells." While Mr. Cuyler was having some success with his painting, they lived in comfort; but long before the last of their five children was born it had become a struggle for them to make ends meet. Nevertheless, a certain style of living persisted. Mr. Cuyler never dreamed of resigning from the Nassau Club, where he spent several evenings a week playing poker; and for weddings, funerals, and other festive occasions his dress was not only correct but splendid, if a little threadbare.

Part of my early prejudice against Mr. Cuyler was based on the false notion that he didn't live with his family and had in effect abandoned them. The fact was that, from economic necessity, the Cuylers sometimes lived in two or three different places at the same time. During the summer they were all together at the Farm, an old frame house a mile out of Princeton, with a couple of empty barns and a few acres of weed-grown fields. When I first knew the place, the only remaining livestock was one goat and a coach dog, but there had been an ancient horse (named Eight, because Mr. Cuyler had bought it for eight dollars at an auction) and a cow that had died of neglect. Mr. Cuyler had undertaken to milk the cow but found it inconvenient to keep regular hours, and sometimes, returning from a late poker game, would milk it at three o'clock in the morning. When the vet was called in, too late, he said, "Well, if that cow was a woman, I'd say she died of nervous prostration."

There was no electric light at the Farm, but there was an electric pump in the cellar for the water supply, and a furnace of sorts. These rather rickety gadgets were too much for Mr. Cuyler, who was short on mechanical skill. The only man who could repair the pump lived at Dutch Neck, a hamlet about ten miles away, and his services were expensive. On one of his visits all he did was pick up a screw that had fallen out of the pump and put it back in place.

But it was the inadequate furnace, and the repeated catastrophe of frozen pipes, that finally convinced Mr. Cuyler that the Farm was not a winter house. Once, when he was hopelessly struggling to thaw out the pipes in the bathroom, he was heard to exclaim: "You nickel-plated sons of bitches! You'd freeze up solid in the middle of August if there was a glass of ice water in the room!"

Besides the Farm, Mr. Cuyler owned a rooming house for undergraduates, on University Place. There were not enough university dormitories in those days to house all the boys who came to Princeton, so a good many of them had to find rooms in the town. If Mr. Cuyler let all the available rooms in his house, which he invariably did, the rent went a good way toward supporting his family. But the September days that brought the new crop of freshmen, some of them escorted by their pernickety mothers or fathers, were always an anxious time for Mr. Cuyler, and he was not at his best then.

He had a studio apartment for himself at the back of the house, and there he would sit and wait, in increasing indignation, to interview his prospective tenants. If they asked too many questions or wanted extra pieces of furniture, he made short work of them. To one mother who inquired whether he would supply soap for her son, he roared: "No, madam! And I won't tuck your little darling into bed at night, either!"

Once the hateful chore of letting his rooms was finished, Mr. Cuyler forgot about it for another year and settled down to an enjoyable fall and winter. His studio had two great advantages: it was not big enough for anyone besides himself and Mrs. Cuyler, and it was next door to the Nassau Club. It was also only a few hundred yards from the rectory, where his wife and children spent the winter.

Dr. Alfred Baker, the rector emeritus of Trinity Parish, was allowed the use of the rectory during his lifetime. He was Mrs. Cuyler's uncle, and known to all the family, including Mr. Cuyler, as Uncle Alf. He was over eighty when I first knew him, and the general opinion was that he would last to a hundred. Though he was widely regarded as a saint, he was set in his ways and as stubborn as a mule: it required great patience and really saintly tolerance (both of which virtues Mrs. Cuyler possessed) to live with him.

Dr. Baker was so out of touch with the contemporary world that he was quite unaware of Prohibition, then in its miserable heyday. He was accustomed to a glass of wine with his dinner, and it was Mr. Cuyler (and a friendly Italian bootlegger) who supplied it. Though he got no credit for it, he was always pleased when Dr. Baker quavered, in his slow, hollow, old man's voice: "This is very nice wine, Julie. Did you get it at Bamman's?"

Age had withered and shrunk the old man, except for his feet, which seemed tremendously outsize. He walked with an inching shuffle, taking a considerable time to cross a room, and his almost daily expeditions to the post office required hours and were fraught with danger. When he snailed across Nassau Street he brought traffic — in those days, luckily, not very heavy — to a standstill. He insisted on going to the post office to mail his letters, of which he wrote several every day, because he answered all his second-class mail. Again and again Mrs. Cuyler would point out to him that an advertisement from Realsilk Hosiery or Wearever Shirts was not *meant* to be answered. Dr. Baker was unconvinced. "This young man has taken the trouble to write to me, Julie, and it is only courteous that I should reply to him."

In the Cuyler family, Christmas presents were always exchanged on Christmas Eve, in the back parlor of the rectory. One Christmas Eve, Mr. Cuyler saw Dr. Baker starting a purposeful shuffle in his direction, clutching a flat parcel in his hand. His heart sank — both because he knew without being told that he was about to be presented with a copy of *Keeping the Faith*, a recently printed selection of the old man's sermons, and because he had forgotten to buy Dr. Baker a Christmas present. He just had time to turn to Mrs. Cuyler, who was unwrapping a small silver bell, a present from one of her nieces, hastily rewrap it, and hold it out with a hearty "Merry Christmas, Uncle Alf!"

It was Dr. Baker's settled practice to say family prayers after dinner, and the whole household was expected to attend. This requirement was often a nuisance to those who wanted to go to the movies or play poker. And family prayers tended to take an increasingly long time, partly because Dr. Baker was growing slower of speech and partly because he kept adding more and more prayers. When Mr. Cuyler was present he was usually alert to this after-dinner threat, and just as dessert appeared he would rise from the table with a look of pain, sometimes holding his stomach, and say, "Julie, is there any soda in the house?" (Everyone knew that he had a bad stomach and dosed himself from time to time with bicarbonate of soda.) Then, whether Mrs. Cuyler said that there was or merely gave him a reproachful look, he would make his getaway, clutching his stomach, and be off to the Nassau Club and his poker game.

But sometimes, when the dangerous moment arrived, he would be in the midst of telling a story or would just plain forget, and he was caught. Then he would look so discomfited that his children could hardly keep their faces straight. Reluctantly he would join the procession to the front parlor, plump down on his knees, and pillow his head on his arms as comfortably as possible on the seat of a chair. As he did, he would often catch the eye of one of his sons and give an enormous, woebegone wink.

Mr. Cuyler's code of behavior included a certain amount of conformity in religious matters. It was part of his code to go to the funerals of friends, and he rarely missed a wedding; otherwise he went to church only on special occasions and to keep the peace with Mrs. Cuyler. His agnostic attitude did not prevent him from being a bit of a religious snob: he was apt to equate all Roman Catholics with "lace-curtain Irish," and he despised Presbyterians as canting hypocrites whose manners in church were common, to say the least. He particularly abominated their habit of pseudo-kneeling by bowing their heads while remaining seated — "smelling their hats," he called it.

Though he was not religious himself, religious people and their beliefs occasionally roused his curiosity, sometimes his wonder. Rather late in life he became aware of the hard New Testament saying "For he that hath, to him shall be given: and he that hath not, from him shall be taken away even that which he hath." Mr. Cuyler would repeat this last phrase with rueful amazement, screwing up his face at the injustice of it but at the same time twinkling with appreciation of its hard-hearted truth: *"Even that which he hath!"*

One day he was coming away from a funeral with Bert Green, a Princeton bootlegger, and said to him, "Bert, just what *is* your idea of the Holy Ghost?"

"Well, Mr. Cuyler, to tell you the truth, I've always thought he was some kind of goblin."

This same Bert Green was also the author of an aphorism often repeated by Mr. Cuyler: "As soon as you get out of bed in the morning, it's ten to one against you."

If Mr. Cuyler was not exactly a philosopher, he was a lifelong collector of memorable statements or comments on the human condition. Though he usually attributed them to others, I suspect that a good many were original with him or that he had polished them into their final form. "The only perfect climate is bed." That, I think, was his own. But when he and some cronies at the Nassau Club decided to put out a magazine called *The Sad Bird*, what was his contribution? He never said. Only one number of this paper appeared, and the only thing that Mr. Cuyler could remember from it was the summary statement of a professor named Algy Kennedy: "Life is monotonous in its milder moods and terrifying in its fiercer aspects."

When Mr. Cuyler's spirits were high, he sometimes liked to sing, and he remembered the words to several French songs. He was completely tone deaf. Whenever he sang at the Nassau Club it was put on his bill — thirty-five cents. The Nassau Club was the center of Mr. Cuyler's social life, but in his golden season he went to weddings far afield and to all the parties that Princeton offered. He liked pretty women and he loved to talk, and he was a most agreeable companion. One thing he couldn't stand was a bore. One of the greatest bores in town was a tiny, dapper old bachelor named Willy Agnew: he was perfectly polite but never very interesting, and when he had drunk his fill his conversation became inordinately monotonous and lengthy. When Mr. Cuyler once encountered him in this condition at a party he took him firmly by the shoulders and turned him around. He said that Willy Agnew didn't notice and went right on talking, but at least to a different audience.

At an out-of-town wedding reception Mr. Cuyler was introduced to a pretty woman and was talking to her with his customary animation, at the same time eating a plate of lobster salad. His daughter, standing nearby, was watching him fondly when to her horror she saw him spit a small blob of mayonnaise straight onto the lady's nose. The lady blinked but stood steadfast, too mannerly to embarrass Mr. Cuyler by wiping off the mayonnaise. On the way home his daughter upbraided him for his behavior. He said simply, "She looked better that way."

Mr. Cuyler must have known that he was a failure as a painter. He was also a failure at making a living, if "making a living" means earning enough money to support your wife and five children. If he needed more money than his rooming house brought in, why didn't he get a job? He did. He held it for years, and it nearly bored him to death.

One of his good friends was Dr. Charles Browne, a rich retired doctor who was the perennial mayor of Princeton. Dr. Browne appointed Mr. Cuyler borough clerk. Besides keeping the minutes of the meetings of the Borough Council, the clerk had to be on duty for some hours every day at the Borough Hall. There was not always very much for him to do. But whenever some citizen called in at the Borough Hall to make a complaint or a suggestion, it was usually Mr. Cuyler whom he saw.

The cupola on top of the Borough Hall had been struck by lightning some time before and leaned at a drunken angle. Mr. Cuyler became so used to people coming in to report this fact that he said he got to know by the look on their faces what they were going to tell him. Before they could speak he would say, "Just a minute. I know exactly what you're going to say. We like it that way."

A salesman came into the Borough Hall one day, trying to sell rubber pads for hard chairs. The clincher to his sales talk was that the rubber pads would keep the seats of the councilmen's trousers from getting shiny. Mr. Cuyler said, "Young man, you've hit upon the very thing I care least about in this world."

Mr. Cuyler's spirits were mercurial, and they were also affected by the season. In spring and fall they were apt to soar, and at those times he simply could not stand the boredom of the Borough Hall: He would pay Jerry Sullivan five dollars to sit in for him, and off he would go to the countryside, fishing or shooting with one of his friends or calling on a friendly Italian farmer who made wine from his own grapes.

He would sit with the farmer and his sons around a table in a pergola, with a glass of red wine in front of him and a cigar in his mouth. There was always a nice fat baby, placid and not squirmy, to be passed around the

circle. This complex of pleasures, Mr. Cuyler declared —
a mouthful of wine, a pull at the cigar, a squeeze of the
baby — was hard to beat.

Mr. Cuyler was a devoted husband in his way, if not the
best of providers. His devotion to his wife did not prevent
him from finding other women attractive. His flirtations
were open, talkative, and usually of long duration. In the
midst of one of them he went duck-shooting with his friend
Charley Browne. On the drive down to Chincoteague Bay,
Mr. Cuyler regaled Dr. Browne with descriptions of the
latest lady.

"I don't like her," said Dr. Browne.

"Why, Charley, you don't even know her!"

"I don't care; I don't like fine women."

This tickled Mr. Cuyler right to his solar plexus. The
minute he got back from his duck-shooting he went to his
daughter's house to report this anecdote, and they spent
an entire evening going through the Princeton telephone
book, checking off the "fine women" — and occasionally
the "fine men." This led Mr. Cuyler to ask himself the
question Whom would I bite first, if I were a dog? Mrs.
Pierce? No, on second thought he wouldn't *bite* her; he
would chase her up a tree, and every time she made a
move to get down, he would growl.

Now and again, though at rarer and rarer intervals, the
spirit moved Mr. Cuyler to a burst of painting. Once when
he was hard at work and did not want to be disturbed,
there was such a racket outside his studio and even on the
roof that he finally flung the door open and stuck out his
head, his moustache bristling with anger. There was a
small crowd in his little courtyard: his wife, his daughter,
and several small boys, one of whom was trying to shinny
up the drainpipe to the studio roof.

His daughter said apologetically, "The fish has fallen
in the gutter."

"*What fish?*"

Eventually they were able to explain to him that a half-grown cat had climbed the tree at the corner of the studio and couldn't get down; Mrs. Cuyler, seeing its predicament, had sent a small boy to the fishmonger's to get a fish head, which she then stuck on a fishing pole, hoping to lure the cat. Unfortunately, the fish head had fallen off the pole and landed in the gutter. That was the situation at the moment.

Incredible as it may seem, the same thing happened several times, with different cats. Mrs. Cuyler's first move was always the fish head — although it never worked. After that she would find a small boy who was willing (and light enough) to climb the tree. As the cat usually kept retreating to a higher branch, this required an exceptionally light and quite courageous small boy. If the boy failed, the last resort was the fire department, which brought a ladder. On each of these occasions, as luck would have it, Mr. Cuyler was painting. He got it firmly into his head that it was always the same cat, driven by some sort of crazy cat death wish. The last time it happened, he charged out of his studio with a despairing cry: "How can I paint when this damn cat keeps going up the tree?"

Like the rest of his family, Mr. Cuyler slept in different houses, according to the time of year, but otherwise his bedtime habits were conservative: he snored, he wore a nightshirt, and he suffered from insomnia. For this fairly common complaint he had developed a remedy. In the bookshelves at the rectory there was a ten-volume set of Ridpath's *History of the World*. One night when he couldn't get to sleep Mr. Cuyler began to read volume one, and a few pages sent him off. The efficacy of this sleeping pill increased with use: soon the mere opening of the book acted as a soporific. Then he had only to stretch his hand out toward the shelf. Finally all he had to do was think of the title.

Impecunious though he was, Mr. Cuyler owned several cars in the course of his life. He never learned to drive well, but he had only one accident: he hit the side of a culvert on a country road, and got off lightly — a crumpled fender and a cut on his nose. He neither understood cars nor wholly trusted them. You can always tell what a horse is going to do, he used to say, but you can't be sure about a car.

When he was driving down a street, he went so slowly that traffic would pile up behind him; if he turned a corner, he put on a burst of speed and swung in a sudden wide arc, usually without signaling. One of my sisters started a nursery school in Princeton and dragooned Mr. Cuyler into fetching and taking home a family of four small children, the Pullens. For safety's sake, Mr. Cuyler made them all sit on the floor in the back of his car. On the straightaways their little heads could just be seen; when Mr. Cuyler swooped around a corner, the heads all disappeared as the children toppled over. He was amazed at himself for taking on this daily chore, which he did only because he had a soft spot for my sister.

"When I get to the pearly gates and Saint Peter asks me what I did to get into heaven, I'll say, 'I took the Pullens!' "

Mr. Cuyler didn't like to back his car: he couldn't or wouldn't turn his head to see where he was going. When he had someone else with him to do the looking for him, he didn't mind much. One summer day his car was parked, head to the curb, on Nassau Street; he had to back out to get under way. Just as he was about to back, his daughter, who was keeping a lookout, said, "Stop, Dad, there's a truck coming." "There shouldn't be," said Mr. Cuyler, "not in August."

Mr. Cuyler's closest friend and boon companion was Dick Stockton. His colonial ancestor, one of the signers of the Declaration of Independence, had built Morven, still

the handsomest house in Princeton. At one time the Stocktons had owned a great deal of land, and the sales or rent-
als of the dwindling remnant supported Dick Stockton: he
never had a job. He lived in a small house on Bayard Lane
with his three spinster sisters. A favorite with both men
and women, he was a bachelor all his life.

Tall, stooped, and lanky, not handsome, but with a long,
lined, kindly face that everyone took to, he looked like a
remnant himself, an early American remnant. You could
easily imagine him in eighteenth-century dress, in the uniform of a Continental officer, or in buckskins and fringed
leggings, toting a squirrel gun. And in fact he was a dead
shot, a charter member and mainstay of the Gun Club.

John Cuyler was peppery and volatile; Dick Stockton,
easygoing, even-tempered, and lazy. Both liked their drink
and loved an argument. According to a family story, they
had gone to New York to see the parade in honor of Ad-
miral Dewey, returning in triumph from the Spanish-
American War; John Cuyler had rented a hotel room overlooking the line of march. While waiting for the parade
they fell into an argument over some engagement in the
Civil War and grew so heated that the parade went by
without their noticing it.

Dick Stockton deeply disliked any sort of bother or fuss
and would go to any length to escape such a thing. A constant potential source of trouble was his tenants. Princeton
in those days was a great place for moving houses, as it
was sometimes cheaper to move a house than to build a
new one. It was a not uncommon sight in the summer to
see a frame house blocking the middle of the street, being
nudged forward on rollers. Dick Stockton owned several of
these transplanted houses and rented them out. They never
quite fitted their new cellars, and after a heavy rainstorm
infuriated tenants would telephone to their landlord, asking what he proposed to do about their flooded cellars.

"Well, what *do* you do?" John Cuyler once asked him.

"I do one of two things. I either go to New York or I go to Philadelphia."

There was a period when John Cuyler persuaded Dick that it would be a good idea to brush up on their French. The two of them would sit in Mr. Cuyler's studio, taking turns at reading a French novel aloud, translating as they went.

It was not long before John Cuyler noticed something odd about Dick Stockton's translation: all the verbs were in the past tense.

"My God, Dick, you don't know whether your characters are coming or going! You don't know one tense from another."

"When was this novel written?"

"I don't know — quite some time ago."

"Exactly! So everything in it has happened, hasn't it?"

Reading aloud is dry work, and there were always drinks at these literary sessions. When John Cuyler refilled Dick Stockton's glass, he would set it down on a table, just too far for Dick to reach it without getting up. Finally even that easygoing man's patience was exhausted.

"John, why do you always put my drink just out of my reach?"

"I like to see you move."

In 1917, when most Anglo-Saxon Americans saw that the United States would inevitably get into war against Germany, there was a rush to enlist. Dick Stockton was well over military age, but he was a single man and determined to get his share of the fighting, if he could. When he went to the headquarters of Company L, Princeton's unit in the National Guard, John Cuyler went with him to see how he made out. Together they pored over the questionnaire that recruits had to fill in: it was reasonably plain sailing till the question "Can you drive a car?"

To John Cuyler's surprise, he saw Dick Stockton write "Yes."

"Why, Dick, you know you can't drive a car."

"If Helen Howe can drive a car, I can."

Mr. Cuyler loved parties. He loved going to them and he loved giving them. When he did give a party, which wasn't often, because he couldn't ever really afford it, it usually had a simple but heavily emphasized idea behind it. Once he gave a "strawberry festival": the center of the festivities was a brimming punch bowl, with one strawberry floating in the middle. Another time he put on a show of his paintings in which there was only one picture. If you had a lot of pictures, he said, people were apt to give them a cursory glance and not really look at any, whereas if you had only one picture, they couldn't miss it.

When he was in a cheerful mood he was always putting on a show, of a kind. He was a famous storyteller, and perhaps it was because he didn't mind repeating himself that his stories became so word-perfect. When he had a mind to tell a story, nothing and nobody could stop him: he was deaf to all pleas that his listeners had heard it before, had even heard it often. But sometimes he would check himself, saying, "Ah, but you've all heard me tell *that* old story" — and at those times he had to be reassured and urged on. Then, almost invariably, he would come out with something new.

Mrs. Cuyler, on the other hand, was incapable of getting a story right: she would ramble on in her vague and gentle way, and sometimes even forgot the point. She seemed to be talking with half an ear, as if she were listening to some interior conversation. If Mr. Cuyler was there too he didn't interrupt or correct her: he merely sighed, took out his watch, and put it on the table in front of him.

He got his diversion, by and large, out of the battle of daily life — or perhaps it would be truer to say out of his own gallant or mocking comments on the battle. To a friend who was dreading the onset of winter Mr. Cuyler said, "If you want the winter to go fast, just take out a note at the bank." He heard of a mother whose three children were so dawdling and dreamy at the nursery table that they never finished a meal. She tried all sorts of things: one expedient was to put an alarm clock on the table and, when the alarm went off, to take away their plates. Even this drastic dodge was unsuccessful. Mr. Cuyler commented, "The best way to get children to eat is to have a large family and not quite enough to go round."

Though he never had much money, Mr. Cuyler always hoped for a lucky strike that would make his fortune. He was an avid poker player, but calculated that he broke about even in the course of a year. Though he always bought tickets in the Irish Sweepstakes, he didn't really expect to cash in. The thing he dreamed about was making a pile by inventing something. One of his forebears had been a successful inventor (the family legend was that he had been the first to build a steamboat, though Robert Fulton somehow got the credit), and Mr. Cuyler felt that the knack was in his blood.

His daughter could always tell, by the faraway look in his eye, when the inventive spell was on him; he admitted to her that in those moments he was figuring out how to spend the first million dollars his royalties would bring him. Most of these ideas never materialized, but some got to the stage of a working model.

Once when his daughter met him on Nassau Street, limping painfully, and asked him what was the matter, he pulled up his trouser leg and showed her his latest invention: two thin steel bands, one on either side of his leg, the bottoms in his shoe and the tops fastened to his sock. This was intended to be a substitute for garters. Unfortunately, the bands hurt his feet and pinched his leg.

Mr. Cuyler suffered all his life from a bad stomach. He never did much about it, aside from dosing himself with bicarbonate of soda. His feeling seemed to be that all stomachs were uncertain, and that if you had one as uncertain as his, you simply made the best of it. This practice did not include getting the advice of a doctor: in his prime Mr. Cuyler regarded doctors as an unnecessary expense, except in an emergency, and I think he avoided doctors in later life for fear of what they might tell him.

Mr. Cuyler's stomach bothered him more and more. He had never been a hearty eater, though he loved good food, but now a few mouthfuls were enough for him. He took to saying that food was only a foundation for smoking. Eventually, when his pains had become so frequent that they were almost continuous, Mrs. Cuyler prevailed on him to see a doctor and have a thorough going-over. The verdict, which the doctor gave Mrs. Cuyler but kept from his patient, was incurable cancer. There was a family conference, at which it was decided that Mr. Cuyler should be told. It was she who told him, one evening in his studio, with all his children around him. She told him very simply and straightforwardly.

He didn't last long, but it seemed a long time to everybody. Mrs. Cuyler was with him constantly, and his children came to see him nearly every day. He was a good patient and didn't complain much. Toward the end he hardly spoke, and then in a rasping, almost inaudible whisper. Once his wife heard him murmur something that raised her tireless hopes. She leaned over him.

"What did you say, darling? 'Body and soul'?"

"No, goddammit, Julie — I said, 'Bicarbonate of soda.' "

⁜ CHILI MEYERS

CHILI MEYERS was the chief of police. (There were only two other policemen in Princeton in those days.) He was a small, dark, burly man who looked half Indian. His uniform was always as rumpled as if he'd slept in it. Besides being chief of police, he was a professional biter-off of puppy dogs' tails, and was said to be an expert at it.

One Sunday morning, shortly before the eleven o'clock service at the Second Presbyterian Church, a number of empty liquor bottles came flying from the window of an apartment above Bamman's grocery store and smashed on the sidewalk among the churchgoers. Several of them, angry and alarmed, went to fetch a policeman. Chili Meyers came in person and, bidding the crowd stand back, stalked into the house, his hand on his gun holster.

Upstairs he found Charley Arrott, the gentle young man who ran the Brick Row Bookshop — a model of courtesy when sober but a very different kettle of sharks when he was drunk — and a blonde, who said she lived in Trenton. Charley had been drinking most of the night and was now ready for sleep. Chili Meyers cautioned him about throwing bottles out the window, took the blonde back to Trenton, and stayed with her for a week.

⚬⁘| THE OLD COMSTOCKS

⌒⟨ OLD MR. COMSTOCK and his wife were one of the sights of Princeton. They were usually to be seen walking down Nassau Street together; that is, not exactly together, but in tandem: Mr. Comstock was always two or three feet ahead of his wife. He was dressed in old-fashioned plus fours and brogues and carried a walking stick. She wore a little bonnet and walked as though she were carrying a muff. He had a long, suspicious face, with eyes close together and straggly moustaches. Her face was pretty and mischievous, but she was almost stone deaf. Both of them were small.

Now and then Mr. Comstock stopped and glared back at his wife. Then he bawled, "How are your *legs* — NOW?" Mrs. Comstock made a face and shook her head coquettishly; she wouldn't answer him. This was a love passage, like the dance of two birds in mating season.

Mr. Comstock adored his wife, and she accepted his adoration. At home in the evening, when it was time for her to take her pill, she always hid behind a newspaper or a book. He shouted at her, but she pretended not to hear him. At last he rolled up a piece of paper and threw it at her; it hit the book and she jumped. He pointed angrily at the pill bottle on the table beside her, jabbing his finger. She pursed her mouth, closed her eyes, and retired again behind her book.

⚬❙ WALTER RODEFELD

⌐◝(WALTER, MY FATHER'S CHAUFFEUR, was an indispensable member of the household, and not only because of his unfailing good humor. Once, when he was ill, the quality of the coffee at breakfast fell off notably, and my father noted it. An investigation was ordered. Although Walter's wife, Dolly, was the cook, and a first-class one, it turned out that for years it was Walter who had made the morning coffee.

Walter liked his glass of beer, but he never smoked; he chewed tobacco. He often warned me earnestly against the habit, which he characterized as "filthy" but couldn't give up. Nevertheless, he could and did exercise great self-control: he told me proudly that he never spat while he was driving my father; he just waited till he got the chance. On a trip that lasted several hours the waiting sometimes got too much for him, and then he would stop the car, get out, and look under the rear wheel, climbing back into his seat a moment later with a cheerful "Thought there was something wrong with my shackle, Bishop!"

Walter spent so much of his life in cars — when he was

not on the road or in the kitchen, he was always to be
found in the garage, sitting in one of the cars, reading the
baseball news or snoozing — that he tended to identify
their anatomy with his: he spoke of "my exhilarator" or
"my tires." Those who didn't know this habit of his may
have misplaced their sympathy when they heard him say,
with a worried frown: "Something wrong with my pump.
Don't seem to act right." He drove my father faithfully for
nearly forty years. In all that time he was never in a bad
accident. I always felt this was due more to character than
skill. Walter never became an accomplished driver; in particular, he had a habit of jumping on the brake. If his passengers were not prepared, they were likely to be thrown
forward. My father and mother, who were accustomed to
Walter's driving, always slipped an arm through the pad-
ded loops that hung down beside the back seat, so that
when Walter was surprised (as he always was) by a red
light or a stop sign, exclaimed "*Oh*-oh!" and jumped on
the brake, they merely bowed slightly.

In his later years he did tend to get drowsy as he drove.
But my mother sat where she could watch him in the driving mirror, and when he nodded she would speak to him
sharply and then keep him talking till he was wide awake
again.

My father had a succession of cars, and usually two at
a time, of different makes. Walter always had his favorites.
There was a Marmon, whose smoothness and power he approved of, but the cushion on the driver's seat was curved
in such a way that the edge pressed into Walter's short legs
at the thigh and cut off the circulation. When I asked him
how he liked the Marmon, he said it was all right, but that
"after you been driving all day you feel like going to the
chiropodist."

At one period in my father's life he took to motorboats.
The first was a modest cabin cruiser. But the second, which

he bought from a Mr. Pernod and which was named *Absinthe* (my father promptly changed it to *Sakonnet*) was all of seventy-five feet and needed a crew of three. Walter and Dolly were pressed into service: she presided in the galley, and he wore a white jacket, masquerading as a steward. On crowded occasions at home, like Thanksgiving dinners, Walter had sometimes lent a hand, but he was a hard-breathing waiter, given to bursts of audible dismay (*"Oh*-oh! Forgot the spoon").

Walter took his new duties in his cheerful stride. But, like me, he was a fair-weather sailor. When my father transferred his household to Florida for the winter, most of the *Sakonnet*'s cruising was confined to the placid Inland Waterway. After a while, however, this became monotonous, and my father decided to voyage across Florida and into the Gulf of Mexico. In the Gulf the *Sakonnet* rolled and pitched like a bronco, and Walter responded. After the event, with his usual cheerfulness he told his friends: "First I got the sweats. Then I says to Dolly, '*Oh*-oh, here she comes' — and there she was."

Walter was completely loyal to my father his whole life long (at South's garage he was known to his fellow chauffeurs as "Bishop"). He had other loyalties too. When I was an undergraduate, in the loose days of Prohibition, I once borrowed a family car to transport some jugs of bootleg wine. One of the gallon jars left a telltale ring on the floor mat, and Walter was up half the night scrubbing away at the evidence — not on his own account but to cover up for me. By the time my father called for the car next day Walter had succeeded in removing most of the traces. Walter was certain that if my father had been alone, he wouldn't have noticed anything amiss. But his sharp-eyed secretary, Helen Emerson, was with him. As Walter disgustedly reported, "Then that goddam Miss Emerson had to go and put *her* face into it."

No sooner had she settled herself in the back seat than she spied the ring-shaped mark on the mat.

"Bishop! What's *that?*"

My father leaned and stared. "What's this mark, Walter?"

"Dunno, Bishop."

"Mr. Tom had this car out last night." (Miss Emerson again.)

"Did he, Walter?"

"I dunno, Bishop."

And thanks to Walter, that was the end of that.

ARTHUR HINDS

HE WAS A BLACK MAN and poor all his life, and he never made a success of anything he turned his hand to. In fact, it was his ludicrous failures that gave him a large part of his reputation. But not the essential part. Though he could never triumph over the slapstick adversary that bedeviled him, he never gave up, either, and as a result he wore a kind of dignity — something of the air of a Charlie Chaplin hero.

Hinds was an odd-job man: he beat carpets, put in screens in the spring and took them out in the fall. He polished floors, even acted occasionally as butler. When his luck was in, he did these jobs not well but without disaster; when his luck was out, as it was more often than not, the results were catastrophic. He must have put in screens and taken them out of hundreds, maybe thousands of windows, but he never quite got the hang of it. Whenever my wife saw the deep gouges in a window sash caused by Hinds, in his desperation, having jammed the window up with its lock sticking out, she swore she would never employ him again. But of course she always did.

Hinds was a small man, with none of the protective bluster that small men often have. He seemed timid, but I don't think he was: he was exquisitely polite, and his politeness had in it much more natural gentleness than timidity. He hated to bother people or make himself a nuisance. I am sure that many of his wrong decisions came from this excessive tenderness. Failure always embarrassed him, and when he was embarrassed he giggled — not because he thought there was anything funny in the situation, but because he couldn't help it; it was like an agonized lie.

My wife once put him to work polishing floors. The polishing brush she gave him was an attachment that fitted on the nozzle of a vacuum cleaner. She explained the contrivance to him, showed him how to work it, and went off to her own jobs, satisfied that for once all would be well. But when she came back in half an hour to see how he was doing, she saw to her horror that he had put the wrong stuff on the polisher: instead of shining up the floor, he was removing the varnish.

She rushed at him (a mistake), crying to him to stop. Alarmed, and bursting into nervous giggles, Hinds fell back a step, dropping the vacuum cleaner; it knocked over an open box of camphor balls, and dozens of them rushed up into the sucking nozzle. The rest of the morning they sat side by side on the stairs, plucking out the camphor balls.

One of Hinds's longest terms as a butler was at the rectory, where old Dr. Baker, the rector emeritus, was spending his last years. Mrs. Cuyler, his niece, kept house for him, and during the Christmas holidays, when her daughter and four sons came home from school, she got Hinds to wait on the table at dinner. One night, as Hinds was reverently changing Dr. Baker's plate, half the plate came away in his hands and the other half remained on the table. Dr. Baker, who was very old and almost as polite as Hinds, ap-

parently noticed nothing amiss, or decided not to notice.
Hinds, with a terrible look on his face and the delighted
eyes of the boys upon him, carefully carried the half-plate
to the kitchen. Everyone agreed that this mishap could not
possibly be blamed on Hinds but that it couldn't have happened to anybody else.

My mother once had Hinds to help out at an evening
party, splendid in white tie, boiled shirt, and tail coat. Just
before the first guests arrived, Mother backed Hinds, gig-
gling nervously, into the pantry, where she went at his
shirt front with a table knife. Somehow he had managed to
get strawberry jam on it.

Between his occasional jobs, Hinds peddled things, lug-
ging a huge and heavy sample case from house to house.
The objects he peddled were ingenious but unlikely, and
he himself had small faith in them. One I remember was a
large, flat cigarette case, meant to resemble silver but evidently made of flimsier and baser metal, and already
dented. As Hinds exhibited this gadget, he pressed a button
and a limp cigarette half-emerged. Hinds explained, gig-
gling despairingly, that the cigarette was *supposed* to jump
out and light itself, all in one, but the case wasn't working
very well.

Another of his wares was a small perforated container
to be hung in a clothes closet: the mysterious properties of
the stuff inside it, said Hinds, would not only keep moths
away but impart a sweet odor to the clothes. Mr. Cuyler,
who took a chance and bought one, reported that moths
loved it and you could never get rid of the smell.

One day, driving back from Princeton Junction, I overtook Hinds; for once he was not burdened with his sample
case. As we drove into town I asked him what he was doing
out here in the country. He had been looking cheerful, but
now he giggled. He told me that "a kind of country club"
was being started on the highway to Trenton, and that he

was to be its major-domo; he hastily and earnestly added that he wouldn't advise me to become a member. And sure enough, the club soon failed.

Every Christmas Hinds sent us a Christmas card. It was always the same: a deep chocolate brown with "Merry Christmas" lettered in silver tinsel, and inside was his signature, Arthur Hinds, written in the most beautiful copperplate hand.

⁓⁑ MIMI

⌒⟨ MIMI WAS THE LAST and best of our governesses. She was English, but she had lived in America since she was a girl and had long ago lost her British accent. And she did not, like some of her predecessors, regard us as little provincials, though she did laugh at us and call us "oddities." We liked Mimi on sight, and by that time we had become experts at sizing up new governesses.

We did not call her Mimi at first: that was a diminutive wished on her later by my youngest sister, her favorite. Her real name, Miss Agnes Miller, suited her much better. She looked like a thin sister of Mr. Punch, or a nutcracker: she had a long British face, with nose and chin to match, and as she grew older her nose and chin seemed to get longer and to lean closer together. I don't remember our kissing her when we were children, but we did when we were grown up. You had to bend your head and go at it sideways. Mr. Cuyler's first remark when I became engaged to his daughter was "Will I have to kiss Miss Miller?" She taught us our letters, but her main job was "taking care of us," and we loved her, though we didn't know it at the time.

When I was nine Mimi gave me a terrible scare. She and I had bedrooms on the top floor, with a bathroom between. Since I still had a babyish fear of the dark, the doors between our rooms were kept open so that I could see a reassuring patch of light on the floor as I fell asleep. One night I woke, roused by a fearful sound. As I lay rigid with terror, my heart pounding, it came again: a horrible low snarl, rising to a slavering growl, then mumbling sounds, and silence. A moment later the snarl began again. The noise came from Mimi's dark room, and I knew instantly what it was. A tiger was in there. It had killed Mimi and was mauling her corpse, now and then chewing a morsel. When it had finished with Mimi, it would be coming in for me. Suddenly I realized that Mimi was snoring.

For a long time Mimi pretended to be younger than she was, perhaps from a fear of being considered too old to be useful any longer. It would have been a natural fear, but if she had it, she reckoned without my mother. Long after she had ceased to pretend about her age, Mimi continued to live in my father's house. She fretted about not earning her keep; she grew suspicious and occasionally complaining, sometimes tearful; she must have been hard to live with. Nevertheless, she was lived with; and when she was feeling well, she was still lively. If something struck her as an "oddity," her old Punch's face screwed up into a squint of laughter and tears of joy ran down her cheeks.

When Mimi got into her nineties, she began to fail. She suffered from rheumatism and could no longer get about the way she used to. Finally she took to her bed; it was the only place where she could be comfortable. My mother and father, who were old themselves by now, were going south for the winter. My mother didn't like to leave Mimi, bedridden and increasingly helpless — and by this time with her wits occasionally wandering — in the half-shut house, with only a caretaker and his wife. So they sent her off to a nursing home.

The nuns who ran the nursing home liked her; they thought *her* an oddity — in that collection of oddities — and I think Mimi was not altogether unhappy in her years there. But she never was reconciled to being away, and she always looked forward to coming home again. I used to go and see her, though not nearly as often as I might have, and sometimes took one of my little sons with me.

Mimi's room was cheerful: it looked out on a garden, and there were always flowers on the chest of drawers. (My father had them sent every week.) She had a roommate, a shapeless old woman with a round frizzy head who was usually sitting in a rocking chair, motionless and humped under blankets. Once I whispered a question to Mimi about her. "That old mermaid!" said Mimi loudly.

Our conversation on these visits always followed the same pattern. Mimi was so glad to see me that she laughed with delight, laughed and laughed, stammering with pleasure, squeezing my hand and pressing it to her old cheek, sometimes kissing it. She always knew who I was and called me by name. As soon as she recovered from her pleased surprise at seeing me, she began to pitch into me for not coming sooner, not writing to her, neglecting her in general. She frowned at me fiercely, managing somehow to smile at the same time, and growled, "You're *bad!* You're *bad!*" That was the only sentence she could still get right.

Sometimes this talking-to went on a little too long and frightened her. Then she would weep. But I could usually cheer her up again by changing the subject. Our conversations must have sounded completely dotty. It wasn't gibberish she talked, for most of the words she used were real words; it was just that they had no observable connection with each other. Some members of the family thought she was gaga, but I was sure she wasn't. When she was trying to tell me something, I sometimes understood or partly understood what she was trying to say. One thing she always tried to tell me, I'm sure, was that she wanted to come home.

At the first sign that I was going to leave, Mimi would get panicky. She clung to my hand, saying wildly, "No! No!" I would pat her hand, promising to come back soon, and gradually extricate myself. And as soon as she realized I really was going, she acted like a good child and stopped pleading with me. She always blew me a kiss as I turned at the door and waved.

The great event of her last days was her hundredth birthday. The nuns gave her a party, with a single candle on the birthday cake; all the family sent flowers; and the local paper carried a paragraph about her. She showed me the clipping with great pride on my next visit. It was the first and last time in her life that her name was mentioned in a newspaper.

HELEN EMERSON

HELEN EMERSON was a pretty little spinster with a voice that would rasp the dead. She was the last of my father's secretaries, and the most durable. By the cruelly level appraisal children make, without even thinking about it, she was not the one we liked best. That one was Ella Charls, who was tall and dark, with a deep harsh voice. We considered her beautiful. But I don't think she was ever actually my father's secretary; she just had something to do with the cathedral where he was dean. The first secretary I can remember was Miss Whetstone, who married the organist, and there were several after her. Then Miss Emerson came, and she lasted a lifetime.

She adored my father and was terrified of him. When he barked at her, as he often did, she would literally jump with fright. She was also, in quite a different way, afraid of snakes — and who but a herpetologist isn't? She thought of herself as fierce, but she was too small to frighten anybody, and her incessant yapping was more a nuisance than a threat. Like many well-meaning people, she meddled and interfered when she only wanted to help. Her last years were spent as a too-close neighbor and tenant of my brother-in-law Buzz Cuyler, whose long-suffering wife, Margery, had to take the brunt of Helen's ceaseless advice and criticism. As my sister Mary Ann remarked, Helen was enough to try the patience of a Margery.

Helen's adoration of my father included, to a somewhat lesser degree, the rest of his family: she was fiercely, belligerently loyal to all the Matthewses and knew more about them — and what was good for them — than they did themselves. As the only other Matthews male, I held a place in her fealty not much below my father's. This allegiance to our family did not preclude the right (the duty, as she saw it) to give constant advice on what to do next — or what not to do — and outspoken criticism of what you were doing or had already done. Her energy was apparently inexhaustible, and she needed it, for she never rested from busybodying herself with everybody else's affairs. In a sense she was almost completely selfless, for her insatiable activity came from her deep desire to meddle *helpfully*. Even when she was at her most annoying, you could see that.

Her opinions were violent and vehemently expressed; her prejudices had the force of innate conviction. Like most people who want to undo everything and then tie it up again in knots of their own making, she thought of herself as a conservative. To remold the world nearer to her heart's desire, she would willingly have had millions of people hanged or shot — or so she gave you to understand. If it came to the pinch I doubt that she could have steeled herself to mete out any harsher penalty than sending the culprit to bed without his supper. (But this may be a sentimental notion on my part. If she *had* been the ruler of the world, she might have put half mankind to the sword without batting an eyelash. I wouldn't like to bet on it, either way.) She was an antifeminist who venerated the male sex and scorned the trousered woman. She was anti-black, anti-Semitic, antilabor, antiforeigner (except for the English, who were her own forebears). She wouldn't have dreamed of voting — except to abolish women's suffrage.

As a girl in Patriot, Indiana, where she was born, she must have been a very pretty girl, "a cute little piece." She was vain about her tiny feet. She must have had beaux. Why did she never marry? Perhaps nobody was quite good enough. Although she seemed to have no sense of family outside ours, she was proud of her kinship with Ralph Waldo Emerson, and traced her ancestry to the English town of Bishop's Stortford.

What could she have been like as a secretary? She didn't know shorthand, and she wasn't much of a typist. But I think she had worked for a time in a bank, and she was good at figures, which generally tended to muddle my father. She kept his checkbook balanced and taught me to do the same with mine — for which I have always blessed her memory. She also kept my father's desk reasonably uncluttered, which enabled him to claim that he might not be neat but that he *was* orderly.

Helen was by no means a drinker, but she came from Bourbon country, where women as well as men are brought up to regard that kind of whiskey as the elixir of life. When drinks were going round, Helen would be asked, "How do you like it, Helen?"

"Oh, just fill it up with Bourbon, and a dash of water on top."

She would grasp the tumbler in two small hands and take a mouthful. Immediately, her eyes screwed shut behind her rimless glasses, her feet swung rapidly to and fro under her chair, she would shake her head and cry, "*Brrrr!*" Then her eyes would open wide, as if in astonishment, as she shouted, "Whew! That's enough to make a rabbit spit in a bulldog's eye!"

Would she like a little more water in her drink? No, that she wouldn't.

Helen liked to lord it over other members of the household whom she considered inferior to herself — and over all workmen from outside. She was never happier than when she had some sweating hulk of a moving man (or preferably two) to chivvy about in her glass-shattering voice.

After my mother died and my father retired from his diocese and spent long winters in Florida, he did not include Helen in his household there. At long last she began to have a life of her own. She acquired half a dozen woman friends and at least as many Princeton undergraduates, whom she delighted to feed and fuss over. Helen could never resist a helpless male — and all such "young 'uns" she considered helpless. As a family we observed this gregariousness of Helen's with a slight curl of the lip. Nobody could accuse members of the Matthews family of liking people, and we didn't really like her liking them. We had become accustomed to the fierceness and (we supposed) singleness of her devotion to us. Was Helen evolving into a different person from the one we had known and put up with all these years? These new "friends of hers" didn't seem to realize that there *was* anything to put up with!

Then my father died, and the provision in his will for Helen was, we thought, so shockingly inadequate that we clubbed together to make it better. Perhaps we overdid it a little. At any rate, Helen was transformed from an undernourished legatee to a lady of leisure. It was not that she didn't have enough to do — with her ferocious energy she was never idle — as that she had more money than she quite knew what to do with. Her affluence became more obvious when she had to give up her flat because of a monstrous increase in the rent and my brother-in-law Buzz soft-heartedly invited her to become his tenant, at a nominal rent. He must sometimes have regretted that gen-

erous impulse. Helen's prejudices were as rigid as royal
edicts: there were some things and certain people she
simply would not put up with, and some of these things
and people occasionally enjoyed the easygoing hospitality
of the Barracks, Buzz's house. Helen apparently believed
that when Buzz and Margery were away, the mice came
rushing in and staged orgies. Her disapproval of such
goings-on became so intense that she refused to speak to
some of the young habitués of the house, whom she suspected of instigating these saturnalia, nor would she
darken its door when they or their like were under the
roof.

Although she was, as she sometimes described herself,
"a bundle of nerves," Helen never shirked an encounter
nor slunk out of the race, and she prided herself on her dubious capacity to lick her weight in wildcats. All the same
she was, as I have said, really terrified of snakes. Everyone
who knew her was aware of this phobia, for she advertised
it to such an extent that it sometimes sounded almost like
boasting.

Legaré Cuyler, a nephew of Buzz's, was a merry little
devil with dancing black eyes and an affinity for mischief.
As a small boy he was what Helen called a "limb" — short
for "limb of Satan." His mother scolded him helplessly,
and helplessly adored him. One summer at Boothden, our
summer house on the Rhode Island shore, Legaré, his parents, and Helen were visiting us. On a shopping expedition
to nearby Newport, Legaré discovered and wheedled his
father into buying a toy snake, so cunningly made that it
fell naturally into very lifelike curves. Legaré made no
bones about why he wanted the snake: he wanted it to
frighten Miss Emerson. No doubt his doting mother and
father should have prevented him, but they didn't. Before
dinner that evening he stole into Helen's room and left the
snake coiled on her pillow. Then he went downstairs and
waited.

The sound he was waiting for came soon — so piercing and terrified that it was not pleasant to hear. A remorseful Legaré and his father and mother did what they could to calm Helen's sobs and soothe her subsequent anger, but I think she never altogether forgave them.

As she grew older and more affluent, Helen traveled a good deal. She seemed to be increasingly drawn to England; it may have been partly because I had settled there, but I think only partly. She was a member of the English-Speaking Union, stayed at their clubhouse in London and made forays by hired car into the countryside, including an expedition to Bishop's Stortford to look for traces of her family.

Pamela Peniakoff (who later married me) used to drive Helen down to East Anglia in her bubble car and, like the inveterate missionary to Americans that she is, would try to rouse Helen's interest in some of the historical sites and houses along the way. Helen would look up briefly, nod, and resume her impassioned chatter about the vagaries, misfortunes, and triumphs of the Matthews family. The only thing that could divert her from this all-engrossing topic was chimney pots. They and they alone could catch her attention and hold her eye. She became an addict, a chimney-pot watcher, a collector.

Helen took a great shine to Pam's mother, who lived in East Anglia, at the end of one of these bone-jarring journeys, and that lady in her cool Irish way seemed to accept Helen as an amusing apparition from overseas. On the rare occasion of a BBC broadcast by me, all three of them listened to it in Mrs. Firth's sitting room. As soon as it was over, Helen shrilled like a thousand cicadas: "I *wish* you could have heard the *Bishop!* Now *he* had a *beautiful* voice!" I don't think she was merely contrasting my father's public speaking with mine, although that was surely part of her intention; I think she was in effect trying to put the best Matthews foot forward by pointing out that, whatever *my* shortcomings, one of my family was famous for his forensic power and grace.

Helen was over eighty when she died. Her death was not the easy one she had counted on or, at least, had hoped for. She was a fighter, and she fought long past the point when it would have been better for her to give in. When the terrible struggle was over, and arrangements had to be made for her funeral, it turned out that she had left directions that her body was to be cremated and that she was not to be given a church funeral. Her instructions were duly carried out, as far as the cremation was concerned. But then her old landlord and friend, Buzz Cuyler, abetted by my nephew Peter Spackman and my son John, decided that Helen's ashes should be buried in the family plot in Princeton, in the graveyard on Witherspoon Street.

The other two accompanied Buzz to the graveyard, where it turned out that they all felt the need of some sort of ceremony before burying the canister of ashes, so they made up an impromptu funeral service. They recited the Lord's Prayer, and Buzz read Newman's prayer: "O Lord, support us all the day long until the shadows lengthen and the evening comes, and the busy world is hushed, and the fever of life is over, and our work is done. Then of thy mercy grant us a safe lodging and a holy rest and peace at the last."

When he had read this prayer and scratched a hole in the turf big enough to hold the canister of ashes, Buzz squatted down and buried it. The position reminded him naturally of gardening and of the many times when Helen had urged him to greater efforts as a gardener. As he got up, red in the face from his exertions, he gave a Buzz-like smile and said, "Well, that's the last squat Helen'll ever get out of me!"

Had she been within earshot, it's not hard to imagine what a whoop and cackle she'd have given.

°⧙ JAMES BOLAND

⌣⧙ IN THE SPRING OF 1953 I went to London to do a last job for *Time*. The consensus was that it might keep me busy for six months, so I needed a place to live. By good luck "a set of chambers" in Albany fell into my hands. In those days as in these, Albany was a very good address, besides being a delightful place to live. Originally a duke's town house, with its attendant stables, Albany lies between Piccadilly and Old Burlington Street. London's taxi drivers, unlike the illiterate and ignorant boors who guide the jalopy taxis of New York, are not licensed until they can pass an exam on the ten-thousand-odd streets in London's West End, but I was surprised at how often my taxi driver didn't know where Albany was.

Its Piccadilly entrance is a narrow alley leading into a small courtyard; the porter's lodge and the grander apartments of Albany are contained in the building that seals off this court. Beyond this lies the spine of Albany: a roofed pavement (the Rope Walk) between two facing, three-story buildings, their doorways lettered from B to L. Except for the flats at the far end, overlooking Old Burlington

Street and Savile Row, never a sound penetrates the still-
ness, though we are now in the loud-beating heart of
London. This hush at times brings out in some people an impulse
to make a noise. A friend of mine who lived in Hampstead,
which he regarded as superior to all other parts of London,
was on his way to see me and was "spoken to" by the porter
on duty at the lodge, because he was whistling. Taken
aback, he said the first thing that came into his head:
"Blackbirds whistle."
"Not in Albany they don't!"

The flat — sorry, "set of chambers" — I was to have was
K-5, halfway down the Rope Walk, on the third (British:
second) floor. It consisted of a tiny hallway (also used as a
dining room), a large, high-ceilinged living room, a large
bedroom with an enormous double bed, and bathroom with
water closet attached. The bathroom had gold taps made
to look like swans' necks and beaks; you twisted their necks
to make the water flow. The loo was old-fashioned but
grand: a flat wooden platform with a large hole over a
china pot decorated like a willow-pattern soup tureen; it
would have graced any dining table. Up a miniature stair-
case was another much smaller bathroom and a bedroom — for the servant.

This furnished fief was mine for a rent that by New
York standards was cheap, but it was a sublease that would
expire in less than a year. And there was one drawback:
there was no servant, although there should have been. My
predecessor, Prince Rospigliosi (known to his friends as
Bill), was Vatican correspondent for *Time*. He looked like
an Englishman but apparently had an Italian temper and
for some reason, shortly before I took over his lease, had
fired the maid who came with the flat. So I badly needed
someone to cook and clean for me. I applied to a helpful
firm called Universal Aunts. Expensive (you had to pay

by the hour) but prompt: next day a girl arrived and set about dusting and sweeping. She also talked — while smoking; a lighted cigarette always dangled from the side of her mouth. I learned that she was writing a novel. I wondered whether I should rise when she came into the room. This was not what I wanted. After two days, I telephoned Universal Aunts and canceled her.

Next day, as I was going out past the porter's lodge (the porters at Albany wore livery, including top hats) the head porter, Mercer, said that he understood I was looking for a servant. Yes, I said, and asked him if he knew of anyone. He said yes, he did.

"Can you recommend him?" said I.

"No sir," said Mercer. "I can guarantee him."

This Mercer was a fine, upstanding, reddish man, a sergeant-major type whom at sight I would have trusted with my life. So of course I said to send the man along. Next day he appeared: a smallish, nondescript Scot named James Boland, with a pronounced burr but an anonymous face, a kind of unobtrusive Alec Guinness type. Trying to be businesslike, I asked him for references. With a look of pain, he said he could, if necessary, produce them, but that he had had only three jobs in his life and was not accustomed to flitting about. I decided that references were unnecessary and engaged him.

In the two and a half years we were together, James and I never ceased from mental strife, nor did our swords sleep in our hands. Not that there was any open disagreement; but even as Jeeves bent Bertie Wooster to his will, so James tried to bend me. The difference between us and a Wodehouse story was that, on balance, neither of us gave an inch.

It started with morning tea. James asked me if I required it. I said no. The very first morning, when I was only half conscious, there it was. I found it easier to let the daily rite continue than to lock horns with James over a small matter that I (wrongly) presumed was also minor. So I suppose you might say that James won that one. Then there was the toothpaste. I used Crest, not only because I liked it and believed in it, but out of family loyalty: it was a Procter & Gamble product. James was not openly anti-American — one of the most cryptic people I have ever known, he was not open about anything — but I soon discovered that the only artifacts of any sort that he approved of were invariably British. The toothpaste *he* believed in was McLean's, and a tube of McLean's duly appeared beside my wash basin, the cap suggestively removed. My tube of Crest was not exactly hidden but was partly concealed by the shaving mirror. I never touched the McLean's, and after a time the cap was replaced. James never, however, removed his candidate. I consider that I won that one.

There was a large gray area, a no man's land, in which most of our skirmishing took place. It would be hard to say who won these ignorant clashes, or even whether they were always actual engagements. The London *Times* (but to James, who recognized no other *Times* but this, it was simply the *Times*) was, in James's unyielding code, the only possible newspaper for a gentleman to read. When he discovered that my favorite paper was the *Manchester Guardian* (utterly beyond the pale, in James's book) he arranged with the newsagent in Old Burlington Street — whose name, believe it or not, was Mrs. Napoleon — to deliver the *Times* as well, with the *Guardian* so wrapped up in it that no prying eye could spy it. That round was James's. And when it came to shops, he knew so much more than I did that it was no contest.

James knew everything there was to know about men's furnishings and where to go for them, so when I wanted shirts I went to the shirt-maker he sent me to; the same for shoes. And I would be the last to deny that on occasion he could be extremely useful. There was, for instance, the

party I gave for the Cambridge boat. In the Oxford-Cam-
bridge boat race that year, Cambridge was generally
thought to be outclassed. I hoped that was so; I always
wanted Oxford to win. But the young Harvard man who
rowed number 6 in the Cambridge boat, Louis McCagg,
was engaged to the daughter of an old friend of mine. I
thought it would be a nice gesture to give the Cambridge
crew a consolation party the day after the race. So I invited
them; they accepted, asking if they might bring their
"poppies" (current undergraduate slang for girls).

James and I were going over plans for the party. He had
been horrified to discover that I was thinking of having
Fortnum & Mason do the catering; he said he could do it
much cheaper himself, and just as well or better. When we
had gone over the lists, James gave a deprecating cough
and remarked, "You know, sir, it might not be a bad idea
to invite Captain Adams."

"James," I said with conviction, "you're a genius!"

Captain Adams was the little pussycat who was then
secretary of Albany. He was a mincing snob and disliked
women; I don't know how he felt about Americans, but he
had told me, without evincing much sympathy, that when
my sublease on K-5 ran out, nothing further was to be had.
James knew all this. I took his suggestion and invited Captain Adams.

The party turned out to be a victory party, not a consolation, and was a great success. The Cambridge oarsmen
were all bright-eyed and good-looking; Louis McCagg was
for the moment the hero of England, and his fiancée,
Cathy, and the other poppies were as pretty as popular
pictures. Captain Adams enjoyed himself and must have
been favorably impressed. Next day I got a note from him,
thanking me for the delightful party, and adding: "By the
way, I understand you are looking for another set of chambers. It so happens . . ."

G-2 was something of a comedown from K-5. Instead of

being in the middle of the Rope Walk it was at the far end, overlooking Savile Row, and the noise of traffic was obtrusive and almost incessant. It was also one floor higher, which meant more of a climb. And it was listed as "war-damaged," which somehow meant that Margaret Leighton, the actress, had swiped James's bathroom, or the space where James's bathroom should have been. I offered to let him use mine, but that horrified him. I don't know how he managed, but he did.

Mercer's guarantee of James must have applied solely to his professional character, and I found no reason to disagree; but his personal habits seemed to me less satisfactory. He was not only stubborn as hell (morning tea, toothpaste), but as a cook he was a dyed-in-the-wool conservative: his school of cooking was brutal British. One word was sufficient to describe James's cuisine: fried. And although I never actually saw him drunk, I was sure he drank like a fish. He was often green in the face from hangover when he brought my breakfast, and for that wild Scottish courage I gave him credit. I suspected but wasn't sure that, as a cleaner, he tended to sweep everything under the carpet. But he was always impeccably dressed and did his damnedest to see that I was too.

I remember one evening when I was going to a white tie dinner. I didn't possess a white tie, and my tail coat, if I'd still had it, would have been much too tight for me. I went to Moss Bros. and rented the whole outfit. It should have been James's night off, but I was worried about my tie and asked him to stay and see me off. Just as I was leaving, he said, "Don't you worry, sir; everybody there will be from Moss Bros."

James did not like to work with women; as for working *for* a woman, he simply wouldn't do it. Our partnership lasted, as I've said, two and a half years. The thing that ended it was my getting married. James inspected the house we were to live in and seemed to admit that it was "a good address"; it was carefully explained to him that the cook and two other maids would be under his authority (or at least of lesser rank). My wife and I both thought that James was reconciled to the change.

A Christmas party I gave in G-2 encouraged our misunderstanding of James's intentions. There were six of us, including a very small boy (the adopted son of the lady I was marrying). James cooked the dinner and served it. As he left the little dining room to fetch the coffee, there was a tremendous crash. I went out to see what had happened and found James, smiling happily (he had certainly been at the bottle), and picking up fragments of china.

"Trod on a toy and went flying!" he said.

Shortly before the move into the Chester Square house, James told me he had taken on a half-time job elsewhere. This didn't so much take me by surprise as shock me. I told James he should have consulted me before taking such a step, and told him he'd better make his new job full time, as he wouldn't be working for me any more.

We parted with little warmth, and I never saw him again, though some years later I got a request from him (at second hand) for some information he needed for a document connected with his work record. Did we miss each other? No. Did he like me? I doubt it. Was I fond of him? A *little*.

❄FLORENCE BATES

SHE WAS A SMALL, PLODDING WOMAN with a stare. The stare didn't so much illumine the track ahead as signal that she was close behind. When she laughed, she sounded surprised and not really convinced; her laugh was more applause ("Well, what do you know!") than amusement. She laughed frequently, but only at TV comedies or in reply to something that seemed to call for a defensive noise. I don't think she thought anything was really funny but that some things, beyond human understanding, were only worth a hoot. Anyhow, that was all she had for them.

Her name was Florence Bates. Everyone called her Flo. She lived with another old spinster, Phillips, in the Old Lodge at the gate of Cavendish Hall and was our "daily." Phillips was older and gentler than Flo, and a bit shaky. They had worked all their lives for Mrs. Brocklebank, the fussy and formidable lady who had lived at the Hall before us.

Flo loved animals. A great many people in the British Isles *like* animals, but not nearly so many really love them (or why does the RSPCA exist?). The ones who get on best

with animals are those who hardly seem to notice them
and treat them like barely tolerated slaves. Flo was not of
that sort. She simply brimmed with love for any animal
she saw. She never encountered a tiger or an elephant in
the lanes or fields of Suffolk, but if she had, she would have
hugged it, or tried to.

She was constantly talking to the creatures she encountered or who tagged along with her. She talked to them on
their level, in a crooning mixture of endearments, chiding,
and passing-the-time-of-day. She was always well supplied
with chocolate drops, which she passed out with a lavish
hand, like a Tammany boss giving his ward heelers a little
something extra.

In the old days, when Phillips was still alive, they took
adoring care of their mistress's Yorkshire terriers, an aged,
wheezing, imperious couple who behaved like crowned
tyrants. You could view their royal progress every morning, early: two elderly women in Wellingtons, one pushing
a carpet-lined wheelbarrow in which sat the two small
dogs, the other humble human attendant trudging alongside. When taxed with pampering their charges and scout-
ing the whole point of a morning walk, they would explain
that the ride in the wheelbarrow was a temporary fraction
of the walk (it wasn't), the object being solely to keep the
royal paws dry and free of mud.

For their annual holiday, invariably spent in Scotland,
Flo and Phillips hired a taxi to take them there and back,
asserting that it was almost as cheap as going by rail and
that it gave the little dogs, seated beside the driver, a better
view of the countryside.

Then old Mrs. Brocklebank died, grudgingly followed
by the aged terriers. Now only one dog was left in the Old
Lodge, a wheezing King Charles spaniel, Flo's own. When
this last survivor died, Flo could not be comforted. My
wife, Pam, who has a sharp eye for helping people, saw an

ad in the local paper about two King Charles puppies for sale. The woman who owned them lived some sixty miles away, and by the time we got there one of the puppies had been sold. Never mind; we took the remaining one and headed for the Old Lodge. When we got there, Pam, for wily woman's reasons, sent me in with the puppy. Flo was not in a receptive mood; she growled that she never wanted another dog as long as she lived, and refused even to look at this one. Just then the puppy stretched its neck and licked her nose. That did it.

Flo named this little creature Sharnell (a spondee). When we discovered that she spelled the name Charnell, we inferred some misspelled reference to Coco Chanel, though we couldn't see the connection. Not at all; Flo knew exactly what she meant: Charles II and Nell Gwynn.

When Charnell got her growth, she revealed a striking resemblance to another celebrity, the dog in the Muppets TV show who plays the piano *molto con brio*. Flo saw this likeness herself and was rather proud of it. But there was really not much *brio* in Charnell's nature; as she grew older, she became more and more like an asthmatic spinster, and the coddling she got from Flo did not tend to ennoble her or give her backbone. She seemed a housebound kind of dog. Only two things roused her to something approaching alacrity — the prospect of a Good Boy (chocolate drop) or the invigorating sight of a cat, which immediately sent her into hot pursuit.

The cosseting Flo lavished on Charnell was almost beyond belief. After she had been taken for a walk or had had a bath or simply when Flo considered that she might find the night air chilly, she was wrapped tenderly in a blanket, seated in the most comfortable chair in the room, and placed where she could get the best view of the telly. On occasion, and when Flo felt she had cause, she would speak harshly to Charnell or even go through the motions of slapping her; these moments were as rare as they were dreadful.

On her daily trudges up to the Hall (four or five a day: the first about seven-thirty and the last well after dark), she was apt to address any animal she might see, and often went out of her way to give pieces of bread to the donkeys or a piece of her mind to a marauding squirrel. In the days before Pushkin, our new cat, came in from the cold and was living rough outdoors, hunting field mice and small birds and being chased by our dogs whenever he came in view, Flo would bring him a saucer of milk every afternoon, and rigged up a protective shield (two panels of wire fence) for the burrow by the haystack where he slept. When they heard her cough as she opened the back door, the little dogs in the Hall came alive for the day and crowded around her, rejoicing, leaping up to lick her hand.

Flo seemed to eat nothing herself, but she went on the assumption that all animals and most people are hungry most of the time and always ready to be fed. She had been the cook at the Hall in Mrs. Brocklebank's day, and her sandwiches, cakes, and puddings were justly famous. An invitation to tea at Flo's was a bidding to a feast.

She was not a native of Suffolk, and that may have been why, although she was neither a recluse nor unneighborly, she had so few human friends. I never heard of her going to anyone else's house for tea, and only two or three elderly women were ever invited to hers. She never went to church or attended a meeting of the Women's Institute or the Conservative Association; she stayed away from meets of the Puckeridge and Thurlow hunt and from the village ceremony on Remembrance Day. If she had any politics, they were so private as to be invisible, and I would be surprised to learn that she ever voted.

But she lived in the world, and she had enemies. Two, to be exact — and they were her nearest neighbors. Let's call them the Salteenas (if Daisy Ashford wouldn't mind). Who began this enmity? Alas, it may have been Flo. But the root of the trouble went all the way back to Mrs. Brocklebank. One of the kindest words that could be applied to that high-handed lady would be *frugal*. Instead of leaving annuities or a cash settlement for her faithful domestics, she gave her butler a cottage (with the title deeds) and left the Old Lodge to Phillips and Flo for their lifetime — but without a scrap of paper to prove that she had. More and worse: some time before she died, Mrs. Brocklebank had "sold" to Mr. Salteena, for a trifling sum, the title to the Old Lodge, so he was now the unfriendly owner. A thunderous situation.

Phillips, who resembled a benignly ugly duchess, was wiser in the ways of the world than Flo; she saw trouble ahead and even foresaw what form it would take. She feared Flo's temper and mistrusted Mr. Salteena's. Phillips hoped that as long as she was alive she might be able to keep the peace, but she was grimly certain that once she was gone Mr. Salteena would find some excuse to evict Flo. And sure enough, that's what happened — or began to happen — shortly after Phillips' death.

There was a row between Flo and the Salteenas. Flo was "pert": she had small respect for either of them and said something she shouldn't have. Mr. Salteena flew into a rage and swore he'd evict Flo. Flo was scared but didn't apologize, and vowed that she'd never do a lick of work for him again. At Pam's behest I wrote him, reminding him that the power was all on his side and urging him to hold his hand. I also offered to buy the Old Lodge. His only answer was "Mind your own business!" and we stopped speaking.

The terms of the truce imposed by the Salteenas were humiliating to Flo and calculated to ruin her: a fence — really a wooden wall — put up between the Old Lodge and the Salteenas' house, and she would have to pay for it. (She couldn't, so we did.) The wooden wall was duly built, and the Cavendish war went rumbling on. As the months went by, a ground swell of disapproval of Mr. Salteena began to gather in the village.

I had no idea of the force of this ground swell until one fine day Mr. Salteena unexpectedly capitulated. I had a note from him saying, in effect, "All right, you've won; I quit." (If push had come to shove, he would have had to appear in court and be cross-examined by a lawyer. The pro-Flo, anti-Salteena party would have made sure of that.) "I can't have my darling Fluff's [Mrs. Brockle-bank's] name bandied about in public. I'll not only sell you the Old Lodge [at a figure about two hundred percent higher than he'd paid for it], but my own house as well, and move away. But if you don't accept my price with no bargaining, I'll sell to someone else."

I didn't want his damn house, but what else could I do? I borrowed the money and bought the house, the Salteenas pulled up stakes and went to the West Country, and we never saw them again.

Flo never breathed a word of thanks for what we had done. But every day and all day long she laid down her life to thank us. I have never seen anybody work so hard or so devotedly as she did. Her working day began before dawn and went on long after the sun had set. She never took a day off. The last summer of her life, when we real-ized that she hadn't had a holiday in years, we bullied and coaxed her into going to the seaside in Devon for a fort-night. We had to make the arrangements, as she stub-bornly resisted the whole idea. We rented the only house in Salcombe whose owner allowed dogs, paid the rent in advance, and arranged to have Flo and Charnell driven there by a friend of ours who would stay with her to keep an eye on her health.

Pam and I went to America that summer, and I stayed on for a month after she went home. Before we left for America, Flo taught me an extremely useful way of finding lost objects. (Up till then I had spent hours every day looking for things I had hidden from myself — usually pieces of paper.) I had lost a list of things I meant to pack and complained about it to Flo, who looked at me quizzically and said, "Perhaps you packed it?"

"Flo!" I cried. "You should be the head of the detective bureau! Of course I packed it!" And I knew exactly where: in my black dispatch case, right on top. And there, sure enough, it was. Since then, instead of *looking*, I stop and think, "What would Flo say?" And usually she tells me.

Flo never got her holiday. Pam's letters to me cover the rest of the story:

"Aug. 17 — I didn't tell you before we left, for if things turned out to be OK, there seemed no point in giving you worry. But the day we left Flo went in for an X-ray. Last week she was summoned to see the specialist, and he wants her in hospital — mentioned something about pleurisy to her. I rang Dr. O'Brien, who says she has shadows on her lung X-rays, so they are going to do a complete scan. He isn't very merry about it. She looks rotten, worse than when we left, and is in pain, which painkillers are helping to control. She is very upset, though she doesn't know about the X-ray evidence. Hates leaving her dogs and hopes to be away for only a few days. I take her in tomorrow morning.

"Aug. 27 — Fetched Flo from hospital yesterday, looking dreadful. The nurses at the hospital were so casual. When I asked if they had given her a supply of painkillers, they said with surprise, 'Hasn't she got some?' All she has is Disprin. I can't think she can live for long. In the ten days she has been away she has deteriorated. The liver is obviously far gone, and she looks like a severe case of jaundice. Thank God all our visitors have left.

"*Sept.* 1 — She is weakening very rapidly, and each morning when I see her I am shocked by the deterioration in the short space of seven or eight hours. Dr. O'Brien has just been in and says it's a matter of days. Tonight the district nurse is going to come and give her an injection, which the doctor promises will give her a good night's rest. She is very breathless due to liquid on her lungs. Flo is all eyes. Everything around them has fallen and melted away. It will be wonderful if she does die soon. She is quite bewildered by the sickness, illness, and pain she is experiencing. It's a blessing, if such a word can be used about someone in her state, that her illness is so far advanced that she will not be subjected to radium or other miserable treatments.

"I telephoned last night to cancel Flo's holiday. I didn't do it before, as it seemed underhand and mean to do such a thing behind her back. However, she brought up the subject herself with Dr. O'Brien, who told her it wasn't possible. She said she had agreed to go only because you were so keen about her having a break and had worked so hard to make the arrangements, but now that she couldn't go, she was longing to. It's just too bitter. And one can hardly bear to think of how she drove herself while we were away. She must already have been feeling wretched, but nothing could stop her. The downstairs of the house was spring-cleaned from floor to ceilings, including the top of the pelmets. We will never have anyone so spikily loving and loyal again.

"The district nurse asked Flo if she wanted a bath. 'No thank you!' snapped Flo. This was the day before she died. After the nurse had gone, Flo asked Mary to run her a bath. She had decided to have one — 'in case.' Mary did as she was asked and offered to help Flo from her bedroom to the bathroom. 'I can manage, thank you!' And she did, by hanging on to chair backs, door jambs, and any bit of handy furniture on the way. She refused to let Mary help her undress, which took her ages. But eventually she got her nightgown and vest off and somehow made it into the bath, where she painstakingly washed herself from top to toe. (Mary was outside the door, watching through a chink.) But when she tried to get out of the tub, it was too much for her. Mary gave her several minutes and then sang out from the kitchen, 'Do you want a hand?' and Flo said, 'Yes, please, Mary,' quite dispassionately and firmly, and allowed herself to be heaved up and dried. Later I saw her back in bed and said, 'What a pretty nightgown!'

" 'Yes, it's my favorite,' said Flo.

"*Sept. 8* — Your postcard to Flo got to her the day she died and she took it in when it was read to her. Although she could hardly speak, and seemed half asleep, her mind was alert and she understood everything. Dr. O'Brien came in to give her a painkilling injection, and she told him she was much better today. Defiant to the end.

"I'm thankful she didn't linger on, fighting for every breath. Her will asked that on her death Charnell should be painlessly destroyed. Luckily, a few days ago, I told her how well Charnell adapted to being with us, ate and slept well, and loved the walks. She said, 'Oh, I *am* glad. Because I left instructions that if anything happened to me, she is to be put down. But now I know she's all right, it won't be necessary.' "

She stood about five foot one and she wasn't strong, but she'd tackle anything. I never heard her say thank you. She never mentioned God or ever went to church, but she was a saint with an imp inside — something like St. Francis and Xantippe grappling in the same person, with St. Francis predominant — sometimes just barely.

I CLASSMATES AND OLD MASTERS

CLASSMATES AND OLD MASTERS

⌒◁ SHATTUCK, THE MILITARY SCHOOL in Minnesota that I entered as the youngest cadet and where I stayed for two years (1913 to 1915), could be rated only second class at best, and in some ways was not much better than a reformatory. I loved it. St. Paul's, in Concord, New Hampshire, supposedly the best school in America (sometimes compared with Eton), where I was doomed to go because it was my father's old school, I hated for most of the two and a half years I was there. Yet at Shattuck I made only one lifelong friend; at St. Paul's, several. More, of course, at Princeton.

o   o   o

"Pa" Dole had been on the staff at St. Paul's in my father's day. He was a worried-looking man with reddish blotches on his face, who held himself erect and seemed ageless, but he must have been well along. In his prime he had been a games master and gym instructor, and he still gave new boys their physical examination. My almost imperceptible chest expansion and my small size distressed him.

⟦107

Often he forgot my name and called me by my father's. "Paul," he would say — or sometimes, looking more worried than usual, "Dear Paul" — and then impart useful rules of thumb for growing taller and stronger. After my shower, he told me, I should always dry myself hard and rub the towel *up* my legs and *up* my arms "to get the blood flowing toward the heart." And he implored me to *stretch* when I first got up in the morning: raising my arms and stretching up as far as I could go. "That's the way to get your growth."

o   o   o

"Stiffy" Howard taught Greek and looked like the bust of Homer, except that he wasn't blind and had a moustache instead of a beard. He was a large, bullocky man, kindly but distant, and moved with the majesty befitting a housemaster; he presided over an echoing, barrackslike building called the School, which housed most of the third and fourth forms. Mr. Howard's tongue crowded his mouth; this gave his deep voice a dignified thickness. He would occasionally pause in midsentence and go through a convulsive series of hawking, throat-clearing, and swallowing sounds. The phenomenon was known as "Stiffy hocking an oyster through his nose."

At meals in the School dining room he sat at one end of the long head table, on a dais a step above the rest of the room. The liveliest and most popular boys were given seats at Mr. Howard's end. On Saturday nights he conducted prayers in the library, a room more ponderously Victorian-Gothic than any other in the building, and never used for any other purpose. Mr. Howard read a few collects from the Prayer Book and we sang the "Saturday night hymn," one of the gloomiest memories of my youth, which for some reason we always began at the second verse.

My days unclouded as they pass
And every onward rolling hour
Are monuments of wondrous grace
And witness to Thy love and power.

The invariable Saturday night fare was baked beans and
Boston brown bread.

o   o   o

"Gurga" Knox presided over the other, less desirable end
of the head table in the School dining room. I never knew
what Gurga's nickname meant; it may have had something to do with his belching. He was an old man, somewhere in his seventies, with a yellowish-white beard,
rheumy eyes, and a sardonic habit of speech. No one liked
to sit next to him because of his sarcasm and his bad breath.

He had taught Latin and Greek but was now retired. I
suppose he was still at the school because he had nowhere
else to go; in those days superannuated masters were not
always forced to leave. A debonair boy named Ross Smith
was once showing a girl around the school; he pointed out
the old man shuffling across the grounds. "That's Gurga
Knox," he said. "You can do the giant's stride on his
breath."

CHANLER CHAPMAN

HE WAS THE MODEL (or, more accurately, the armature) for the "hero" of the funniest if not the best novel Saul Bellow has written: *Henderson the Rain King*. Bellow's Henderson was not a finished portrait of Chanler Chapman, but he was a recognizable likeness. While Bellow was Chapman's tenant for a year or so at Barrytown on the Hudson, in a small house on the big place Chanler's father had left him, he must have taken some good long looks at Chapman; I doubt if Chapman had bothered to look nearly so hard at Bellow. As a dedicated egocentric, he didn't notice other people much: his whole life was devoted to feeding his hungry persona. Henderson's cry was the same as his: "I want! I want! I want!" Chapman must have known about the book and heard that the chief character was modeled on him, but when he was asked by a friend if he had read it, he replied, "Never read that trash."

I first knew him as a schoolboy at St. Paul's. His term there was lengthy and troubled; mine was comparatively brief but perhaps no happier. So it was natural that we should notice one another, and we became friends, like two lifers in Sing Sing. He was in the form below mine but already a scarred school veteran when I first met him. Later he wrote an engaging and candid book about his schooldays (the only book of his, I think, that was ever published), called *The Wrong Attitude*. I can vouch for the truthfulness of his account, and especially for one central episode in it, for I was an appalled and fascinated eyewitness.

Chapman badly wanted a motorbike, and that cost a lot of money, which his father refused to give him. He thereupon determined to raise the money himself. His reading of history and of his own experience had convinced him that most people will willingly pay to watch a brutal and degrading spectacle. He decided to offer one: himself in a fight to the finish against a skilled boxer. Chapman had never boxed in his life. A public assassination. The event should be a sellout. He picked as his opponent a cool and cruel middleweight, reputed to be the best boxer in school, sold as many tickets as he could at fifty cents apiece, and advertised the coming entertainment by quiet, wildfire word of mouth — next Sunday after chapel, in the Gym.

It was a brutal spectacle, sure enough. And bloody. From the first round, when Chanler charged out of his corner, bellowing and flailing his arms, his opponent feinted, jabbed, feinted, punched, and made a gory mess of him. The fight lasted seven rounds, as Chanler remembers it. (I would have said three.) In the last round his nose was broken and he was knocked unconscious. It was quite a show.

So noisy and well attended an event was bound to come to the attention of the Rector. He summoned Chapman, pried the facts out of him, and told him he must disgorge the money he had fought and bled for. But only a few were soulless enough to accept a refund, so Chanler cleared more than a hundred dollars (nowhere near enough to buy his motorbike). He was also dishonorably discharged from the school battalion for going absent without leave. In order to give his customers value for money, he had skipped two days of drill and gone running in the woods, with the notion of getting himself in better fighting shape.

In a school famous for its prowess in ice hockey, both Chanler and I were outstanding disgraces. In those days St. Paul's played no outside games except in ice hockey — and those only against college freshman teams. In all other sports the games were entirely intramural, among three clubs: Delphians, Isthmians, and Old Hundreds. In my sixth-form year I played on the 10th (and lowest) Old Hundred hockey team: the fact that I was appointed captain only underlined my infamy.

Chapman, an even more hopeless hockey player than I, if that were possible, was captain of the 10th Delphians. He could hardly stand up on skates, and either misunderstood or completely disregarded the theory and practice of ice hockey as a game. His idea of his role was to seek and destroy: to encounter the opposing captain in the center of the rink and there to fight it out with hockey sticks or anything that came handy. I remember his sidling, crablike, along the high boards of the rink, shouting at me to come out and fight, and brandishing his hockey stick like a battleaxe. His conversation even in those days was of an unequaled gusto; original, explosive, and unexpected, it seemed to most of his schoolmates as wild and senseless as it was forceful. Groping in vain for a nickname to fit him, they hit on one that was derisive yet grudgingly admiring: Charlie Chaplin.

Chapman inherited his heated temperament from his father, John Jay Chapman, who had a reputation in his day as a classical scholar, littérateur, and social gadfly, and who knew most of the celebrities of his time and admired very few of them. In our own day Edmund Wilson wrote of him with respect. One of the sensational tales that clung to him was known to us at St. Paul's: that once, having in a passion struck one of his dearest friends, Mr. Chapman had followed the classic example of Mucius Scaevola, thrusting his offending hand in the fire and holding it there until it was burned off. When Mr. Chapman next visited the school and Chanler took me to breakfast with him, in spite of my best efforts to see what this terrifying man was hiding up his sleeve (and which sleeve?), I failed to discover whether he had an artificial hand or the charred stump I hoped and feared to see.

The Chapmans were an old American family, related to other families equally prestigious. To my Midwestern eyes, however, they didn't look American at all, but Italian. Chanler was swarthy and black-haired; he sweated profusely and often; and grimaces and explosions chased each other across his face. Even in his calmer moods, his brow wrinkled and his lips writhed. I particularly remember him in chapel at Evensong, his eyes closed, an ecstatic smile on his face, his lips murmuring the words of hymn or anthem, drunk not only with surreptitious sherry smuggled from Concord but with the sound of the familiar music.

After his five-year struggle through St. Paul's, like all his family Chapman went on to Harvard. Whether or not he got his degree there, I don't know and don't suppose it mattered much to him. Our paths didn't cross again for some years. In New York, where I was beginning to break into journalism and he wanted to do the same, I remember two scenes, one dim, one clear.

The dim memory is of running into him on a midtown street. He had two girls in tow, both of them, he said, unemployed harpists. They were young and rather pretty. He pointed out that, though they had both been out of work for some time, their fingertips (feel them!) were still cal-

loused. I think I took them all into the Coffee House Club
for a drink and found the bar wasn't open. Chanler looked
wistfully around, saying that his father had been a charter
member but that he himself had been blackballed — I suppose because his behavior was unpredictable and alarming.

The clearer memory is of a dinner party at the Chapmans' in New York. His wife, Olivia, was a James from
Boston, who seemed (though perhaps she wasn't) as proper
and cool a character as Chanler was volcanic. This must
have been in the late forties, for Chanler was home from
the wars. He had not waited for the United States to be
pushed into action by Pearl Harbor but had straightway
taken up arms for de Gaulle and the Free French. His first
foray had been to liberate (singlehanded, I believe) the
tiny islands of St. Pierre and Miquelon, off the coast of
Newfoundland. He might very nearly have brought it off.
The natives were much closer to independent-minded
Québec than to cowed Vichy France; Chapman spoke fluent
French, was a born rabblerouser, and might have bellowed
the sparks of local patriotism into a blaze. At the last moment, however, the U.S. State Department, which was then
cozying up to the Vichy government, withdrew its tacit
support, and the scheme was shelved.

This adventure having fizzled, Chapman decided to enlist in the Free French army, if he could find it, and went
to look for it in Africa and points east. He sailed from
Boston on a freighter, in a convoy that foolhardily split up
when it reached the Caribbean. The U-boat wolf pack that
had been shadowing the convoy from the start then tor-
pedoed the unprotected ships at will. When Chapman's
ship went down, he found himself in a lifeboat heading for
the coast of South America. For the next ten days, on short
rations and very little water, they rowed and drifted south.
Chapman volunteered for the most unpopular job in the
boat — steering from dusk to dawn — because in effect

that gave him the boat to himself: he could sing all the hymns and songs he knew at the top of his voice, curse the waves, and defy the elements without fear of being interrupted. When at last they made their landfall on the coast of British Guiana, he wrote to his wife: "Dearest Olivia, I never had a better time in all my life . . ." For some reason he sent me a copy of this letter. I passed it on to *Life*, which was then being edited by another old St. Paul's boy. *Life* published it and sent Chapman a handsome check.

As a husband, Chapman went his own gait, but Olivia was not the kind of wife who would obediently fall into step. On one of his reappearances, Chapman found he had been relegated to a small room in the attic. He must have told me this himself, no doubt roaring with laughter. On this evening, which I remember so clearly, all was apparently serene — the dinner good, the company congenial. Perhaps Chapman considered that he was not getting his share of attention. At any rate, he disappeared for a few minutes and came back with a carpenter's nail, at least six inches long. He said he would show us a trick he had learned in a bar in the Far East, when he was with the Free French. He thereupon began to push the nail through his cheek (at this point the women began, gratifyingly, to scream) and then, with strenuous grimaces, through the other cheek. He then pulled the nail out, leaving two bloody holes. The women were now all screaming in unison. Chapman seemed well pleased with the effect of his "trick."

I suppose there were other such incidents. Not unsurprisingly, Olivia at length divorced him. He married again, this time a journalist named Helen, and retired to his family estate on the Hudson. He started a monthly paper, the *Barrytown Explorer*, and sent me a sample copy. It was very like him: loud, self-centered, opinionated, and (in small doses) entertaining. The motto of the paper was

"When you can't smile, quit!" Chanler wrote a monthly column or *Spiel*, and the last page always featured a drawing of two spotted dogs, the mouthpiece for schoolboy jokes in the form of appalling puns. He frequently included sonnets by himself, long on platitude and sometimes collapsing into doggerel. I can't imagine that the *Explorer* ever broke even, but it may not have cost him more than he could afford.

Helen managed to keep the *Explorer* from capsizing while she was aboard. But she died, and after her death Chanler and the *Explorer*, both incurable amateurs, slowly foundered. He married once more, a brief and quarrelsome alliance with an elderly psychiatrist. His final years were increasingly muddy and dark, and it was evident that he took small pleasure in them. But at last he was letter-perfect in his bombastic curmudgeon's role, however little satisfaction he may have got from playing it. At the outdoor wedding of a friend's daughter, where the ceremony was simple, moving, and culminated in a lengthy silence, the celebrant standing with bowed head, the hush was shattered by Chapman's hoarse cry: "Jesus Christ, the son of a bitch has croaked!"

It was a Frenchman who, after meeting Chapman at Barrytown, summed him up in a sentence: "That is a storm of a man." When the sun was out in his private heaven, Chapman could be charming and absurdly funny; he reminded one Englishwoman of an eccentric duke. He was equally at home on blasted heaths with the thunder cracking. Then you heard him at his rodomontadinous best, growling the soliloquies of Lear or shouting his own spur-of-the-moment diatribes. At its best, his speech was like lava: implacable, fluent, and searing. He loved to read aloud, with gusto. When he read "The Ancient Mariner" (entire), his audience was captivated.

Of his three sons, the two by his first marriage, Jay and

Robert, went warily in his presence; Victor, his favorite son, was like his father but much quieter, gentle, and exceptionally intelligent. He and his father were very close, although neither of them could bear that proximity for long. At Chapman's funeral, Victor spoke a tribute to his father; the other two would not — one of them declaring that he could not say anything good of his father and would therefore say nothing.

Chanler's nature was warm to the point of fury but was also capable of affection, and he roused great devotion in others. He once drove fifteen miles to a friend's house to give his four-year-old son a silver dollar wrapped in a handkerchief. He whirled in, presented the silver dollar to the small boy, saying, "Four's a good age, God bless you!" and blew out again.

In *Henderson the Rain King* Bellow makes his Chapman character more incoherent than he actually was, but does not exaggerate the force of his desires. He wanted everything and he wanted it now. Chanler was also an aristocrat, and his *noblesse* obliged him to treat all commoners alike. At his New York club, the Knickerbocker (much grander and more stylish than the Coffee House ever dreamed of being), he was on familiar terms with the club servants. In Barrytown he was a farmer among farmers. And when his oldest son, after graduating from Harvard, went to Puerto Rico, became a postman in San Juan, and married a black woman (considered by one of his friends to be the only altogether sane member of his family), Chapman rejoiced in his black grandchildren and visited them often. He loved music and wrote about it with love.

Brave and obtuse as a lion, he led a thwarted and unhappy life but was too insensitive to notice. The only form of writing that he practiced with any constancy was the sonnet. Drunk and sober, he wrote so many sonnets that he developed a glib facility but did sometimes hit off a line or a couplet that rang like an unexpected gong. In general, however, he appeased his small appetite for matters of the mind by quoting and rereading the same books he read and reread all his life. Never stopping to think or to ponder, his inflated ego kept him afloat long after he had ceased to be seaworthy. He feared and failed to understand his father, even as his sons feared and failed to understand him.

Alas, poor Chanler.

HIRAM HAMILTON HACKNEY

⤳❬ WHAT SORT OF PARENTS would saddle a name like that on a defenseless infant? Formidable, you say. Yes, they were formidable. I remember seeing them only once and thinking that they *couldn't* have been as severe as they looked. They were rich and rigid Presbyterians. Mrs. Hackney was a Hogg, of Texas, and the Hoggs were said to have inflicted even more outrageous names on two daughters — Ima and Ura.

The Hackneys were formidable in more than their ominous humor, if humor it was. They were fearsome parents, and their two sons, even after they were grown up and married, continued to hold them in awe. When the elder Hackneys came on a visit, all ashtrays in the house were hidden and smoking stopped. They did not approve of smoking; they were also against ginger ale, because it might lead on to champagne.

Both the Hackney boys went to St. Paul's, and each in turn was nicknamed "Monk." But Hiram, who was in my form, was the one it stuck to. Both brothers had mournful, long-upper-lipped Irish faces, and freckles and sandy hair.

⟦119

Everyone liked Monk Hackney; nobody could help liking him. He had an explosive sense of fun, but he was a gentle person, kindness itself, and he himself liked nearly everybody. The few people he didn't like generally amused him, so he got some fun out of them anyhow. He was sentimental about people but not about facts. When I once made the fatuous remark that oysters make the heart grow fonder, Monk corrected me: "No, no. They put lead in your pencil."

He loved St. Paul's and was distressed that I didn't. He was always trying to convert my antipathies, which he couldn't understand or really believe in. The same process continued when we got to Princeton, where he was even more popular, and where I found as much or more to be antipathetic to. Ours was the last class, I think, to be subjected to the "flour picture," a traditional indignity inflicted on the freshman class, dating back to the golden nineties. Immediately after the freshmen held their first class meeting, to elect their president and other officers, they grouped themselves on the steps of a neo-Greek temple that housed one of the two debating societies. The sophomores, who were waiting for them, bombarded them at point-blank range with rotten eggs, vegetables, flour, and water, and after all this ammunition had been expended their picture was taken by the official Princeton photographer.

Shortly after this mock massacre I encountered Monk in one of the washrooms of our dormitory, peering at his egg-streaked face in the mirror and laughing quietly to himself.

"Caught an egg in the ear," he said. "Like to laid me cold."

At times Monk affected a certain swagger and the side-of-the-mouth tough talk that went with it, but this fooled nobody. Much more characteristic of him was his ambition to learn how to spit through his teeth (he never did learn) and to pronounce the name of his old school properly — *Sunt* Paul's, not *Saint* Paul's (he never got that right either).

His older brother went to Oxford for a postgraduate year, at Trinity, and had a high old time there. When Monk wanted to follow his footsteps and applied for a place at Trinity, he was told — this was his story, at any rate — that not only would Trinity never again accept anyone of the name of Hackney, but that it would be some time before another American would be admitted. So he shifted to Cambridge, where several of his friends were also going. He was very proud of his college, Jesus, and of its athletic prowess, which he helped to further by rowing in one of the college boats. The reason Jesus usually went head of the river, especially in the winter races, he told me, was that it used the "Jesus system": its oarsmen were taught to treat their fixed seats as if they were sliding. This Spartan technique, Monk explained, gave them a longer stroke, at the price of blisters and calluses on their bottoms.

After he came home from Cambridge, Monk went to law school and was admitted to the bar in Maryland, but his heart wasn't in it: the law was not human enough for him. If he had remained a bachelor in Baltimore, where the easygoing life exactly suited him and where everyone in town was his affectionate friend, he might have had a happier time of it — perhaps too happy. Anyhow, he didn't remain a bachelor for very long, and his wife, who loved animals, got him away from the city and on to a cattle-breeding farm.

Cold Saturday was the name of this farm: its name and title deeds went back to the colonial days of Queen Anne. Monk settled down to be a farmer, "raising feed for my wife's cattle," as he put it. They bred pedigreed stock, Black Angus, and Monk took great pride in the herd and in the blue ribbons they soon began to collect. He would point to one of his small, square bulls and say, "Look at him! Pure filet mignon, all the way through!"

When I was running the National Affairs department on *Time*, Monk wrote to tell me that Cold Saturday had just paid a record high price for a champion bull, that he knew I would agree that this was news of national importance, and anyway, as an old pal would I please see that the transaction was given plenty of space in *Time*? (I don't remember getting many such requests, but each one was a shock.) I replied that news was partly a matter of opinion and that he was welcome to his, but that in my opinion this item was not worth mentioning, certainly not in *Time*. He was outraged. What was the use of having a friend on *Time*, he said in his next, if the friend wouldn't do you a good turn when asked? I replied stiffly that journalism had its own code of ethics, no matter what farmers might think.

He went on and on; he wouldn't drop the subject. I couldn't get it through his head that what he was asking for was in effect a free advertisement; he couldn't get it through my head that friends should bend rules backward to do each other favors. He finally embarked on a campaign of barefaced emotional blackmail. He was supposed to have his tonsils out, but kept putting off the operation, which he dreaded. Now, as a last desperate expedient to win me over, he threatened to go to the hospital and submit to surgery. I made no reply. A few days later he sent me a telegram: FIRST THING I SAID ON EMERGING FROM ETHER WAS DID TOM CRASH THROUGH?

Some time after this I paid a visit to Cold Saturday. Monk had told me to take a train from Baltimore; he would meet me at Asbestos, their nearest station. (The name has now been bowdlerized to Finksburg.) It was one of those old-fashioned trains whose conductors seem to know all the passengers by name, and there were antimacassars on the backs of the seats. At Asbestos, which turned out to be a small way station, no one was there to meet me. In fact, there was nobody there at all, except a hobo asleep on a baggage truck.

I picked up my suitcase and started up the road. Fifty yards from the station I passed a parked car, with a half-grown girl in the front seat. She didn't look to me like a Hackney, and she didn't speak, so I walked past. Then I hesitated: she might be one of Monk's daughters, after all. Anyhow, she might be able to direct me to the farm. I walked back and asked her if by any chance she was a Hackney or if she could tell me how to get to the Hackneys' place. She gave me a bold and jeering look, and said, "Ain't never heard of 'em."

I apologized and walked on, in some embarrassment. A few moments later the same car overtook me, with Monk at the wheel and the half-grown girl behind him. He was delighted at the success of his trap: he had been the hobo, asleep on the baggage truck, and the girl was his daughter. I had to admit that I had been completely taken in.

Farm life suited Monk but wasn't enough for him: he wanted to do something more. One of his Baltimore friends, Jake Waxter, was then judge of the juvenile court. Monk had done some work in legal aid (defending clients too poor to afford a lawyer). Jake, whose whole life was given to welfare work, was about to get a bigger job, and he persuaded Monk to take over the juvenile court. There was one slight hitch, it turned out: Monk would have to be appointed by the governor, and the hard-and-fast political rule was that the governor must appoint a member of his own party — which Monk was not. That was easy; he would just change his party. And he did. As luck would have it, this was on the eve of an election that the governor unexpectedly lost — and Monk found he had turned his coat to no purpose. He came in for a good deal of delighted mockery. Whether he changed his party again or had to wait for another election, I can't remember; anyhow, he did finally become judge of the juvenile court.

He was so conscientious and so tender-hearted that the job nearly did him in. He could never get free of the memory and the worry of these endless, hopeless, sordid cases that crowded through his court. They preyed on his mind and gave him sleepless nights and horrifying dreams. He was only too well aware of his own helplessness and the impotence of the law to do anything much or even right about the human puzzles he had to deal with daily. He came close to having a nervous breakdown, and after several years he resigned. He was not tough enough to be a judge.

∘⟦ WILLIAM ELLERY HALE

◝⟨ HE WAS THE SON of a distinguished father, an astronomer so highly regarded by his colleagues that the great observatory at Palomar was named after him. Bill himself had one of the noblest heads I ever saw: well shaped, majestically large, with a brow like Socrates'. And this head of his was not hollow, though it was deceptive: he was neither an intellectual nor a scholar but a bonhomous companion. I would rather have "wasted time" talking to Bill Hale than to anyone else I knew.

In college, where we met, we talked a lot; several times all night. And we didn't need drink to keep the talk going, though I remember one all-night session in which the two of us sat for hours straddling the ridgepole of the unfinished skating rink, passing a gallon jug back and forth between us. At dawn, when the jug was empty, we slithered down from this perch — in daylight, and sober, I could never have got up there or felt easy if I had — and looked around for something to undo, let loose, or destroy, those being the feelings that well up in an undergraduate after a lengthy bout of drinking while sitting still.

⟦125

On that occasion we tried to take the brake off a freight car that was standing by itself in the yards near the station. The tracks sloped down to the lake, and we pictured our untethered monster gathering its sleeping momentum into a roar and a plunge that would astound the countryside. Luckily for us, we couldn't budge the damn thing.

Another time Bill and I called on a girl he knew in New York. We were not sober, but we flattered ourselves that we behaved with deceptive sobriety: sitting bolt upright on the edge of our chairs, spinning elaborately polite conversation in a mincingly articulate tone. When we felt we had made exactly the correct impression, we took our leave — and the moment we were outside the door burst into self-congratulating drunkenness. It was an old-fashioned apartment house, with a section of fire hose folded neatly into a rack on the wall of each landing. Without a word spoken, we looked at each other, raced to the top floor, seized the brass nozzle of the hose, and carried it downstairs, unwinding the miles and miles of hose as we went. By the time we got to the lobby, we were so uplifted that it seemed the natural next thing to go into the first church we came to — it was St. Patrick's Cathedral — and sit there for ten minutes to cool off or give thanks for everything, I don't think we knew which.

In our last year at Princeton the class passed the traditional judgment on its members, voting for "the most brilliant," "the most likely to succeed," et cetera. Some of these choices were a close race, but Bill and I each won our accolade hands down. I was voted, overwhelmingly, "worst poet," and Bill was easily elected "most desperate fusser." In Princeton lingo this meant "greatest ladies' man" and was considered an honor — unless, as sometimes happened, it was bracketed with "thinks he is." Bill's vote was not so qualified.

In a homelier field he was also regarded as a nonpareil.

At some point in our college careers some idle talent made the fascinating discovery that farts are inflammable. Immediately, competitions sprang up to determine whose could produce the most brilliant flame, the furthest reaching, the longest lasting. In my set, Bill emerged the undisputed champion, a human Bunsen burner.

It must have been after we left college that Bill developed his famous cat fight. It was irresistible. It started off with a sinister, snarly challenge, given and received, and worked up to such a concatenation of spitting, yowling screams that you would have sworn three or four tomcats were murdering each other in an alley. To produce this crescendo of sound, Bill went through a series of facial contortions that were the comic equivalent of the noises he made. So many demands were made on him to "do the cat fight" that he finally decided to make a record of it. Shut in a soundproof recording booth in a Los Angeles shop, he was in full cry, intent only on his performance, when he happened to look up and see a crowd of people watching him through the window from the street outside, their faces frozen or slack-jawed in expressions of fascinated horror.

![T] THOMAS COVINGTON McEACHIN

~(WHEN HE CAME TO PRINCETON, in sopho-
more year, he was a lean, sandy Scot who spoke with an in-
congruous Southern accent: his father or grandfather had
emigrated to Florida. His name was still pronounced in the
Scottish manner: McCann. He was ambitious, cool, and
able, and he knew what he wanted. What he wanted, and
got, was the chairmanship of the *Daily Princetonian*. Besides the prestige, the job brought in about $1,500.

In senior year he came close to being kicked out of college. He loved to play bridge and played nearly every
night till a late hour. Then he was very likely to oversleep
and miss his first lecture. His cuts mounted up to such a
figure that the dean put him on probation and told him
coldly that, chairman of the *Princetonian* or not, one more
cut and out he would go.

His friends got together and formed a Committee for
Waking McEachin. I served on it one morning a week. An
hour before his first lecture I burst in on him, cursed and
shook him awake, left him sitting on the edge of his bed,
closed his bedroom door, and ostentatiously slammed the

door of his study, as if I had gone out. Then I tiptoed to the bedroom door and listened. Sometimes there would be a sigh, a yawn, and the creak of the bed as McEachin settled back into it. I would burst in again and repeat my rousing performance. This time I wouldn't leave till I was sure he was safely past the point of no return.

None of us, the dean included, recognized that this apparently invincible laziness of McEachin's was not at all in character and was in fact a symptom of illness. For by this time he had long ceased to be lean and had become unhealthily fat. And the fatter he grew, the more listless he became. He won a Rhodes Scholarship, but his life at Oxford lasted only a year and was not happy.

In the spring vacation, which was six weeks long, we went to Paris together to lead the simple life and get a lot of reading done. We were sure we would not be distracted by the fleshpots, because we had only enough money to get us there and keep us going for a week or so. The reason we were so short was that we had both lent more than we could afford to an English friend, a member of my college at Oxford. This man solemnly swore he would send everything he owed us within a week, and he knew we were counting on him.

We traveled by the slowest and cheapest route: third class on the overnight boat from Southampton to Le Havre. The third-class passengers were confined to a large cabin in the stern crammed with double-decker bunks. McEachin and I tossed a coin for the lower berth, and he won. As I clambered up to my bunk, I noted the naked electric light bulb, which couldn't be turned off, just over my head. When we pulled out of the harbor at midnight, a steward clumped around, putting battered tin basins alongside every pillow.

Soon the boat was bucking like a bronco, and the cabin was thick with the noise and smell of vomiting. A queasy sailor, I hate being sick, so I crawled down from my bunk and hung on to an upright to fight it out on my feet. McEachin was lying on his side with his eyes tight shut, one hand holding his nose and an arm over his ear. After a short struggle I reached for my basin and joined the retching chorus. When we landed at dawn the next day, I felt as empty and fresh as a new-born soul. McEachin, who had managed to keep the victory, was grumpy.

In Paris we took a room apiece on the top floor of a sleazy boarding house on the Left Bank; the house was at the end of a blind alley called Impasse des Deux Anges. It was decrepit and dirty, and the food was depressing. We didn't mind at first, for we had visions of better things when our money came. We gave our indebted friend a few days' grace and then hot-footed it to the central post office. No money. We told ourselves that this facer was only temporary. Soon we fell into a daily routine: a walk to the post office (we couldn't afford the Métro) and back again, stopping at a café, where we ordered a *bock* and called for the backgammon board. There we would spend two or three hours, sharing our single glass of beer and playing game after game of backgammon.

Why didn't we go back to our rooms and get some reading done? I don't know. We would probably have said that between work and worry, worry came first, and that we didn't have time for both. In the first weeks, before hope died, our common problem gave us much to argue and speculate about. When there was nothing more to say, we fell back on the daily routine and silence. On our regular walk to the post office we stopped at bakeries and pastry shops and sniffed (but never bought anything), and we called in at Morgan Harjes to search the register for some new arrival whom we might know well enough to borrow from.

Most of our time was spent playing backgammon, in complete silence. Our tempers grew short; we both hated to lose; and we were getting so much on each other's nerves that we could no longer trust ourselves to speak. Sometimes, of course, we had to. If I had a run of luck, McEachin couldn't resist some bitter remarks on the inevitability of a player winning who threw nothing but doubles. This drew a rejoinder from me, and the upshot was that McEachin insisted on keeping a careful and complicated record of every game we played, showing the number of doubles each of us threw, the number of times we could play only part of them, the number of times we couldn't play them at all, et cetera. He seemed to get a certain satisfaction from this, and it helped to fill in the time.

Once we had a windfall: a chance encounter with another American from Oxford. He not only lent us a little money but bought us a good dinner, and McEachin piled up so many saucers of cheap brandy that he had to be taken home in a taxi. That was the one bright spot in a long month. McEachin didn't open a single law book; I did no better. But at long last our daily prospecting at Morgan Harjes hit pay dirt. In the register appeared the name of a man who, I knew, would lend me enough to get back to Oxford. He did; I abandoned McEachin, returned to England, and then wired him the price of *his* ticket.

And the cause of all our woe? Well, when it came to dealing with that, McEachin was wiser and more generous than I. He simply wrote off his loan as a bad debt. I was both angry and hurt that a friend should have lied to me (and why should he have?) and also felt myself responsible for McEachin's fleecing. So I cornered my erstwhile friend and debtor, listened scornfully to his stammered explanations, and demanded to know whether or not he could pay up. For the nth time he swore he would and could; we set off together for the bank. Halfway there he stopped and admitted that he hadn't the money. I told him to go to hell and turned on my heel. That scene has been on my conscience ever since, for in effect he obeyed me. If he took a degree at all (at one point he had been regarded as "a sure First"), it was a poor one. He got some sort of job in India at a branch office of the Oxford University Press, and the last I heard of him he had been dismissed for incompetence, or worse.

At the end of the summer term McEachin chucked his scholarship and went desperately back to Florida to be a banker. There, a few years later, he died of pneumonia — or from a heart weakened by his hugely overweight body.

It was a sad thing to see, the thin man in him struggling to escape, for the struggle grew perceptibly feebler. When I first knew him he had been a stimulating person to talk with; he was the only Southerner I knew who could state the Southern feeling about blacks with calmness and common sense. He had had a tough wit and a steely judgment. The one remark of his I remember from Oxford days was like a tragicomic travesty of himself. He had been spending the evening in my room; near midnight he heaved himself up from his armchair and shuffled to the door. There, he turned with a ghastly fat grin and said, "Well, big boy, what does it all add up to?"

JOHN TILLOTSON WAINWRIGHT

◟◞◟ HE WAS THE BRAVEST BOY and became the bravest man I ever knew. But the first thing I remember about him was how he wrote his name.

The classroom at St. Paul's in which we endured fourth-form algebra seemed old-fashioned even then: the master's desk on a little platform, our own scarred desks riveted to the floor, and all four walls lined by a wooden blackboard. When the master sent us to the blackboard to do a problem, each boy signed his last name in chalk at the top of his section. Jack Wainwright always printed his, starting each letter at the bottom and slashing it right off the top of the board. None of the rest of us wrote his name that way.

Everything Jack did was dashing and jerky. He had very poor muscular control; he was stone deaf in one ear and had a cast in one eye, and he had absolutely no sense of rhythm. Though he was thin and gangly, he bore himself jauntily. His hair was unruly and jutted out or stood up in shelves and cowlicks. His features were indeterminate and didn't fit together very well, and he had a retreating chin. Some masters made the mistake of treating Jack as a butt, a figure of fun. There was one in particular, Mr. Sears, head of the science department: a large, stiff, dour man known as "Sourbelly." He had it in for all of us in the classics division, suspecting, quite rightly, that we took small interest in science. He liked to hand us heavily wrapped sarcasms on our supposedly "classical" view of the world, and he singled out Wainwright as a favorite target. Once, Sourbelly undertook to explain to us the properties and uses of a Leyden jar. Holding this uninteresting object aloft for our inspection, he looked at Jack and said, "Wainwright, this is a Leyden jar."

"Good!" said Jack.

Jack was a posthumous only son. His mother had been a beauty and a great lady in New York and Philadelphia, where she had married again (a Biddle) and had a house in Rittenhouse Square. She and Jack adored each other. Although she was always perfectly turned out and he usually looked like a scarecrow, they had an odd similarity; and they understood each other so well that Jack said they could often finish one another's sentences. She used to knit him ties: they were loosely constructed to begin with and, from Jack's nervous habit of pulling at them, they soon dwindled to the thickness of a shoelace.

Woe betide the boy who dared to comment on Jack's tie, for he took it as a reflection on his mother. He would cheerfully accept any amount of jeering at his appearance or his other failings, but not a word about his ties. On this subject he was so like Cyrano, in fact, that even a glance at his neck was likely to be considered an insult. And anyone who insulted Jack had a fight on his hands. He would fight anybody at all, any time, any place. One of his fights took place in the zinc-lined shower room at the Middle, in fifth-form year. His opponent was Ham Williams, who was at least twice his weight and a cool and sadistic boxer. Jack never had any notion whatever about boxing: he always came rushing in, flailing his arms like a windmill. Ham Williams counterpunched and sent Jack hurtling back against the zinc wall, whence he rebounded like a ball for another hopeless attack. The fight was stopped. Jack himself would never admit defeat.

I remember only one fight that Jack actually won, and that was a boxing match when we were at college. In our third year at Princeton, to his friends' dismay he entered a boxing tournament. He was matched against a classmate, Ollie Rodgers, who looked like a Greek god and was an experienced boxer. We expected Jack to be chopped into chowder or to be knocked out in the first round. At the bell Jack shot out of his corner and swarmed all over Rodgers in a frantic blur of arms, legs, knees, and elbows. Rodgers ducked, covered up, gave ground, and waited for an opening. You could see that he was annoyed and a little disconcerted. He found Jack's unorthodox style — if you could call it a style — extremely difficult to handle.

Jack's aggressiveness saved him from punishment in the first round, but we were sure he would catch it in the second and would never be able to last out the full three rounds. We reckoned without Jack's spirit. Every now and then Rodgers hit him, but Jack never let up; he kept whirling in like a bewildering windmill, and Rodgers was so bothered that his skill and experience went for nothing. Jack was awarded the bout on points.

Another of Jack's famous fights was a draw, although it started out to be a "duel to the death." This time his opponent was Schuyler Jackson, who was no more of a boxer than Jack but was stronger and much better coordinated. Though they were both friends of mine, they had a deep and unspoken antipathy to one another. This antipathy finally came out into the open on the evening after my wedding, at which Schuyler had been best man and Jack one of the ushers. After the wedding was over, these two,

arm in arm and bottles in pocket, meandered down Prospect
Street, going into all the undergraduate clubs and demanding that the members drink the health of the bride and
groom. They were quite drunk.

A quarrel blew up between them, God knows about
what. But it must have been on a point of honor, for both
agreed that the only way out was a duel to the death, to be
fought with bare hands and stark naked, and that a suitable dueling ground would be the deserted golf links,
where they would not be seen nor interrupted.

Arrived at the site and stripped to the buff, they sprang
at each other. All that Jack could recall later was the sensation of being seized by the legs, lifted from the ground,
and whirled: he remembered the lights of the Graduate
College revolving about him, upside down. Next day, besides numerous bruises, he also had a sore throat, so presumably Schuyler had tried to throttle him. Jack must have
given as good as he got, for both survived and eventually
staggered home to bed. Schuyler had been wearing borrowed wedding clothes, from cutaway to Ascot tie; next
day bits of this costume were found scattered along the
route.

Apart from his duels (all Jack's fights were really duels),
he was the gentlest soul alive, and his manners were of
such an old-fashioned courtesy that to the boors of our un-
polished day they sometimes seemed laughable. He treated
everyone alike with the same elaborate politeness, whether
he was asking directions from a stranger in the street or
getting a light from a waiter in a restaurant. People don't
bow much nowadays, except in courts of law or to royalty
or on state occasions, but Jack did, whenever he met a
stranger, a lady, or an older man.

Several times he disguised himself as a hobo and rode
the freight trains. His ragged and dirty clothes might pass
muster but his exquisite manners never. Once he worked his

passage to Europe as a coal-passer (stoker's assistant), the lowest job in the stokehole of a coal-burning ocean liner.

Jack's ingrained chivalrousness was instantly at the service of any underdog, and of course this applied to dogs themselves. In our undergraduate days there was a stray mongrel, whose left foreleg was crippled, that used to roam the Princeton campus. Jack adopted him and named him Tripod. Some of his roommates didn't much like Tripod, and one of them, a spoiled rich boy, in Jack's absence once got the dog drunk. Jack was furious but somewhat mollified by Tripod's own settling of the score: he was sick all over the rich boy's bed.

One of Jack's settled principles was that a man should get drunk once a month: this catharsis, he firmly believed, was good for the blood, the brain, and the character. Sometimes his command-invitation to join him in a white night came at an inconvenient time. Even without the booster of drink, his extraordinary energy was exhausting to less energetic men. A friend of his once reported a weekend visit from Jack, adding, "I had such a nice time with him. He was tired."

When my first son was born, in New York, and I was still recovering from the ritual celebration, Jack arrived from Philadelphia, announcing that he had come to drink my son's health with me, and that we would make a night of it. I tried to explain that I just *had* made a night of it; Jack was adamant. While my wife was in the hospital I was living in a small single room with one narrow bed. Jack and I got back to my room at a very late hour, having drunk all and more than all the requisite healths. I tried to persuade him to take the bed, but of course he wouldn't; he insisted on the floor, where he said he'd be most comfortable.

He had to catch an early train back to Philadelphia, so I groaned out of bed when the alarm went off, and shook him awake. The blanket I had given him, and his overcoat, had worked up during the night so that his head was swathed in them and his legs bare. I knew by the frightful goings-on in my own skull what his must feel like. Prone and cocooned as he was, and knifed by hangover as he must have been, he managed to bob his head in a bowing motion while his muffled voice announced in tones of great conviction: "Delightful evening, Tom. Delightful. Never felt better in my life."

Jack was accepted for the diplomatic service, and his first post was in Brazil, at São Paulo. He had looked forward to the foreignness of South America, but he said São Paulo was a dull, characterless metropolis; he might as well have been in Chicago. He put in for a transfer. I don't suppose the State Department much likes a man on his first post to apply for a transfer. Jack got one — but it was to Guayaquil, a fever port on the humid coast of Ecuador. He was delighted.

The normal route to his new post was by sea; Jack elected to go overland, on foot, across the Andes. He packed his top hat, cutaway, Bible, and all such ceremonial trappings in several boxes to be shipped by sea. For his trans-Andean journey he collected an ample supply of canned goods, blankets, and other necessities to be carried on burros. When his little expedition made camp the first night, Jack discovered that the two consignments had somehow been switched. For his journey across South America he was armed with top hat, cutaway, and Bible, but no canned goods or blankets.

Nevertheless, he got to Guayaquil. In the several years he spent there he never complained about the heat, the fever, or the boredom. It was foreign; it was exotic; it was much more like his idea of South America than São Paulo had been. The State Department must have noted that he took his punishment like a man (though Jack, of course, didn't regard it as punishment), and his next post, Cuba, was a step up.

On his home leave he took an even bigger step: he was married. His wife was the daughter of a general in the Marine Corps. When Jack first saw her, she was buying a mule that was being brutally treated by its owner. This immediately enlisted Jack's sympathy, and in a few weeks they were engaged. The wedding was a joyful occasion and thronged with well-wishing friends.

Four months later, almost to the day, some of his friends received the following cable from the embassy in Havana:

ALICE CUTTS WAINWRIGHT REQUESTS I GIVE YOU THE SAD NEWS THAT JACK WAINWRIGHT UNSUCCESSFULLY AT-TEMPTED TO SAVE THE LIVES OF TWO FRIENDS FROM DROWN-ING IN MATANZAS BAY AND LOST HIS OWN LIFE IN THE AT-TEMPT AT FIVE PM SUNDAY AFTERNOON. REQUEST YOU INFORM JACKS FRIENDS AT PRINCETON AND ELSEWHERE.

That Sunday Jack and his wife had gone for a picnic lunch with another couple from the American Embassy. They were not close friends; in fact, they had only recently met. For their picnic spot they chose some high rocks over-looking the sea but some yards back from it. There had been a storm, and a big surf was breaking over the rocks. After they finished their picnic, they sat at a respectful dis-tance and watched the battering seas. Suddenly a gigantic wave shot up and licked off the other man's wife.

There was no possibility that any human being could swim in that boiling sea, but her husband went in after her. Jack immediately jumped in to try to save them both. His agonized wife caught one glimpse of him as a wave flung him up; then he disappeared. His body was found two days later; the other bodies were never recovered.

The funeral service was held in New York, at Calvary

Church, which had been his mother's girlhood parish. It was now one of the headquarters of the Buchmanite group, and, as one of his friends remarked, Jack wouldn't willingly have been seen dead there. The pallbearers were the same friends who had been the ushers at his wedding, four months earlier.

The burial was at Rhinebeck, a two-hour train ride up the Hudson, in the cemetery where his father was buried. His mother had engaged a special car for the funeral party. It was a cold November day, and at the graveyard it was raining. On the return trip his usher-pallbearers, by wordless consent, all gathered in the small smoking compartment of the car. Someone produced a flask. Someone started to tell a story about Jack; it was followed by another and another. All the stories were funny and very like him; it was as if he were there himself, laughing helplessly and protesting. In the midst of all this a stranger appeared in the doorway: one of Jack's family come back to have a smoke. The laughter and the stories ceased, and the sting of death came back.

Some years later I came across a description of Don Quixote by the Spanish writer Ortega y Gasset. It seemed to me that the words might have been written about Jack: "He was a man of heart; this was for him the only reality, and round about it he stirred up a whole world of unhandy phantoms. Everything about him he turned into a pretext for the exercise of will, the warming of the heart, and the spending of enthusiasm."

⟦ HENRY CONSTANTINE WHITEHEAD

⟨ THE PHILOSOPHER Alfred North Whitehead was his uncle; his father was an Anglican bishop in India — Bombay, I think. Henry himself was a mathematician, so mentally he must have taken after his uncle; but some of his characteristics were oddly episcopal. He had a way of standing in front of the fireplace, teetering on his toes and tapping the tips of his extended fingers together, that seemed to me very Church of England. I remember him in this stance in my mother's living room at tea, and also (but this time with a drink in his hand) in my own house, trying to explain the quantum theory so that I could understand it.

Henry had had the best English education — Eton and Balliol — and he went on from there. He came to Princeton to study mathematics under Veblen and stayed at the Graduate School for several years. He took a great shine to my family, particularly to one of my sisters, and developed a deep fondness for Princeton. He must have been a brilliant mathematician, for he was called back to Balliol as a fellow and shortly afterward was given the chair of mathematics at Magdalen.

In those days I had a theory that scientific lingo, even symbols, could be translated into plain English. I think I got the idea from Arnold Bennett. So I said to Henry Whitehead: "If I put a drink in your hand and stand you in front of my fireplace, and stop you whenever you say something I don't understand, can you explain the quantum theory to me?"

"Certainly," said Henry. "But can I have more than one drink?"

He got off to a good start, and all went well for the first fifteen minutes. Then he hesitated.

"At this point," he said, "you'll have to —"

"No, I won't!" I cried. "You put it in plain English! You promised."

In that case, he said, he'd have to make a brief detour — and he began to talk about a Danish physicist named Niels Bohr. Just as I thought we were coming back to the main road again, we ran into a stop sign.

"There's just *one* equation you'll have to accept," said Henry.

"Never!" I said. "Say it in English."

"I can't. It's impossible."

And that's where it ended. But it was a good try; and if anybody could have done it, I think Henry was the man. After that, I decided to leave mathematics to the mathematicians.

Henry and I had other things in common. He was an enthusiastic games player, and he became a member of our Stony Look Squash Rackets and Afterwards Club. As secretary, I had the job of arranging matches with other clubs (always "away," since we had no court of our own) and a party afterward. Our members were of very varying ability as squash players, but as drinkers we could always give a good account of ourselves. On the court we each wore the club shirt: a Medusa's head on the pocket, and the sleeves edged in ribbon with the club colors, black and blue.

Henry was one of those Englishmen who play games with an elaborately casual air, as if they couldn't care less about winning, when in fact they care a great deal and are trying like hell. Squash was not Henry's favorite game (that was cricket), and American squash differs in several annoying ways from British squash, but he was a useful member of the team, and his bulldog spirit often brought him an unexpected win. Win or lose, at the party afterward he did his bit with a whole heart. Though he was vaguely aware that he could not carry a tune very far without dropping it, he loved to sing, especially Gilbert and Sullivan, and on these occasions nothing and nobody could prevent him.

The parties were usually simple affairs, but not always. Once we were entertained at a rich house on the north shore of Long Island, in a large basement room. (Such rooms were called "rumpus rooms" in those days.) A bar was the main attraction, but there were also two slot machines, one that took dimes and the other quarters. Beside each of these machines our host had thoughtfully placed a large bowl, one brimming with dimes, the other with quarters. He may have meant well, but it wasn't much fun to play with somebody else's money. And when a silver platter of hard-boiled eggs, already peeled, appeared on the bar, someone naturally started throwing them. I hope somebody hit the host, but I can't remember.

Henry must have missed his cricket. Once, he managed to scrape together a scratch team to play against Haverford College. He dragooned me as "an old hand," on the strength of my having played once or twice at a prep school in England, some twenty-five years before. Several members of our team had never even seen the game played. The match lasted for only one afternoon and was unfinished; I don't remember getting a turn at bat, which was just as well. But Henry was in his element, and looked it. He arranged us, coached us, encouraged us, cajoled us, and did everything himself. He bowled so furiously (I think from both ends) that before the afternoon was over he had to retire with a sore arm. At that point he put *me* in to bowl. I was allowed several practice shies at the wicket, never having bowled in my life, and couldn't get within six feet of it.

After Henry went back to Oxford, several years passed before we met again. He married and became the father of two sons. He grew a little thicker in the middle, a little thinner on top; but he still played cricket and squash, he still enjoyed an occasional song at twilight. And in a way he "got religion." Though he had always been cold to his father's Anglican faith, he had the same generous warmth of feeling as his philosopher-uncle, and it came out in Henry as sympathy for the left wing. We used to argue about this in a rather halfhearted fashion. I couldn't quite take Henry seriously as a political animal: he was neither active in politics nor committed to a party, and I thought his sympathies did credit to his heart but not to his common sense. And yet I don't think common sense the highest intellectual virtue, especially not in a mathematician.

Henry revisited Princeton and took his wife with him. His old friends there were delighted to see him, and new friends as well. One Princeton lady, with more forthrightness than tact, exclaimed: "But you're a very nice man! I didn't know mathematicians could be so charming."

His wife returned to England before he did to look after their farm near Oxford. And one day on a Princeton street, Henry dropped dead of a heart attack.

⁖⟦ GEORGE McLEAN HARPER

◟◝⟨ In our currency, great men are a dime a dozen — or cheaper than that, if you take the newspaper valuation — but a good man remains beyond price. Like good bread. George McLean Harper was a good man, in that priceless sense.

He wasn't much regarded in the Princeton of his day. He was liked and respected and rated a better than adequate professor of English literature. But he was nowhere near sufficiently admired. Like other scholars of international repute, he was held in more honor abroad than at home. Also, his specialty, William Wordsworth, was out of fashion then, as he still is.

Sixty years ago the acknowledged authorities on Wordsworth were Professor Harper and his French colleague Emile Legouis. When, late in the day, they discovered the shocking fact that Wordsworth in his *sans-culotte* youth in Revolutionary France had fathered an illegitimate daughter, it must have been a sad blow to them, for this most respectable of poets never acknowledged the child, never married her mother, and turned his back on the deepest

⟦145

romance of his life. The revelation of this family scandal, and of Wordsworth's behavior, was painful to Harper and Legouis. All the same, as scholars they were pledged to the truth, and it was better that they should make the announcement rather than some unsympathetic or vulgarizing journalist. So they did.

Mr. Harper was a smallish man, compact and erect; he stood and sat bolt upright. His clipped moustache enhanced his air of serious simplicity; it could also bristle with generous indignation. Behind his steel spectacles his eyes were wide, innocent, and trusting; they could show pain, horror, and honest anger as well. He had started off as an old-fashioned liberal and never got over it. As a young man he had been for a time on the staff of *The Nation*, but journalism was not his trade nor New York his town. He had been a strong supporter and always remained an admirer of Woodrow Wilson.

Though he was a middle-aged man at the time of the Sacco-Vanzetti case, that long crucifixion of justice horrified him as much as it did some of his younger contemporaries. After its tragic end, Mr. Harper went to a university reception, where he unwittingly shook hands with Judge Grant, who had presided over the review of the trial. When he discovered what he had done, he told us in his earnest and husky voice, he had been horror-struck and had seriously thought of returning to Judge Grant and somehow taking it back — "but you can't un*do* a handshake."

He was a great walker, and so was his wife. Their favorite form of holiday was a walking trip. Together they had perambulated the fells of Wordsworth's Lake District, large tracts of Europe, and the western parts of his native Pennsylvania. They sometimes walked hand in hand down the street; I remember once seeing them skipping. Mr. Harper's frequent costume in his classes was a walker's Norfolk jacket, knickerbockers, heavy woolen stockings, and high-laced boots.

It was in his classes, his "preceptorials" (informal classes that supplemented most of the lecture courses), that Mr. Harper was at his unique best. He was a quiet teacher, on the dry side, yet quite incapable of irony or sarcasm; an open and guileless expectancy was his natural frame of mind. Before you had been long in his class, you became aware that he was not only giving you the benefit of every doubt but confidently trusting that you might, at any moment, tell *him* something both original and true. And that he would be grateful for it, but not at all surprised.

In a man whose innocence was less armored by integrity, this attitude would have been fatally vulnerable, an invitation to ambush, but no one took undue advantage of Mr. Harper's simplicity. Why not? I suppose he would have been easy to fool, but I doubt whether anyone could have tried it more than once. It might have seemed at the time as simple as taking candy from a baby, but it would infallibly have left you feeling like a cradle-robbing thief — and there was also the possibility that God might strike you dead in the act.

I never consciously tried to fool him, but I got my warning all the same. I had handed in a paper that led off with a sweepingly sophomoric statement, and Mr. Harper's grave comment in the margin, taking my grandiloquence seriously and in effect thanking me for presenting him with a new and ponderable idea, floored my pretentiousness as if it had been hit with a poleaxe. He treated us seriously and took it for granted that we would respond in kind; perhaps that was the secret of his influence on us. That, and his goodness: a childlike quality that surprised him into sudden shouts of delighted laughter or unself-conscious displays of emotion.

I will never forget the times when he read to us — or tried to read, for he was never able to finish — Wordsworth's poem "Michael." It's a fairly lengthy narrative, in Wordsworth's prosiest blank-verse style, about a shepherd in the Lake country. This old fellow married late in life and had one son, whom he adored and whom he brought up to be as good a shepherd as himself. But before the boy was fully grown, his father was threatened with the loss of half his land, and decided to send his son off to live with a kinsman in town, where he could go into business and earn enough money to save the family acres. As a last task, they began to build a new sheepfold. The boy did well at first in the city; then he began to go to the bad, and finally took his failure and guilt overseas. When the news reached his father, all the heart went out of him. Many a day he went up to the field where he was building the sheepfold,

And never lifted up a single stone.

As Mr. Harper approached this line he would begin to show signs of distress: abrupt clearings of the throat, a frown, impatient shufflings of his feet. When he reached the dreaded words he stopped, glared at the page, set his lips, cast a despairing look at us. He went back a line and tried it again. No go. Once more — and he gave up, huskily apologizing, when he could speak, for his inability.

I remember him "outside of classes," at parties in his white-frame house on Mercer Street. Very sedate parties they were, yet my memory of one of them sticks with me as among the most exciting evenings of my young life. We sat in the garden, in the dusk of a spring day, drinking milk and eating gingerbread, and talking in low and passionate voices about *Paradise Lost*. Through an open window we could hear his daughter Isabel at the piano, playing Mozart.

Was he a great teacher? I don't suppose so, unless you can be a great teacher simply by being a good man.

⁰₈⟦ DR. J. DUNCAN SPAETH

⌁(DR. SPAETH WAS A BIG, bustling, hump-shoul-
dered man with an old-fashioned face: long nose, long hair,
little eyes that could stare, glare, or crinkle. His voice ran
the gamut from a bull-like roar to a mouse's squeak. He
was an accomplished and perfectly unself-conscious reciter
of poetry. (Browning and Shakespeare were his special-
ties.) He was a professor of English at Princeton, and he
also coached the university crew.

Dr. Spaeth and his wife, who was a lovely, serene
woman, lived with their four children in the old fieldstone
house, reputed to be the oldest house in Princeton, called
the Barracks, that was later bought by my brother-in-law
Buzz Cuyler. Across a narrow courtyard from the house,
and looking rather like its whelp, stood a one-room stone
cottage. This was now Mrs. Spaeth's studio and sanctuary,
where she painted strong, childlike pictures, mostly of children. The house was her husband's domain: he roamed up
and down in it or hurled himself from room to room, bellowing Shakespeare or Whitman or Browning or yelling at
the children to be quiet. The studio Mrs. Spaeth had all to
herself.

⟦149

Dr. Spaeth was of German descent, and he was like a Wagnerian warrior. He had played football for the University of Pennsylvania, and rumor had it that once, carried away by the spirit of combat, he had bitten off the nose of the opposing tackle. When the wind was right, people on Nassau Street could hear Dr. Spaeth in his coach's launch a mile and a half away on Lake Carnegie, shouting at the crew through his megaphone: "There is a tide in the affairs of men which, taken at the flood, leads on to fortune — *now give 'er ten!*"

In his packed lectures, when he recited a passage from Browning or Shakespeare, Dr. Spaeth became the character whose words he was speaking. In the scene between Juliet and her nurse he even imitated two quite different feminine voices. This might have been ludicrous, but he always spoke with such force and conviction that, although he was sometimes funny, he was never ridiculous. His audiences sat silent and fascinated.

He had the same overpowering vehemence, outdoors or in, and a small room never seemed big enough to contain him. One day in the Brick Row Bookshop he was talking (shouting) to Charley Arrott, who ran the bookshop, about *Moby Dick*. Arrott was a small man, gentle and polite, and he kept giving way: Dr. Spaeth, advancing his stomach relentlessly and flinging his arms wide, was urging Charley to rejoice with him in the mating scene between the whales — "those great Leviathans!"

If you had the luck to draw Dr. Spaeth as your instructor in a preceptorial, you yourself found how formidable he was at close quarters. Like some other first-rate actors with mobile mouths, he sometimes emitted a fine spume, and if you sat near him, it was nearly impossible to dodge. The thing to do was not to notice; he didn't.

To undergraduates who went to see him at home he was cordiality itself. They might find him on all fours, blowing at a recalcitrant log fire; he would have scorned to use the bellows even if he had had a pair. Except to those who make a fetish of neatness, his desk was an encouraging sight: piles of papers, books, and pamphlets in delicate balance, just short of cascading. No one but Dr. Spaeth could possibly have found anything in that midden, but he had a system: he could always lay his hand on anything he was looking for, and no one was allowed to *touch* his desk.

Wherever he went, he rode an ancient bicycle, getting up such momentum that even cars gave him a wide berth. If he had a bell, he never used it: his stentorian shouts of "GET OUT OF THE WAY!" were as effective as the siren of a fire engine. It was said that a much frailer, pedestrian professor had once disregarded this trumpet blare (or perhaps was paralyzed with terror) and was run over like a rabbit.

The Spaeth children grew up and left home; a younger man succeeded Dr. Spaeth as coach of the crew. Worst of all, Mrs. Spaeth died. He wrinkled up like an old balloon, and the air went out of him.

EMINENCES, VARIOUS SHADES

EMINENCES, VARIOUS SHADES

Of the eminences sketched here, three were friends (Thurber, Chambers, and Stevenson), two were admired acquaintances (Joyce Cary and James Agee). Churchill I met on three occasions, thanks to my job on *Time*. Einstein was a near neighbor in Princeton, seen frequently but never met, although my wife, like other housewives in the vicinity, once nearly ran over him (he was an absent-minded and meandering walker).

∞⌐ JAMES THURBER

◠⟨ WE WERE FELLOW OHIOANS: I was proud of that. But he was famous; he had put Columbus on the map, while Cincinnati and I couldn't even remember each other. Thurber was a great name to me for years before I laid eyes on him. We met one late night in the bar at "21" in New York. He sent a waiter to my table to inquire if I was me, and further flattered my vanity by asking me to join him and his wife. The three of us then went off for a last drink at Bleeck's, which, he assured me, was always open. Bleeck's was shut. We grumbled a little over this mischance and parted.

Our next meeting was several years later, at Kenyon College, in Ohio. Thurber was there to be given an honorary degree and I was there to make the baccalaureate address. The prospect of speaking to a crowd — even though I was reading my speech — made me nervous, and the knowledge that Thurber would be listening made me more nervous still. I had sweated over the opening paragraph, trying to include a veiled but recognizably complimentary reference to him and *The New Yorker*. And I couldn't

manage it: all I could manage was a veiled and uncompli-
mentary reference to Joyce Kilmer (why him?), the author of the well-known sentimental poem "Trees."

In the morning we had a dress rehearsal of the ceremony,
which was to be held out of doors; it was a lovely June day.
We took our places on the platform, and the president of
Kenyon, Gordon Chalmers, put us through our paces.
Thurber's role seemed to me enviably simple. All he had to
do was stand up and listen while his citation was being
read, and then be guided a few steps (his blindness had
become worse) to stand in front of the president and duck
his head while the hood was put around his neck. But it
was obviously not a simple matter for Thurber: he was
quivering like an aspen.

When the rites were over, there was a reception, with
drinks for those who needed them. Thurber came up to me
and said something pleasant about my speech, quoting word
for word the phrase I liked best. And then, without the
slightest change in his drawling Ohio monotone, he said,
"I suppose you know, Tom, that the whole Kilmer family
were sitting in the front row?" For one horror-struck moment I believed him.

Our friendship took another great leap forward when
he and his wife, Helen, spent a summer weekend with us
in Rhode Island. I saw then how much his blindness
(which was not yet complete) handicapped him, especially in rooms that were unfamiliar. His ashtray, his
drink, his butter plate, had to be put literally under his
hand, and even then he sometimes missed them or knocked
them over. Helen was very good with him, steering him
only as much as was necessary, and then leaving him to
his own devices.

He must have worked a great deal, but whenever I saw
him he was talking. At his best he was a marvelous solilo-
quizer, and could go on by the hour, nourished by ciga-

rettes and whiskey. Toward the end of an evening — if the evening lasted long enough — his discourse blurred and turned sentimental. Sometimes he sang, in a thinnish but true tenor, popular songs of his youth, remembering all the words.

It must have been extraordinarily difficult to be James Thurber, but you wouldn't have guessed it from him: he made the accomplishment look casual. To be shut off from the whole visible world by blindness, to be dependent on others to guide you across an unfamiliar room or show you where the ashtray is, or your drink or your plate; scenes and faces invisible, as if the light on the cinema screen had gone out and all you had to go on were incomprehensible scraps of dialogue — to live in this unrelenting and perpetual night and keep cheerful, unhysterical, and sane is enough to certify anyone who can do it as a very good human being. I'm not sure that Milton altogether succeeded, but Thurber did.

Few writers have been so beloved in both Britain and America. He showed that that famous gulf between British and American humor can be disregarded, if you know how to be yourself, and if your self is clear, friendly, and original, as his was. He was American to the quivering tip of his shock of white hair, and his speech never lost the lipless drone of Ohio, but his writing was as unaccented as E. M. Forster's or E. B. White's. I once told him that he and Adlai Stevenson were the two Americans most popular in England, and I think for the same reason: they were understood.

Whoever set the tone of *The New Yorker*, it was Thurber and White who were its first and greatest mainstays. Did they really burst, fully armed, from its aching head, or was their apprenticeship less miraculous? Thurber may have learned as much from Harold Ross as he thought he did, but it is certain that Ross didn't invent him. (It is less certain that Thurber didn't, in a sense, invent Ross.) However he managed to find it, I think Thurber's apparently frail but durable style came, as it must, out of the man himself.

Many Americans are popular with their fellow citizens without being much loved, but in Thurber's popularity affection played a large part. A few years ago, when his wife ("my seeing-eye wife," he called her) was reading to him, she remarked on an odd, crescent-shaped shadow that kept appearing on the page. Thurber, who by that time had painfully learned all about the pathology of the eye, immediately knew what the trouble was — a detached retina. He also knew what eye surgeon was needed, and how urgently. The surgeon was on vacation, somewhere in the Rockies, and couldn't be reached by telephone. When Thurber appealed to friends in the newspaper and radio world, they set up an impromptu network that quickly found the surgeon and brought him back for a successful operation — and not a word about it got into the papers or on the air.

Thurber listed himself in *Who's Who* as "cartoonist, writer, playwright." Surely his drawings, those marvelous doodles of the subconscious in broad daylight, deserve a wilder and more original name than "cartoons." Playwright he was, to a certain extent, smaller than he would have liked. He didn't want to be typed as a humorist (who among those great sad men ever did?); he wanted to be recognized as a serious writer. He *was* serious, and also a very good writer, but how can we deny to his dead face that we love him most for his funny writings? Mark Twain felt much the same way and perhaps wouldn't have believed that the Great American Novel is a book he wrote for boys.

Who will ever be able to think again of Columbus, Ohio, as an ordinary town? It's on a par now with Hannibal, Missouri.

⁂ JOHN McNULTY

⌒(I DID MEET JOHN MCNULTY a couple of times,
or maybe three. I don't remember his saying much of anything, but I never forgot his face. The *Times* obit said he
was "a small, jaunty man, Irish of face and manner" —
and I guess that was all right, as far as it goes. But as I
remember it, it was his clothes that were jaunty (the last
time I saw him, in a bar and grill in Providence, he was
sporting a black-and-white-check jacket and was on his
way to the races); his face had that weathered and watchful look you sometimes see on city children. And that's
what I think he was: an old child, an old city child. It was
also a face that belonged to McNulty; you wouldn't have
mistaken it for anybody else's.

I always wished I'd known him better, and now, having
read his book, I think I do. Anyhow, I defy anybody to
read it without getting personally fond of McNulty. As for
the pieces themselves, I shouldn't be surprised if some of
them are around a hundred years from now.

This collection* is introduced by his old friend James

---

* *The World of John McNulty* (New York: Doubleday, 1957).

Thurber, who knew him from way back, when they were both reporters in Columbus, long before they got to be big names on *The New Yorker*. McNulty was a native of Lawrence, Massachusetts, where his father, a bricklayer, had been killed by a fall from a building, and his mother supported her two infant sons by keeping a small candy store. She bought a piano on the installment plan and made little John practice every day. By the time he was eighteen he was playing the piano at night in Boehm's Café for twenty-four dollars a week and beers. He liked that. And he liked playing the piano in an Andover movie (same pay). Then he must have drifted into newspaper work in New York, for by the time he showed up in Columbus he was getting sixty dollars a week, more than any other reporter in town, Thurber says.

He stayed in Columbus a dozen years, and then went back to his beloved New York, to the street he liked best in the world, Third Avenue. He wrote a lot of pieces for *The New Yorker* about things he had seen, here and there — the Tabasco factory in New Iberia, Louisiana (he got interested in that one by reading the label on a Tabasco bottle; he was a great reader of labels on bottles); Ireland, a place where he had never been but where he finally got back for a visit; a ward in Bellevue Hospital, where he was a patient for several weeks; how a friend of his won a television prize of $24,000 and got $5,780 out of it; famous racehorses he had been introduced to at Belmont and Louisville by the men who lived and worked with them — but he always went back to writing about his own neighborhood, the bars and newsstands and little shops of Third Avenue.

Now and again he tried other jobs, in radio and the movies. Thurber says that when McNulty went to Hollywood, *The New Yorker*'s editor, Harold Ross, gave him a rare but Ross-like benediction: "Well, God bless you, McNulty, goddammit."

John McNulty loved his fellow man and paid attention
to him, especially to those whose words delighted his ear,
which was always cocked and ready. He wrote (why
wouldn't he?) in American — and I think, in his day,
better than Damon Runyon, because he didn't dress it up
the way Runyon did. Sometimes his pieces don't add up
at all, in a commercial or successful sense; more like
Chekhov than Runyon, really. The titles, which are sometimes even better than the pieces, give you the idea. Just
listen to these: "This Lady Was a Bostonian They Call
Them," "A Man Like Grady, You Got to Know Him
First," "Tell Him What Happen, Joe. See Will He Believe
You."

Sentimental? Sure he was; all that Irish in him. He
wrote a letter to his new-born son: "Chances are that you
will be a lucky mick, because I have been a lucky mick,
never really met any bad people, had a lot of fun, owe the
world a lot for how nice it has been to me, and that's about
the way it all sums up." But at his best what he wrote
comes straight from the horse's mouth:

A bar room regular: "He is a cynic, and when he is
drunk he don't believe in anything. You can't tell if he believes in anything when he is sober because then he don't
say."

A horseplayer, protesting against the way the cops keep
arresting him all the time: "Getting married causes
trouble, drinking causes trouble, working wears a man
out, and I see guys all around me dying making successes
out of themselves. Why can't they let me harm nobody just
studying horses and playing 'em when I can?"

A bookie: "The bookie is a Greek runs a flower store, but
he watches the entries and results more than he cares a
damn about the rhododendrons."

A newsdealer, offered a slug of whiskey on a cold morning: "I only took a little sip I wouldn't offend the man."

A handyman in a Third Avenue bar: "The Slugger weighs only about a hundred sixteen pounds, but they call him the Slugger because he talks very ferocious whilst drunk and he has big ideas about who he can lick then. He could lick hardly anybody at all. A customer one time said the Slugger looked like a guy that was maybe a small altar boy and fell into bad company for thirty-forty years. He is frail and got practically no health at all left from ramshackle living. Most of his teeth are gone and he must be nearly fifty years of age. Everybody likes this little guy, never mind his faults, they don't do any harm at all."

That's McNulty.

°⁰⟦ GERTRUDE STEIN

⌐⟋(THE FIRST GLIMPSE you get of her, as she trudges resolutely up onto the lecture platform, is reassuring. This solid, elderly woman, dressed in no-nonsense rough-spun clothes, seems at once smaller and more human than her monumental photographs or Jo Davidson's squat image of her. As she looks out over the audience and thanks us, with a quick low hoot of laughter, for "controlling yourselves to five hundred," we laugh too, in appreciative relief, and settle back in our seats to give her the once-over. This Gertrude Stein woman may not be so crazy, after all. Some of our wariness eases off. She has made a good beginning; there's no denying that.

But why are we here? Well, there are two answers to that question. Miss Stein knows one; we know the other. She knows we have come because we are interested — not so much in her as in her writing. We know better. We are here because we are curious — not so much about her writing, which we have never read, and probably never will, as about herself — an apparently sensible, perhaps really sane woman who has spent most of her life writing absolute balderdash, and then, by gum, a year ago published a book that was perfectly plain sailing and got her on the best-seller lists. We want to see what this creature looks like; we want to hear what she has to say for herself.

Now that we can get a good look at her face, that too is reassuring. The photographs we have seen didn't show those deep black eyes that make her graven face and its archaic smile come alive. Her short-cropped hair doesn't look queer; it looks as right as a cap on a grandmother. And though this is her first visit home in thirty-one years, her voice is as unmistakably American — she says "Amorrican" — as any of ours. As we listen to her low-pitched, harshly pleasant sound, we realize, with further grateful relief, that we were afraid she might have added, on top of her swami-like incomprehensibility, some of the affected patter of the expatriate. But no, we can see right away that she is too stubborn to have done anything like that. Foreign parts of speech have not affected her at all: she talks in as flatly sensible an American tone as any Midwestern aunt. We also notice with approval that she indulges in no gestures, except the natural, grandmotherly one of taking her pince-nez off and putting them on, and we soon discover, with mixed feelings, that she is not a very good lecturer: she drops her voice at the end of every sentence and talks more and more to one side of the room, so that a good third of us have to cup our ears and guess at the words we miss.

She is talking about herself, trying to explain what she has been up to all this time, and how she happens to write the way she does. It all sounds very sensible at first. She writes, she says, just the way she talks, and she tries to prove it by reading progressive examples from her books. But immediately, with the very first example, we notice a difference. That tonelessness that helps to lend an idiotic quality to her writing is emphatically absent from her reading. She reads, indeed, with an exaggerated emphasis, putting back all the italics and commas and dashes she has carefully not written. The passages she reads make startlingly good sense. A great light begins to break over us: by knowing what to accent, where to pause, we too might dig some meaning out of Gertrude Stein. It isn't true, then, that all that work of hers is just a brier patch; there *is* a rose in there, after all. A few of us make a mental note to try reading *Tender Buttons*, say, aloud — in the strictest privacy. Something might come of it.

Quite soon she says something funny. We laugh, not very loudly, and then look aghast. Was it meant to be funny? But Miss Stein doesn't seem to mind; she is even smiling herself. What a relief! We undo another tender mental button, and laugh whenever we feel like it. Toward the end of the lecture a few of us are shaking hysterically, and at the least excuse. But she doesn't seem to notice, and most of us are still sitting solemnly enough. After the lecture she is surrounded by an apparently reverent semicircle of undergraduates, who want to know still further. Her face a little flushed now from so much talking, she answers their questions with dogmatic directness. Yes, she considers herself a genius. No, self-expression has nothing to do with it. No, it is not her job to make people understand what she writes. Yes, she feels just like everybody else; she has often said to Picasso, who is also a genius, "Do you feel any different from anybody else?" and no, neither does he.

The total impression we carry away is that of a fundamentally serious, not to say megalomaniac writer — are all really serious people megalomaniacs? — who has come back home for a visit in the happy consciousness that she has triumphed at last. Her own country, after thirty years of neglect, is delighting to honor her. Later, when you hear her in a fifteen-minute "interview" on the radio, that impression is further confirmed. Miss Stein is having a swell time, wish young Miss Stein could be here too. She loves the tall buildings, the people on the street, she had a grand time at the football game, America is certainly a wonderful country. Miss Stein is decidedly bullish on America; her enthusiasm is delightful — a delighted visitor's enthusiasm. And she really seems to believe that we have hailed her as a genius, not welcomed her as a freak. She tells her "readers" not to worry so much about understanding her. If you enjoy a thing, you understand it, she says; and she wouldn't be read if she weren't enjoyed; therefore her readers understand her. Unfortunately this pretty piece of logic blinks the fact that practically nobody does read her. Some of us may have sat through *Four Saints in Three Acts* (we went either to have a good laugh or to feel snobbish), or we have read what the newspapers have to say about her, or perhaps *The Autobiography of Alice B. Toklas*, or we have taken one horrified or amused dip into one of her serious books — but if we did, we hardly stayed in a minute; the water was too cold and there were too many queer fish around.

There is certainly some grudging admiration in our welcome to Gertrude Stein; even Republicans thought more of Upton Sinclair after the scare he gave them in California. We are Greek enough to reverence (or fear) as well as gibe at what we do not understand. Our intolerant, cocksure skepticism always wavers in the face of quiet certainty. But Miss Stein has been away a long time. She thinks we are polite. She is wrong: we are simply timid, unsure of our ground, unsure of hers as well. There are a lot of things in the world we don't know anything about, and she may be one of them. This incommunicable meaning of hers may even be important. Why not? — especially if the meanings we have been able to communicate with have one by one proved unimportant, meaningless, or false. And so we totter reverently from her presence and explode with laughter just outside the door. That doesn't mean, of course, that our reverence is any more fake than our laughter.

What Miss Stein does not seem to have gathered is that our altars to the Unknown God — and they are many — are at the same time sideshows, with the barker-priests always drumming up trade. If she really thinks, as she seems to, that the guarantee of her genius is the popular notice she is receiving here, she would do well to let another thirty years elapse before she tries it again. By that time she may have learned that newsboys don't care what they're shouting about as long as they sell their papers.

▏WHITTAKER CHAMBERS

⌒⊰ I FIRST HEARD about him from his friend Robert
Cantwell, who told me that he was an extraordinarily tal-
ented writer (Cantwell likened him to André Malraux),
an experienced journalist, and a Communist who was about
to leave the party. Cantwell showed me a short story Chambers had written, and it *was* something like Malraux: it
was shot through with the same murky flashes of rather
sinister brilliance. I was impressed.

Shortly after that, Cantwell reported that Chambers had
definitely broken with the Communists and was in hiding,
as he was in fear of his life. It may have been Cantwell
who suggested that I find Chambers a berth on *Time*, or
perhaps I had the idea myself; at any rate, a meeting was
arranged to discuss the possibility.

Chambers was not a prepossessing figure: he was short
and stout, with a large head and a face whose coarse features were enlivened by the intelligence of the eyes and
the sensitiveness of the mouth. His dark gray suit, white
shirt, and black tie gave him a Quakerish, or perhaps lay
brother, appearance. He spoke little, listened with an air

[169

of cynical understanding, and sucked a short pipe. He agreed to come to work for *Time*.

I was not altogether convinced that Whittaker Chambers was his real name, and although he told me almost nothing of himself and his circumstances, there was such an air of suppressed melodrama about him that I should not have been greatly surprised if one day a Communist gunman had shot him down in one of the office corridors. He may have had some such idea himself, for he always walked fast from the elevator to his office and, once inside, always shut and often locked his door. His suspiciousness soon became an office legend.

Sam Welles, later a firm ally and advocate of Chambers, worked in the same department and, being a friendly soul, asked Chambers several times to come out to lunch with him. Chambers invariably put him off, saying that he never ate lunch. After several of these rebuffs, the good-natured Sam Welles got miffed and gave up. Some weeks later, when Chambers had presumably satisfied himself that Sam was a reasonably good risk, he himself suggested one day that they go out and have a sandwich together.

First they took the subway to Herald Square, where they surfaced, Chambers leading the way, and dived into the ground floor of Macy's, a large department store. They walked rapidly to the nearest escalator, went up a floor, traversed its length to another escalator, went down, back into the subway, took a downtown train, got out at the second stop, and came up again to the street. Chambers said, "I think it's all right now," and they went into a sandwich shop and had lunch.

On *Time* Chambers very quickly proved his worth as a journalist. In his first or second week, through bad luck or bad management, he was assigned the "cover story" — the feature article which was normally given only to a seasoned *Time* writer or at the end of a lengthy apprenticeship. Chambers cleared this hurdle not only creditably but with extraordinary style; almost the only fault to be found with his first cover story was that it was considerably too long and had to be cut. Almost all *Time* writers had to resign themselves to having their copy cut and also to being hacked about ("edited") and often largely rewritten by an editor. From the very first, Chambers made it quite clear that he objected violently to this convention and would never resign himself to it.

Whenever I edited his copy, if I cut a sentence or altered a word, I could always expect his protesting presence or, more effectively, an eloquently despairing note (often quoting Dante, Milton, or some German poet — usually in the original) to the general effect that his story was now ruined and, if these indicated changes were made, completely senseless and not worth publishing. In these and other ways he let it be known that he did not feel himself among his intellectual superiors or even equals; and though this feeling of his was shared, with some qualifications, by others on the staff (including me), it did not endear him to most.

For a time he shared an office with James Agee, another lone wolf, though of a very different breed, and the two of them grew to respect and like one another. Both of them preferred to work at night (sometimes all night) when the office was deserted. After a long bout of work they would often disappear for a couple of days. If the habits of the rest of the staff had been like theirs, the paper would never have gone to press. But the quality of their writing more than made up for the inconvenience of not always being able to find them when you wanted them.

Chambers had another quirk that bothered me more. At least I thought of it then as a quirk. On any subject that touched on Russia or Communism, he seemed to me so biased that he could not be trusted to write fairly. Those

were the days when the Soviet Union was our wartime
ally, and Stalin, though not as popular with Americans as
Churchill, was certainly more respected and more popular
than de Gaulle. Yet whenever Chambers referred to Stalin
or the Soviets, he made them out to be not friendly allies
but cynical and treacherous enemies.

This anti-Communist, anti-Russian attitude, which in a
few years was to become common throughout the United
States, seemed in those days embarrassingly peculiar to
Chambers. At first I did what I could to keep this bugaboo
out of his reach, or at least out of his copy. As the climate
of opinion changed, Chambers' view of Russia gradually
came to seem less outlandish. Even then, he remained so
uncompromising and so obviously contemptuous of any
contrary opinion that he became increasingly unpopular
with a large part of the *Time* staff.

Not very long after the Yalta Conference he brought me
a fable he had written, called "Ghosts on the Roof": the
shades of the murdered tsar and his family looked down
from the roof of their Yalta palace on the meeting of
Stalin, Roosevelt, and Churchill and made pungent comments on the situation. As I remember it, Chambers simply
left the piece on my desk, saying that I might like to read
it but that it was certainly not for *Time*, and made no at-
tempt to persuade me to run it. It was not calculated to further friendly sentiments among the Allies. It was not
written like a *Time* story. Nevertheless, I thought *Time*
should print it. I took it to Henry Luce for his opinion: his
eyebrows went up. He admitted that it was a forceful
piece of journalism and asked me what I intended to do
with it. I said I thought of running it in *Time*. The eyebrows went up again; Luce washed his hands of the affair.

Somehow word got around the office about the fable
Chambers had written. I was visited by an unofficial dele-
gation from the staffs of both *Time* and *Life*, urging me

strongly not to print the piece: it would drive a wedge between the Allies, it was biased and bitter, irresponsible journalism, et cetera. I was sufficiently shaken to postpone publication for a week. Then I sent it to press. "Ghosts on the Roof" caused some stir in our small journalistic world, but even there the skies did not fall. And a few years later, when *Time* reprinted it as an I-told-you-so, it seemed in retrospect a mild and orthodox comment, and no eyebrows went up.

But in those days none of us knew why Chambers was so sure he was right about Communism. When he became Foreign News editor of *Time*, he carried things with such a high hand that most of *Time*'s foreign correspondents (and I think all our correspondents in Europe) protested, first to me, and then over my head to Luce, against Chambers' continual disregard or contradiction of the sense of their dispatches. They wanted him removed. It was they who should have resigned, because by this time both Luce and I were convinced that Chambers knew what he was talking about, and that they didn't.

It was a bad situation: a Foreign News editor who despised his correspondents as fools (or even suspected that some of them were knaves), and an increasingly enraged corps of correspondents who considered the Foreign News editor insane or crooked or both. I thought it was a damn poor way to run the Foreign News department, but that was Whit's job. My job was to get the paper out, at the same time trying to see that it told as much of the truth as it could about the events it reported. In those years I was responsible for *Time*'s reputation, and I am only too well aware that *Time* had a reputation for being biased. I had to make a choice: side with Chambers (Communist policy is cynical and sinister) or with his rebellious correspondents (Communist policy is humanitarian and hopeful). My choice was to uphold Chambers.

Though I came to believe that Chambers was completely right about the ruthless and bloody intentions of Stalinist Russia, I still jibbed at what I considered his melodramatic descriptions of Communist methods, especially in the field of international conspiracy. His descriptions of these methods seemed to me both dark and vague. And perhaps they were, of necessity. At all events, when Chambers denounced Alger Hiss as a former Communist spy, admitting that he too had been one, it was a shock not only to me but I think to most of my colleagues on *Time*. This was naïve of us, but it was a fact. We never stopped to consider that membership in the Communist Party necessarily implied taking orders from headquarters, and that headquarters were in Moscow.

Shortly before Chambers denounced Hiss, he told me what he was going to do. I was very far from understanding all the implications or suspecting what a national uproar the case would create, but I could tell from Chambers' agitation and from his broken remarks (one was that "this will be the end of me") that whatever it was he was planning to do was costing him a great effort. Even after his confrontation with Hiss and the Nixon hearings and the complicated revelations brought out in court, I could not help feeling that the whole affair was somewhat melodramatized.

It was a stunning blow to realize that Chambers had been a spy for Russia; it was even more shocking to learn that someone as high in the councils of the government as Alger Hiss had also been a spy. (Hiss's champions, among whom many of my friends were numbered, would never admit this, and some of them believe in Hiss's innocence to this day.) But all this had happened years before: by the statute of limitations both Chambers and Hiss were automatically absolved from any prosecution for espionage. Besides, when they were spies for Russia, Russia was

the ally of the United States and supposedly a friendly nation. Passing state secrets to an ally was surely not as bad
as passing the same secrets to an enemy? And what, in
fact, did those secrets amount to? They seemed pretty
small potatoes and not the kind of thing that could have
helped Russia much or done the United States much harm.
Who can remember now even what they were?

Why, then, did Chambers go to such lengths — the ruin
of his own career, with the attendant notoriety that made
his name a by-word and a hissing, and (worst of all) allow
himself to become the forerunner of the rascally Senator
McCarthy, the tinpot Robespierre who, to the amused disgust of the civilized world, for a disgraceful period became
the dominant voice of his half-ashamed, half-terrified nation — why did Chambers go through all this just to ex-
pose one fellow ex-Communist to the government?

The motives that have been ascribed to Chambers run
the gamut from jealousy to paranoia, and some of these al-
leged motives are sickening or trivial. I believe that, insofar as any man can be believed when he tries to explain his
actions, Chambers' own explanation is true: he was trying
to make amends for his Communist past and hoping to
show his fellow Americans that the international "appa-
ratus" of Communism is a mortal danger to democracy.

Witness, the book he wrote after the trial, favorably
compared by some readers to Dostoyevsky and damned by
others as the sentimental maunderings of a deluded hypo-
crite, elaborates this case by telling the story of his life
and, to my mind, not only clinches the argument but
leaves it far behind. This is the statement of an agonized
soul, adventuring not among masterpieces but among the
brutal and cruel realities of our murderous day. The book
was a best seller and sneered at as such; it was also said to
have made Chambers' fortune and put him on Easy Street.
This is not true. The royalties from *Witness* went largely

to pay his debts. After he resigned from *Time*, he lived the hand-to-mouth life of a farmer, mortgages and all. I believe that *Time*, quite properly, did help him to bear the heavy expenses of the trial. But what eventually rescued him from near-poverty was the advice of a friend who showed him how to make money on the stock market.

The hatred and contempt of Chambers felt and voiced by American liberals was deep and instinctive, and still remains so. Nobody likes an informer — not even the police. Chambers forced himself into that role, and I think he paid the price for it, a far higher price than his enemies will allow. Many of them carry their scorn of him even further: they believe that Hiss was innocent, that Chambers committed "forgery by typewriter," and that he was a malicious or a vengeful liar. (An eminent psychiatrist, called by the defense, who never even interviewed Chambers, but only observed him in court, announced that he was, among other things, "a pathological liar.")

Hiss's conviction, for which he went to jail, was for perjury, but during the course of the two trials Chambers was forced to admit that in his testimony he too had perjured himself. (Was it seven times altogether?) Hiss never admitted anything: that he had ever done anything wrong, ever told an untruth, ever made a mistake. This contrast between the two men, one of whom admitted that he was perfect, the other who admitted he was not, must have had a powerful effect (as I think it should have had) in making up the minds of the jury about who was trying to hide something and who wasn't.

Unless the story that Chambers told in court was essentially true, and unless the reasons he gave for denouncing Hiss were essentially the true reasons, the only possible alternative explanation for his action against Hiss would be revenge or malice. Revenge for what? No hint of such a motive ever found its way into the court record or into the press, for the good reason that it was too far-fetched to make sense. As for malice, not even Hiss's most desperate supporters could seriously advance that motiveless motive, short of accusing Chambers of being dangerously insane. When Chambers first made his deposition about Hiss, did he envisage the train of events that would follow? I doubt it very much. He knew, I am sure, that there would be hell to pay — for himself and his family certainly, for Hiss probably — and that foreknowledge must have made him wrestle with himself for racking weeks and months before he made his decision. It has been said of him that he did more harm to his country than any man of his generation. People who say that mean that he paved the way for McCarthy, that if it hadn't been for the Hiss trial and the influence of Chambers' book *Witness*, the nationwide fear and suspicion of the "Communist menace within our gates" would never have reached such hysterical proportions. I wonder. McCarthyism, under other names, has always been active or latent in the United States. Whittaker Chambers certainly didn't invent McCarthyism, though it must be admitted that he helped to let loose the McCarthyite madness.

Of the various indictments that have been brought against Chambers — that he was an informer, that he deliberately ruined Hiss by committing "forgery by typewriter," that he did his country untold harm by summoning up McCarthy and his evil spirits — I think the only one that is really damaging to him is the last. Damaging, but not damning. I wish he hadn't been *friendly* to McCarthy and his witch hunters, but he wasn't the first, and he wasn't the only one, by a long, long shot. How much harm a man does or whether he actually does more harm than good is a question we can leave to God and the historians.

After the tumult of the Hiss trial, Chambers lived in iso-

lation with his wife and two children on his Maryland
farm. I used to go there to see him. I often wished that the
people who were so sure he was a scoundrel, or those who
had doubts of him, could see him at home with his family
or could meet his wife, Esther. She had no doubts of him
whatever. She was quietly certain that her husband was a
great man — and to her that meant that he was also a
good man. She herself was like one of those fabled wives of
ancient Rome: simple, high-minded, guileless. Suffering
had aged her, and she looked considerably older than her
years.

Neither Chambers nor his family ever drank spirits, but
whenever I came there was always a bottle of whiskey for
me. Esther was a good cook, and those farm meals were
feasts. In his own house, Chambers was not the sardonic,
warily silent character he seemed outside, but hospitable,
relaxed, almost talkative. He and I would settle ourselves
in a quiet room for a lengthy discussion that might start
with the situation on *Time* but always ended with the situation of the world and the human condition.

He did most of the talking, and the burden of it was not
optimistic. Far from it. He saw life as a tragedy, and he
lived it as he saw it. He believed that Communism was the
winning side, that Soviet Russia (or Red China) would almost infallibly conquer the world, and that our role was to
keep the losing fight going as long as possible. This, as I
remember it, was the unvarying general theme. I came
away from these talks and these visits, believe it or not,
invigorated and refreshed.

Why? It wasn't that I didn't take Chambers seriously or
think he didn't mean what he said. Being a bit of a doom-
singer myself, I even tended to sympathize with the general drift of his talk. But although he spoke with conviction
and I admitted the logic of his argument and the force of
his statements, he somehow didn't get me *down*. On the

contrary, I invariably went away from these occasions with head and heart high, like a true believer after a brisk rubdown with a hellfire-and-damnation sermon who walks out of church feeling fighting fit and ready for Monday.

On my last visit Chambers had moved, and I had a little difficulty in finding the new farm. It was not far from the old one, but was even more remote and secluded. The house looked as if it had been recently painted, and indoors everything had a new or refurbished gleam. Esther's kitchen was spotless, as always, but it seemed to have a lot of new gadgets as well. I said to Chambers that the farm must be doing well. No, he said, he wasn't farming the place at all now. Then why, I wondered, these signs of prosperity?

But that could wait. First I wanted to hear Chambers' report on the world — a world from which Stalin had vanished but in which loomed the no less sinister figures of Khrushchev and Mao. I never had to wait long for Chambers to raise the subject, and I thought we had begun when he remarked with a smile that he had just sent in his resignation from the board of *The National Review*, a right-wing weekly for which I knew he had done some writing. He had resigned, he said, over a disagreement on policy: *The National Review* was violently against allowing Khrushchev to visit the United States, but he himself thought the visit might not be a bad idea.

This tolerant attitude — or was it tactical? — surprised me. I waited to hear more, but more was not forthcoming. Instead, Chambers began to talk about a mutual acquaintance, a man who had been on *Time* with us and had now made a fortune in business. This man, it appeared, had given Chambers a tip that had made him a lot of money and, he expected, would make him a good deal more. He described the transaction in some detail.

I was glad to hear that he was in easier circumstances.

But what about man's fate and the fate of our world? Had this lifelong, all-consuming concern, to which he had sacrificed his career, his family, and (some would say) his reputation, begun at last to bore him, and was he now taking refuge in the stock market, of all places? This would have been like a Somerset Maugham ending to a Dostoyevsky novel, a shoddy-clever answer to a tragic question. I thought I knew Chambers too well to suppose that anything could have made him abandon a position so long and grimly held.

And of course he hadn't abandoned it. He was tired and unwell (he had already had several heart attacks and was soon to have a fatal one); he felt himself growing old. Entwined with his clearsighted tragic view there had always been a dark cast of resignation, the Spanish attitude of *no hay remedio*. When we were both on *Time* he had once amazed me by remarking casually that journalism did more harm than good. I had been too shocked — and too busy being a journalist — to pursue the argument. If I had, I think I might have got him to admit that in effect "serious literature" is at least as ambiguous as "journalism."

I think that, at the time of my last visit, Chambers had resigned himself or was trying to resign himself to the fact that he was finished, that whether or not there was anything more he might have done, there was nothing more now that he could do. He was trying to resign himself, but he had not given up. When he had finished telling me about his newfound interest in making money (and he made it an amusing story; he put quotation marks around his "success"), he responded, at first reluctantly but then with something approaching his old smoldering way, to my questions about the volcanic future.

He spoke of leaving the United States, in which he no longer saw any hope — somewhere the nation had taken a fatally wrong turning — and emigrating, perhaps to Mexico; Europe was finished. He even seemed to feel that his old enemy, the voracious Communist conspiracy, had bogged down and might flounder in the mud for some time to come. The prospect did not seem to cheer him: it would be as anticlimactic as it might have been for Leonidas and his Spartans, having combed their hair, prepared themselves for death, and closed ranks, to get the word that Xerxes had called off the invasion and ordered his myriads home.

Or perhaps Chambers felt that the steam had gone out of his old Marxian metaphor, the express train of history. If the train of events could really be likened to an express, something had gone wrong with the timetable or someone was doing a hell of a bad job of running the railroad. Could it be that we were so far out in our calculations that we should have been thinking in terms of dinosaurs, not railroads; that our out-of-joint time is not yet history but prehistory?

I can't remember the words Chambers used, but the effect of them was something like that. And this time, when I said goodbye to him, I went away without my accustomed sense of having been reinvigorated. It was mainly, I suppose, the premonition that we should not meet again. But it was more than that: this time I felt that I had been in the presence of Cassandra, whom for once I had understood, and with whom at last I agreed, and whose foreknowledge cut too close to the bone.

⠙ EDMUND WILSON

◜◜ I T WOULD BE AN EXAGGERATION to say that
Edmund Wilson was the mentor of my youth, but an exaggeration with a modicum of truth. For the four years
(1925–1929) when we were both on the staff of *The New
Republic*, I regarded myself as his pupil, and so, I think,
did he. I also learned to like him and laugh at him (behind
my hand) as one of the eccentric elders in whose company
God or Herbert Croly (*The New Republic*'s founder and
editor), themselves a sufficiently eccentric pair, had put me.

When I first met Wilson I was twenty-four and young
for my age; he was my elder by only six years, but seemed
of a different generation; I considered him and deferred to
him as an older man. I thought him rather disappointing
to look at: a short, sandy-haired youngish man, at thirty
already inclined to stoutness and baldness, with pale, blink-
ing eyes and a high, strained-tenor voice, his profile as
regular as a plump Roman emperor's, but his expression
like an absent-minded, cantankerous professor's. There was
something chilly and withdrawn — *disagreeable* is perhaps
not too strong a word — in the set of his face.

He was not so much shy as uneasy and awkward with people, and his uneasiness held more than a hint of impatience, as if he felt he was wasting his time in such company and was in a hurry to be off. He had no small talk whatever, but when he was holding forth on a subject that interested him, he seemed perfectly oblivious of his audience and would go on and on in his rapid-fire, high-pitched voice, gesturing mostly by jerking back his head or wagging it from side to side. When he paused, always at the end of a paragraph, a hearer might wrongly suppose that he had finished and would sometimes make the mistake of starting a new subject. That this was a mistake was borne in on him when Wilson, having collected his thoughts and regained his breath, broke ruthlessly in at the exact spot where he had left off.

In the first months of our acquaintance I never had any real conversation with him, though I saw him nearly every day. At first he would slip past my office door without stopping, sometimes with a nod and a small whinnying sound meant as a greeting. Then one day he stopped and came in. There was something impressive and something appealing about him — you felt that while his mind was roaming (occupied with very serious matters and in awesomely select company), he might not quite realize that it was beginning to rain, and you felt impelled to open an umbrella over him or guide him to shelter.

He did have friends, and his friends felt that way about him; they respected him, laughed at him, and called him Bunny. And there must have been something about him that appealed to women, for he was married four times. When I first knew him, he was divorced and not yet remarried, and I remember the room he was living in — I think it was on Ninth Avenue — a perfect picture of helpless, squalid bachelorhood: an unmade bed, empty gin bottles on the dirty floor, no carpet, one naked electric light bulb. Women, too — some of them — wanted to guide him to shelter.

Wilson had enemies as well as friends. The printers at the Steinberg Press, for instance, where *The New Republic* was printed, hated him. They had their reasons. Although Wilson had been a journalist, of a literary sort, for years, I don't think he clearly understood or had much interest in the mechanics of printing. Anything he wrote was likely to be rewritten several times before he was satisfied with it; he would cross out paragraphs on his galley proofs and paste in new passages, typewritten if there was time; if there wasn't, he would crowd the margin with his small but legible handwriting, in pencil. (He had a peculiar way of holding a pencil: he seemed to bunch his whole hand about it, using both his middle finger and his forefinger to guide the point.) Worst of all, he would often make drastic revisions on the page proof itself. As anyone who knows the printing process doesn't need to be told, such eleventh-hour corrections entail a lot of highly expensive extra work for linotyper, compositor, proofreader, and foreman, and hold up the stereotypers as well. All hands in a printing shop take a strong view of authors' last-minute alterations.

The printers didn't hold me personally responsible for these outrages of Wilson, as they knew I was only a go-between. But one day at the press, when with a sinking heart I had given the foreman some heavily "corrected" page proofs of a Wilson article, he said to me, "This Wilson a friend of yours?"

That wasn't quite the way I'd have put it, but I said yes.

"Well, let me tell you something. Don't ever let him show his face down here. Why not? The boys would kill'm. That's why."

I think it's a pity that Wilson never knew that, but it was characteristic of him not even to suspect it. I suppose it was equally characteristic of me not to tell him — although if I had tried to, I don't think he would have understood.

Our friendship — if that is not too warm a word (it is certainly not too warm for my end of it) — broke off in about 1940, when we met by chance at Princeton Junction and he dumbfounded me by picking a quarrel, the reason for which at the time was quite incomprehensible to me. He began by accusing *Time* (on whose staff I had then been for some ten years) of being "dirty about women," and noted that the higher I rose in *Time*'s ranks, "the dirtier it got." This unexpected attack, by a man whom I had regarded as friendly, if not my friend, left me ruffled, angry, and puzzled.

I finally came to the conclusion that the animosity behind Wilson's outburst must have arisen from his resentment of *Time*'s review of a book by Mary McCarthy, who was then his wife. The review had been written by James Agee, who was incapable of being "dirty" about anybody. I had not read the book, *The Company She Keeps*, but I had passed the review. I now read the book, reread the review, and found myself in complete agreement with Agee.

Later it occurred to me that the underlying reason for Wilson's attack was not merely this particular review. I think he may have felt disappointed by my giving up writing for the anonymous, executive job of a *Time* editor; besides, he didn't consider the writing in *Time* respectable journalism. There was nothing in my accomplishment he could happily take credit for; in a way it was a reflection on himself as an instructor of my youth. He must have felt that the time he had spent on me was quite wasted. I had left school too young and had gone to the bad straight off. As for me, I remember Wilson as one of my favorite professors.

The break in our friendship lasted so long — twenty years! — that I never expected to see him again and felt

free to describe him, in a book of memoirs I wrote, exactly
as he had appeared to me. Then, shortly after the book,
Name and Address, was published, to my surprise and delight I received the following letter:

April 4, 1960

Dear Tom:

I have been reading your book with great interest. You
have turned out to be a writer after all. I think you did
well to decide to do a straight autobiography rather than
the usual autobiographical novel. I am sorry that our last
meeting was disagreeable, and when I heard that you were
leaving *Time*, I had the impulse to wire you congratula-
tions. I hope to see you again in a more cheerful way.

Here are some observations:

First of all, I was surprised to discover that I was only
six years older than you. I had thought of you as so much
younger. The point is that the younger people are, the
more difference a few years make. At first it did not seem
to me plausible that you should have been in England in
1911 — I was there in 1908 and 1914; and that you should
remember the old-fashioned Fourth of July. (You don't
mention that those paper balloons were sometimes in the
form of animals.) I also read Ralston's *Russian Fairy
Tales*, which was in my grandfather's library, and also
thought they were among the most frightening. You know
Gogol developed his story *Viy* — which I think is the most
hair-raising modern tale of horror — from one of those
vampire stories . . .

He then proceeded to cite more points on which he either
corrected me or had some critical comment to make, and
ended on a sympathetic note:

I share your personal reactions to what is going on in this
country: Russia and the United States are getting to be
more and more alike; and sometimes I feel that I have

reached the point when, as the old adage says, good Americans can die and go to Paris . . .

As ever,

Edmund Wilson

This letter made me very happy. It not only conferred on me the diploma he had all these years withheld, but also added an apology for his attack on me. From Wilson, such a statement of regret could certainly be construed as an apology.

I replied warmly; he invited me to visit him on Cape Cod on my next trip to America. In October of that year I went to his house in Wellfleet for dinner. He had told me to come early so that we could have a good talk beforehand. I arrived about six o'clock, and his still-beautiful wife, Elena, showed me into his study. This room itself was not very large, but it was the anteroom to a much larger than ordinary library — apparently a series of boxlike rooms containing serried ranks of bookshelves.

In the twenty years since I had seen him he had changed very little. He was, of course, much stouter, so that he no longer seemed to have any neck; he was shorter of breath (and perhaps of temper?), but he had not become, as so many aging men do, a caricature of his youth. He was impressive.

We sat down and Wilson poured us both large whiskies. After a silence of twenty years there was a great deal to talk about, large areas of time to cover; I was full of comments and questions. But Wilson had always liked to be in charge of the conversation, and in this respect I found him quite unchanged. After a lame beginning, when he was impelled, to my embarrassment, to repeat his apology *viva voce*, I tried to change the subject and also introduce various topics from my mental list. But each time Wilson would say, "Yes, yes, we'll come to that presently!" and imbibe another draft from his glass.

By the time we went in to dinner, I had drunk more than I wanted — but nothing like as much as Wilson. He managed to carve the leg of lamb and serve us all (his wife and teen-age daughter joined us for dinner), then said to me, in that characteristic tone of voice that sounded half annoyed, half surprised, "As you see, I am quite unable to carry on a conversation." It was only too true. Elena Wilson did her best to keep the talk going, and Wilson would occasionally rouse himself and make a drowsy, ineffectual pounce as a phrase went past him. We tried to pretend that nothing was amiss, but as soon as dinner was over, I took my leave. What an anticlimax to my great expectations! And my timetable did not allow another try; that would have to wait till our next meeting.

That meeting, almost a year later, began more auspiciously. As I pulled up in front of his house, the whole family was gathered in the grassy dooryard, under a spreading elm tree, and a camera crew from *Holiday* magazine was taking pictures of them. Wilson beckoned to me, calling, "Come join us! Come and join us!" When the man in charge of the crew asked Wilson who I was, he cried, "My son!" Wilson's only son, Reuel, was in fact there; also his daughter Helen and her mother, Elena. I duly joined them, and a picture was taken.

Wilson was very proud of his son and told me (not in Reuel's presence) what a gifted linguist he was. He gave me to understand that there was a keen rivalry between them in learning a new language; he admitted that Reuel had the advantage over him, in being able to speak whatever language he acquired, but Wilson himself rarely had more than a reading knowledge. He told me he had lately tried to steal a march on his son by secretly studying Hungarian, only to discover that Reuel was there before him. Physically, father and son were much alike, Reuel being also short and square, with sandy hair and a blink like his father's. He was in his twenties; he wore a striped shirt, shorts, sandals, and a cropped beard, and said (at least while I was there) almost nothing.

The photography over, Wilson and I repaired to his study, and on this occasion the flow of talk was not overborne by the flow of whiskey; by the time dinner was over, we had pretty well covered all the topics postponed from the year before.

During the next ten years, which were also the last ten years of his life, Wilson and I met only four or five times. He came more and more to resemble David Levine's cartoon of him as an owl, and many a prancing Squirrel Nutkin had reason to remember him as Old Brown himself. He and I never corresponded to any extent, but I read everything he wrote and sent him several congratulatory letters; I don't remember his ever responding to any of them. I presumed that Wilson must have found these letters unsatisfactory in some way. They were unsatisfactory to me as well: I felt that I could never manage to control my enthusiasms and make them seem *reasonable*. But was I overenthusiastic? I remember writing to him that *Patriotic Gore* was a great book and certain to become an American classic, and I don't think that was far out.

I had been particularly impressed by a passage in his introduction in which he likened the cause of wars to the voracity of rival sea slugs. When I next saw him he told me he had expanded this idea in a small pamphlet, *The Cold War and the Income Tax*, which would soon be published. He also talked darkly about "the government trying to take my houses away from me" — both his house in Wellfleet and the house he had inherited in upper New York State. It sounded to me like the conservatism of middle age; I thought it was perhaps a sign that he was comfortably off at last and was now grumbling about his taxes, like any good Republican. Little did I know!

After reading *The Cold War and the Income Tax*, I understood why he feared that his houses might be confiscated, and I gained some idea of the nature and the extent of his "difficulties" with the government. He had fallen into such arrears in paying his income tax (for nine years he had not even filed a return) that he was liable not only to a large fine but also to arrest and imprisonment. He had gone for advice to a friend and Princeton classmate, high in the legal profession, who told him frankly that the best thing he could do was to become a citizen of some other country. This he refused to do.

The upshot was that after he paid $16,000 — all the money he could lay his hands on — toward back taxes, he still owed the Internal Revenue Service more than $68,000. Besides this, he had unpaid lawyers' bills, an unpaid loan of $10,000, and a mortgage. His despair was only mitigated when the IRS informed him that in fact he could settle his bill for only $25,000, this sum to be paid by their garnisheeing his income for the next three years.

How on earth did he land himself in such a pickle? Sheer negligence, as he himself confessed. In some practical ways he really did need someone to look after him, and most of the time someone did. For him, money and all its appurtenances were only an interruption and a nuisance; his literary labors preoccupied him to the exclusion of everything else. This fact must have become apparent even to the vengeful bureaucrats who pursued him.

In the years of our renewed acquaintance, however, I don't think I once heard him laugh heartily. There was too much on his mind, and I think, too, that he must often have felt far from well. I never knew him to take any exercise — he was obviously much overweight, and he drank more whiskey than was good for him. In spite of these obstacles, he did an amazing amount of work and lived a long life.

Wilson's discovery of the income tax led him to investigate the uses to which the government put the tax money, and his findings horrified him. Most of the money was spent for "defense" — an ambiguous word that can also mean "attack" and can include the secret manufacture and storing of vast quantities of such horrors as napalm and deadly or contagious bacteria. He came to the conclusions that "the people of the United States are at the present time dominated and driven by two kinds of officially propagated fear: fear of the Soviet Union and fear of the income tax"; that "our country has become today a huge blundering power unit controlled more and more by bureaucracies whose rule is making it more and more difficult to carry on the tradition of American individualism; and since I can accept neither this power unit's aims nor the methods it employs to finance them, I have finally come to feel that this country, whether or not I continue to live in it, is no longer any place for me." And he saw what America's image had become to the world at large: "self-intoxicated, homicidal, and menacing."

Perhaps if he had been twenty years younger, he might have carried out his threat to leave his native land. But I doubt it. Where would he have gone? The British would have felt it an honor to welcome him, but he was too deep-dyed a Yankee to return the compliment. The state of Europe only deepened his gloom. His younger love affair with Russia ("the moral top of the world, where the light never quite goes out") had long ago been cured by a lengthy visit to the Soviet Union. He was not the type for Latin America or the South Seas.

In July 1971 I saw Wilson for the last time. I had heard that he was not well and telephoned to ask if he could see me. Elena Wilson let me in and went to fetch him, leaving me in a sitting room. When he shuffled in, in a dressing gown, I was shocked at his appearance: his face was quite

chapfallen and a bad color. But he seemed glad to see me.
He asked why my wife hadn't come. I told him that she
had sent her respects but thought we would do better without her. Elena brought him a whiskey; I chose iced tea.
The whiskey seemed to revive him, but presently he said
reproachfully to Elena: "You see! My speech is affected
[as indeed it was]; I cannot pronounce my words properly." She said to him soothingly that he was talking very
distinctly. But quite often I lost the operative word in one
of his sentences or had to ask him to repeat a name.

He was no longer the ruthless pursuer of a single con-
versational fish; often one sentence would be enough to finish a subject, and he was quite amenable to the shifts and
changes of a rather gossipy conversation. He told me he
had just written a book about his father's house in upstate
New York and hoped to finish several other things — "if
God spares me."

He had lately suffered a bad fall, he said, followed by at
least two strokes, and he was now unable to work more
than two or three hours a day. He was obviously ailing and
exhausted, and I soon took my leave. I felt that I would not
see him again, and I was right: he died the following June.

Wilson was the foremost American man of letters of the
twentieth century. He was also, I think, a great American
sage. He embodied that rare combination of stubborn
skepticism, inveterate innocence, and sturdy, clarifying
common sense that we used to consider peculiarly American — almost an American invention — but whose expo-
nents now are sunk under the horizon, as deep as Atlantis.
Wilson's sort, if it has not quite vanished from America, is
in the fast-dwindling, minuscule minority: although once
dominant in the Republic's affairs, this old American type
is now almost completely disfranchised and disregarded.

I no longer wish, as I once did, that he had been given
the Nobel Prize — except for the material help the money

would have been to him. The honors he deserves and will certainly be awarded will be bestowed by a larger and better informed panel than any Swedish committee: generations of civilized readers. His place in the hall of literary immortals is secure; in fact, he is there already, looking unimpressed by the company, and seated between Sainte-Beuve and Dr. Johnson.

⸨ SIR WINSTON CHURCHILL

⟋⟍ A GREAT MAN must appear to his fellow men as a hero, and not on one occasion only; his heroic quality must be durable enough to maintain a lasting image that is larger than life. George Washington qualifies, and Nelson; Napoleon (alas) and Wellington (hurrah); Robert E. Lee is a clearer case than Ulysses S. Grant; Lincoln, certainly. Martyr a "great man" and you ticket him for the ages. Lindbergh, whose one great deed put him in the running, deliberately disqualified himself by refusing to run one step further. There must have been many "better" men in his own generation than Winston Churchill, but who can we say was "greater"?

I saw him, in close-up, three times. The first two were at small private dinners in New York given by Henry Luce, at which Churchill was the guest of honor. The club at which the first dinner was held was spiritually (if the word can be applied to such a place) much the same as the Carlton in London; materially, it was more like Kubla Khan's pleasure dome.

We met in a large anteroom for drinks before dinner. In

the center of the room stood a table loaded with dishes of caviar, toast, slices of lemon, and the grated whites and yolks of hard-boiled eggs; surmounting this collation was a large eagle carved in ice, with half-spread wings, under the tip of each wing a silver bowl to catch the drip.

When Churchill entered and our obeisances had been made, I watched him to see what he would drink: rumor had it that he lived exclusively on brandy and cigars. Not a bit of it: he called for a dry Martini, and had two more after that one. We flowed slowly into the dining room, where the table decorations surpassed the ice-carved eagle. In the center of the round table a thicket of varicolored flowers stretched out vinelike tendrils; from the thicket itself a concealed fountain jetted arcs of blue-lit water. Churchill took a grinning look at this display and growled, "I hope it doesn't turn *pink!*"

The food was of a piece with the stage setting: every dish so famous and fancy that in effect it exceeded the borders of taste; we might as well have been eating ham and eggs. But it was Churchill we had come for — and we got him. I suppose we all admired him, some of us close to idolatry. Two of the company had recently collaborated on a brief biography of him. (How many such biographies appeared in his lifetime? I'm sure he had never heard of this one.) One of these men, who had the unfortunate mannerism of seeming to be supercilious or challenging even when he was at his most respectful, as he was now, asked Churchill an explosive question. How did it happen, said he, that after Germany had been knocked out of the war, the overlords of Allied strategy had far overestimated the effort it would take to finish off Japan?

Churchill's lip went out, and he looked at his questioner a long moment from under his lowered eyebrows. He mentioned a date and a single fact. Then — it was like a tank getting under way — fact followed fact in a relentless

caterpillar tread until he shifted gear into a roar of peroration and crashed to a stop. He glared again across the
table at his questioner and growled, *"Have I answered you,
Sir?"* The burst of laughter was like a cheer, and Churchill's hapless opponent flung up his hands in surrender
and bowed his embarrassed head. Then someone asked another question.

It was not really a question, although it was politely
phrased as one: it hinted, it suggested, it almost stated that
the first fact Churchill had mentioned and on which his
whole case depended was simply not a fact. In short, it was
a devastating question, and this time it was Churchill's
turn to make a gesture of surrender. Quite unashamed at
being caught out, however, he grinned at the table in general and chuckled, "Good thing I didn't try that in the
House of Commons!"

On that occasion he left quite early. We all knew that he
had an important speech to make in the next day or two,
at Fulton, Missouri. We wondered if he would use (he
didn't) the Churchillian phrase we had just heard him
apply to Russia's rulers: "that ruthless little gang of bloody-
minded professors!" And he let us in on the fact that he
had bought two American dictating machines, and that he
always dictated the first draft of anything he was writing,
before he got out of bed in the morning. With a descriptive
sweep of his arm he indicated his distaste for the out-dated
drudgery of putting pen to paper: "All those dirty little
words!"

A year or so later Churchill was in New York again and
came to another dinner given by Henry Luce. This time he
had his son Randolph with him.

After dinner we went into the next room, where there
were little tables. In a few minutes Luce sent for me to
come and sit at the table where he and Churchill were. In
characteristic elaborate Lucean style he reintroduced me

as "the head of the English Fifth Column on *Time*." Churchill, who either didn't understand or didn't care, said, "Huh."

Throughout the evening, he gave the impression of quite frequently not being in direct communication with the person he was talking to. Or perhaps it would be more accurate to say that the person he happened to be addressing, the questioner he happened to be answering, seemed merely the current representative of the thousands, the hundreds and hundreds of thousands, he had addressed and answered in his time. He sometimes misunderstood or disregarded the particular point or intention, but he always met the general question behind it squarely.

His physical appearance and behavior were of a piece with this large and somewhat removed mental attitude: he seemed partly blind and partly deaf to the actual presence of the people around him. His eyes twinkled at times with good nature or gleamed with delighted anticipation when he was about to say something funny or flooring, but at other times they stared glassily at nothing; then they looked less like eyes than like warm brown bruises.

He also exhibited considerable hardness of hearing. Here too, of course, there were mitigating circumstances: he was surrounded by the greatest little collection of mumblers ever concentrated under one roof. When one of them asked a question, the old man would cup his ear and lean forward and invariably ask him to repeat.

The performance he gave as a conversationalist was of championship caliber. But it was an exhibition, not a bout. Occasionally someone would be foolhardy enough to slip into the ring with him; there followed a few foot shuffles and the sound of hard breathing — then, crack! — and the champ stepped back, grinning, while the crowd roared.

In between times, as if to employ his incredible old man's energy, he would balance himself on one finger or practice funny faces. He was certainly no deadpan Britisher: his face waxed and waned continually from a sad, almost sulky old baby's to a mischievous old boy's to a completely captivating crinkled-up, charming clown's. He gave us an imitation of his facial contortions under the ordeal of television lights ("If you're a suckling pig, at least they turn you around occasionally.") He disliked television and thought it a threat to the simple pleasures of domestic life. Somebody objected, "But that's the only way our children would ever see Mr. Churchill — on television." He replied, "But you must always allow for the exceptional case." And when somebody argued that television was proving a good thing for home life by gathering the family together in the evenings, Churchill grunted, "Yes, like a jury in a box."

He spoke of Beaverbrook, "a foul-weather friend." Churchill and his advisers had been much concerned after Pearl Harbor lest all American war production be diverted to American uses, but Beaverbrook had reassured him, "You have not seen a quarter of what the United States can do." He commended Beaverbrook's enthusiasm: "He had an influence on me and I liked that." Although he shook his head over Beaverbrook's defection from the Tory ranks, he said, "Beaverbrook is still for me personally — he wants the jockey to win but not the horse."

He spoke with affectionate admiration of Bourke Cochran, a Tammany politician whom he had once visited, and whose oratorical flow he much admired. He quoted Cochran (apropos natural resources) with appreciative orotundity: "The earth, our great mother . . ." He became so fond of that quotation, he confessed, that Mrs. Churchill refused to go on the platform with him unless he promised not to use it.

He was obviously worried about his forthcoming speech at the Massachusetts Institute of Technology. For one thing, he didn't want to bear down too hard on the cheering fact of Britain's recovery, because that would give the Labour government ammunition in the next general election. And I got the impression that, although he was apprehensive about stirring up the same sort of angry clamor as he had by his Fulton speech, he was perhaps almost equally apprehensive that he wouldn't — because, as he was at great pains to make clear to us, he did not favor a showdown with Russia just now, and, in short, he had nothing very startling to say. He thought things were going just about as well as they could, and he gave the distinct impression that if the Russians kept their strength and their pushing ways, "the fraternal association" of the English-speaking peoples would soon become a very solid fact indeed — up to and including a common citizenship, which he said was bound to come, "not in my time but in yours." His explanation of Kremlin policy: "They fear our friendship more than our hostility." His answer to that policy: "We must make them fear our hostility more than they fear our friendship — then we may be friends!" (A pity he didn't use this in his MIT speech, two nights later.)

He was very strongly in favor of the United States admitting "a million or two DPs — vetted, of course" — this, with our "breeding habits," would be a "rich addition."

At one point Churchill leaned over the table to Luce and said, in a tone of satisfaction mingled with almost awe: "My prestige is *enormous*. Workmen along the road salute me and wish me well."

He would not be drawn out about his opinion of Truman. He had liked him at Potsdam but thought he was a bit uncertain of himself then. Now, however, "Who has done more?" (in taking a firm line with Russia). Churchill said that he himself never misunderstood the proposed Vinson mission to Moscow: Vinson would have gone not as an appeaser, but as an earnest messenger of U.S. intentions to use the bomb if it became necessary.

Asked which of his schools had had the most influence on him, he replied (perhaps deliberately misunderstanding the question): "I was not happy at Harrow. I patronize the school now, but I don't know which I disliked more, the games or the lessons; I think the games." How did he like Sandhurst? "I passed in at the bottom [I think he said] and ended eighth from the top. I liked Sandhurst. It was there I first began to feel that I might not be altogether a failure."

Speaking of the scientists among whom he would find himself at MIT: "I shall give them a crack or two . . . Scientists were made for man, not man for scientists . . . Scientists are servants." (He seemed to mean it in the menial sense.)

He ended by quoting from Tennyson's "Locksley Hall" — which reminded him that one of Tennyson's most admired phrases, "Better fifty years of Europe than a cycle of Cathay," was batted back to the poet at a weekend house party. Someone asked Tennyson if he knew how long a cycle of Cathay was. Tennyson said, why no, come to think of it, he hadn't looked it up. A cycle of Cathay, said the critic, is exactly fifty-two years. This so troubled the poet, said Churchill, his whole face one crinkled chuckle, that he went upstairs and didn't come down for the rest of the weekend.

Like all men who have presided successfully over great affairs, Churchill regarded the human answer to life's questions as essentially simple: the clever men, the scientists, the intellectuals, complicate the issue needlessly and hopelessly — "all we have to do is our duty." (In other words, those with perfect moral pitch — among whom he would have stoutly numbered himself — have no difficulty in hearing clearly the "stern Daughter of the Voice of God.")

As he toddled from the room, at a quarter to twelve,

smiling and nodding benevolently to the whole company,
he paused by the door where his son was standing, and I
heard something like this:

Churchill: "Why, you know America; you have been
more places in the United States and know the country
better than I do."

Randolph: "Yes, but they don't make so much fuss over
me."

My third and last sight of Churchill was at his country
house, Chartwell, in Kent. It was an early spring afternoon, and fine weather (that is, not raining). It was also
an auspicious moment: Churchill's newly acquired race-
horse had just won its first race. After his greeting at the
front door, he retired into his study and I was left with
Mrs. Churchill and her daughters. As we waited for her
husband to join us for tea, Mrs. Churchill told me of a time
during the war when Mr. Churchill had been taken ill on
a trip to North Africa. She was flown out to be with him,
in a special RAF plane. They flew at night and the plane
was unheated, so she and her two companions, a WAAF
and an aide-de-camp, lay down on the floor of the plane,
covered with layers of heavy blankets. The two young ones
were soon asleep, but Mrs. Churchill was wakeful. From
where she lay on the floor she could see a pile of crates and
boxes and, on top, a bunch of bananas. She thought she
would like a banana, and tried to struggle up from under
her blankets to get one. But the blankets were too heavy:
she simply couldn't move. She could shout, however, and
did — and woke the aide-de-camp. He brought her a
banana — "and," said Mrs. Churchill, "I et it and felt much
better."

Churchill joined us, and we all sat down at the tea table.
He gave me my choice of whiskey and soda or tea. I chose
whiskey. This may have given me the nerve to ask Churchill a question. (I was told afterward that that was a mis-

take: he didn't like to be asked questions.) An old friend of mine had told me that when she was a teen-age girl she and Sarah Churchill had both been members of a children's ballet troupe that used to perform at church bazaars and such affairs. They didn't regard themselves as amateurs, but they didn't make much money. Once, they put on their show at a village nearby and were invited to swim afterward in the pool at Chartwell. This time the audience had been so large that they thought they must have made a profit, but when they counted up the takings, they found they were five pounds short of breaking even.

They were sitting on the edge of the pool, trailing their legs in the water and feeling glum, when Churchill and several other men emerged from the house.

"Why so disconsolate, little girls?" said Churchill. They told him.

He turned to one of his companions and said, "What would you bet I wouldn't jump in the pool?"

"With your cigar?"

"With my cigar."

"Five pounds!"

In he jumped with a tremendous splash, slowly heaving into view again with his quenched and shredding cigar still clenched in his teeth.

I repeated this story (I must have had two whiskeys) and asked Mr. Churchill if I had it right. Instead of answering me, he rumbled out that "the meanest peer in England" (was his name Lord Monboddo?) had once bet him five pounds that he wouldn't jump into the pool with his clothes on.

"He was *asking* for it," growled Churchill — and the incident was closed.

After tea he took me on a tour of the house and grounds. A sizable room was filled with his paintings; I peered at several and said nothing, which seemed to satisfy him. We emerged from the house into a walled courtyard: on two sides the court was half-roofed and on these walls Churchill's nephew, John Churchill, was painting scenes from the life of their famous ancestor, the first Duke of Marlborough. Churchill paused and looked out over the sweep of countryside. He pointed toward the Weald of Kent.

"There should be mountains there," he said. "But there aren't."

We were joined (at a military three paces to the rear) by a tall man in mufti with sweeping moustaches — Churchill's bodyguard. At our first stop, a small fishpond, this individual handed Churchill a tin can, from which the old man poured out several handfuls of something that looked like caviar, sweeping it out over the fishpond with a sowing motion, at the same time shouting, "Hike! Hike!"

As the carp rose to the surface and went for this stuff, Churchill said, "And some people say that fish can't hear!"

I ventured to ask what it was that he was feeding them.

"The very best maggots obtainable."

Next stop was the pool. Churchill informed me with satisfaction that it was heated, and that the water flowed down into a lower pond and was piped back to be used again and again. We stumped down to this pond. It was stately with swans. It was also ringed with searchlights set on high poles: he had lost some birds to marauding foxes and intended to lose no more. Close inshore, penned in by chicken wire, a black Australian swan paddled moodily to and fro. Churchill pointed his stick and said, "He doesn't get along with the others. We call him Tito."

The moustachioed guardian stepped smartly forward and presented hunks of stale bread. Churchill took a couple. I took one. The swans sailed toward us.

"Don't be afraid," said Churchill. "He won't nip you."

I broke off a bit of bread and gingerly held it out to the nearest beak. There was a muffled oath behind me. I turned to see Churchill wringing his fingers.

"He gave me a *hell* of a nip."

We trudged on and came to a farmyard. Large grunting pigs in a sty: Churchill looked at them benignly and scratched their backs with his stick.

Chartwell takes in both sides of a narrow valley, with the farm at the bottom. To get back to the house we would have to climb a fairly steep hill. I asked myself how the old man was going to manage it. But at this point a station wagon was waiting: we clambered in and were driven back in style.

I wondered what sort of memorial Britain would raise for him after his death. It would have to be a big one — bigger than the Nelson column. But what more could be added to the memorial he himself had already built: the tremendous Churchillian monument of his own words?

ADLAI EWING
STEVENSON

⌇⟨ I F WE HAD KNOWN THEN how he would turn
out, who he was to become, we might have paid more attention to him. We'd have looked at him with more curiosity, anyhow. But we were too young to make the right
sort of surmises about the future. Full of misapprehensions
of ourselves and of our friends, we thought a football hero
would remain a great man all his life, and we judged our
classmates by the small goals and simplified laws of our
undergraduate world.

I first met Adlai Stevenson in our freshman year at
Princeton. We had entered college in September 1918, but
not as civilians, except for the few who were physically
unfit: as soon as we passed the doctors, we were issued uniforms and assigned to a company of the Students' Army
Training Corps or to the Princeton Naval Training Unit.
We were members of the university, but the Army and
Navy were our masters "for the duration," and the university could not enforce its rules on any of us. The one course
we were all required to take was called War Aims, of
which I can recall only the final prophecy in our textbook,

written by a Princeton professor of German descent: that there would never be a revolution in Imperial Germany.

In the Naval Unit there seemed to be no regulations at all and more perquisites than you could shake a stick at. These sailor boys apparently got up when they felt like it, wandered uptown for a late breakfast at Renwick's, drilled hardly at all, and were the objects of our scorn and envy. Adlai Stevenson was a member of this easygoing outfit.

I seem to remember him in his sailor's uniform — or is it only a photograph I remember? Perhaps we didn't meet till after the Armistice, when we were demobilized and had become proper freshmen. Then we donned a different sort of uniform, strictly observed in those days: a little black cap (known as a beany in other universities, but I don't think we called it that at Princeton), corduroy trousers, a black high-necked sweater, or a shirt with a black tie. Did our shoes have to be black too? I can't be sure, but I remember that anything "collegiate," anything more than drab, was forbidden.

This penitential costume was our traditional wear until some rite of spring, whose name and date escape me, freed us from it. Meantime we observed other time-honored customs, on their last legs then, and quite dead and forgotten now: "rushes" (riots usually engineered by the sophomores as a means of keeping the freshmen in their place), the "cane spree" (a formal contest with the sophomores, with picked contestants at different weights; this often ended in a riot); the "flour picture" (the first official photograph of the freshman class, taken after we had endured a quarter of an hour's pelting by the sophomores with rotten eggs, flour, water, and garbage).

We were a big class, larger than any freshman class before us, and some of us never even got acquainted, but Adlai and I drifted into the same group. He was a slight, dark, nervously lively boy with a quick, lemony laugh; his ready mockery had a tentative air and was never wounding because it somehow included himself.

The social system in the Princeton of our day was well defined, but its clear definition was not apparent until the club elections. These took place in the spring of our second year, in an intensely emotional few days known as Bicker Week. In our time, the twenty-odd undergraduate clubs took in each year about three quarters of the sophomore class; those who were left out were regarded as mavericks or misfits, so the system was considered fairly democratic, on the whole. The standing and characteristics of each club were well known and passionately discussed for weeks before the fatal day by all sophomores, except those lucky few who were sure of being invited by the club they wanted to join.

The best (that is, the most socially desirable) clubs usually got most of the list they invited; the other clubs had to fight each other for the doubtful remainder. This meant that they went after groups rather than individuals — in practice, the key individuals of a group — and this in turn meant bargaining: the group wanting more friends included, the club committee wanting to draw the line somewhere. These negotiations, which had to be concluded by the end of the week, often became tense and sometimes bitter.

It was my first taste of politics, and although I didn't much like it, I found it interesting and revealing. Groups split, necessarily: friendships were strained, sometimes to the breaking point. The group to which Adlai and I belonged went several different ways: some to a good club, a few scattered among the not-so-good, the rest of us to the definitely mediocre. As the leader of a patched-up group (some friends, some mere acquaintances), I ended up in a club that was near the bottom of the mediocre category. Adlai and about a dozen of my other friends landed in a club ranked just above it. When the dust from Bicker Week had settled, I took the tally of my friends and privately put a small black mark against some of their names, for opportunism. Adlai was one of these. Why didn't it occur to me to give myself the same mark? But it didn't.

That summer about a dozen of us went to Europe together as if Bicker Week had never happened. It was the first summer of Prohibition: Europe was "wide open" and seemed the delightfully appropriate place to go. We traveled by different ships and made a rendezvous in London. Somebody had told us that the Regent Palace Hotel, off Piccadilly Circus, was the place to stay. We could see that it was central; it also seemed a touch underworldly, but so did Piccadilly, so that didn't bother us.

When we were all there, we held a meeting to decide what to do first. Adlai was all for going to the British Museum. I was against it, on the grounds that it was sightseeing, which was not what we had come for — anyway, not what I had come for. Adlai won, and led a sizable contingent off to the B.M. The rest of us went to a pub. The next round, I think, was mine. Six of us took a house in Oxford for a week, at an incredibly small price. Adlai, who really did like sightseeing, or thought he ought to, "did" all the colleges, or as many as he could. I said there was too much to see in Oxford in a week, and proposed to spend the time avoiding historical information, mooching about the town, lying on the grass, and perhaps trying to master a punt. Most of the others followed my lazy lead.

At the end of our week in Oxford we set out on a walking tour. The first day's goal was Banbury, twenty-two miles away. One of the party, Jack Wainwright, set a hot pace — we walked the first twelve miles in three hours — and by the time we shambled into Banbury, Bill Tucker was tottering along on tiptoe, leaning on two borrowed walking sticks. Next morning he and Adlai and I agreed that we had shot our bolt: we told the others to trudge on without us, and we made the rest of the trip by train. So that round was a draw.

It was not so much that Adlai and I were in competition, for as undergraduates we went after different things; and, measured against the "big men on campus" of our class, he was medium sized and I was small. In our senior year he was managing editor of the *Daily Princetonian* and a member of several solemn committees; I was chairman of the *Nassau Lit* and on the board of the Théâtre Intime. But both of us felt, I think, that there was an element of mutual criticism in our friendship. Anyhow, there was something defensive in his attitude toward me, as if I were always taking exception to what he did or how he did it — and this attitude carried over, to some extent, into our later lives. I think he felt also, however (and if he didn't, he should have), that if I was critical of him, it was because I liked him and expected a better performance from him than he sometimes gave.

Like the rest of his friends in college, I thought him then "a bit of a politician." This aspect of him seemed to me, as I think it seemed to them, partly a joke: as an undergraduate he was not a very *successful* politician. During his last two years in college he had seven roommates, who would probably have said that they knew him better than anyone; and their opinion of him was perhaps only a slight exaggeration of the general opinion. As one of its last acts, the outgoing senior class passed judgment on its members by voting on them under various time-honored categories: "most brilliant," "most respected," "biggest gloom," "most desperate fusser" (ladies' man), "thinks he is," et cetera. As far as I can remember, there was no such category as "biggest politician," but if there had been, Adlai would not have won it. He would have been a more likely choice for "thinks he is."

Just the other day I encountered a Princeton classmate on whom Adlai's undergraduate politicking had made an indelible impression. It was the accepted practice, when you passed an acquaintance on the college paths (and all classmates were presumed to be acquaintances), either to raise a hand in silent greeting or to say "Hi!" (plural: "Hi, men!"). The thing Adlai had done that shocked this classmate so that he still remembered it, with a slight shudder, more than forty years later was to say "Hi, Al!" Though Al knew who Adlai was, he himself would never have dreamed of saying "Hi, Adlai!" And the reason this incident made such a disagreeable impression on him was that he felt Adlai was somehow after his vote.

None of us in those days ever called him "Adlai." If we had, no doubt some of us would have mispronounced it, as many of his followers did for years after he became a national figure: *Ad-lie* instead of *Ad-lay*. Most of us called him Steve or Ad. His roommates called him Rabbit or the Rabbit. This was obviously not respectful, but like many nicknames it was based on something singular: he did have a nervous habit of wrinkling his nose, and he did have a kind of rabbitlike wariness.

His seven roommates had more in common with each other than with him. He was the only Midwesterner of the lot. Six of them were St. Paul's boys (Adlai's school was Choate): two were Californians, the other five Easterners. Only one of them besides Adlai distinguished himself after college, and that was in the manner of his death: Jack Wainwright was drowned in a characteristically gallant attempt to save two other people in a hopelessly stormy sea. It was Wainwright who was the beloved butt of his roommates, but their baiting of him had definite limits. Everyone who knew him respected his fierce integrity and knew he would literally die for his quixotic beliefs. They liked Adlai, but he was near the bottom of their pecking order.

By good luck or finagling they had acquired a suite of rooms at the top of Patton Hall, which furnished them with a bedroom apiece and a couple of sitting rooms. On one of the walls of Adlai's bedroom one of them had drawn a crude sketch of a horse's rump — "just to remind him who he was" when he woke in the morning. Adlai's family — his father, mother, and sister — had taken a house in Princeton for the four years that Adlai was there, and his mother used to come to his room every week to fetch his dirty clothes for the laundry. When she saw this rude sketch, she asked him what it was, and he had to make up some sort of story to explain it.

Did he actually declare his intention of going into politics? I seem to remember his saying once that he would like to be governor of Illinois. In any case, we knew he had political leanings, and that his grandfather, after whom he was named, had been Vice-President under Grover Cleveland. This fact was joyfully italicized by two of Adlai's roommates, who returned from one of "Buzzer" Hall's eight-thirty (A.M.) history lectures and woke Adlai up to report that Buzzer had said his grandfather was the crookedest Vice-President the country had ever had. (I doubt very much whether Professor Hall, a kindly, blunt liberal of the old school, said any such thing; what he may have said was that Stevenson, when he was assistant Postmaster General in Cleveland's first term, had faithfully administered the "spoils system," under which the incoming administration handed over all federal jobs to members of its own party. The practice dates back to Andrew Jackson, I believe, if not to Jefferson.)

After graduation we scattered to different parts and careers, and my meetings with Adlai were occasional and fortuitous. It must have been on a visit to Chicago that he told me of his attempts to build up the local branch of the Foreign Policy Association. I met his wife, a Chicago belle and an heiress, and heard that he was becoming a successful lawyer and was making a reputation in isolationist Illinois as a citizen-evangelist of America's role in the world.

But it wasn't until 1948, when he ran for governor of Illinois, that we began to write to each other and meet more frequently. During the campaign he sent me one of his speeches, with a characteristic note saying that if he had to give that speech one more time, he would vomit.

To many people's surprise, including mine, he was elected governor by a record-breaking majority. I remember his sending me a copy of his inaugural speech, and perhaps one or two others. I think he was a little nettled by my cool response to these speeches; I thought them dull and ponderous, and may have said so.

At any rate, when I went to visit him at the Executive Mansion in Springfield, he played me recordings of some speeches he had made on nonpolitical occasions. They were an extraordinary improvement on the campaign harangues and state papers he had sent me. He never became a great speaker, but he was now much easier and more graceful.

During the two days I spent with him he had only local engagements, though I gathered that he spent about a third of his time traveling, mainly by plane, all over the state. He was already a compulsively hard worker, with a long day's timetable. At Springfield he spent most of his waking hours at his desk, a huge table in a basement office in the Executive Mansion. The only time he could have had for reading was after he had gone up to bed. His wife had left him shortly after he became governor: he had managed to persuade her to stay with him till after the inaugural ball.

On the two nights I was there, we sat up talking till midnight or after. The only other person who lived in this gloomy nineteenth-century pile was his assistant and former law partner, William McCormick Blair. The staff of the mansion all went home at night, shortly after eight o'clock. On my first evening Blair had gone to a movie, so before we said good night, the governor and I made the rounds of the house, turning off lights and locking up.

I asked Adlai what his principal problem was; he answered, "Graft." He didn't expect to clean up the stables in four years, but he was already looking forward to a second term. I wondered whether he wasn't lonely. No, he said, he was too busy; he simply had no time for a private life, and so far, at least, he didn't miss it.

He was never a handsome man, and as his hairline retreated and his waistline grew, he became less handsome with the years, but he had great charm, and he could have married any one of a number of adoring ladies. Why didn't he? Because, I think, he preferred his life as it was: hard work, dinner parties, the society of glamorous and successful people, many friendships, some of them sentimental. He liked women and greatly enjoyed their company, but he always "distributed the risk": he was more than a bit of a flirt.

He had many enduring friendships with women, some of whom took him more seriously than he intended. He left a few middle-aged ladies with great expectations, which invariably proved false. His three sons and his married sister were all the family he wanted. Insofar as public figures are capable of love for other public figures, he loved and was loved by many of the world's great. For the rest, he had his friends.

Many of these friends dated back to college days and included his Princeton roommates. After his first nomination for the presidency, in 1952, I thought it would be interesting to find out how his roommates were going to vote, and as editor of *Time* asked them the question. One of the six survivors refused to answer, but as he was by far the richest of the lot and an unshakable Republican, no reply from him was necessary. The others all answered that they were going to vote for Eisenhower. (One had temporarily wavered, but after attending a Stevenson dinner at the Waldorf-Astoria, where he had been seated unbecomingly far, in his opinion, from the head table, he decided that Stevenson should not have his vote after all.)

Time printed the results of this little poll — and without comment, as I remember; but I had my own opinion. Why wouldn't a single one of his old roommates vote for Stevenson? (If Wainwright had still been alive, I'm fairly certain he would have been the exception.) Their "reasoning," I thought, must have been something like this: "Adlai? For President? Why, we *roomed* with him!" No doubt they rationalized this feeling by saying to themselves, "No, no, we really *knew* him; you can't fool us."

Either they couldn't see or wouldn't admit the possibility that he had continued to grow after he left college to a stature they themselves were incapable of attaining and simply refused to recognize. It was as if they still clung to the belief that the football heroes who towered over him when we were undergraduates were still bigger men than he was.

Adlai himself, I think, was too much inclined to honor their opinion, or at least to let it influence his faith in himself. In the early months of 1952, I am certain, he did not want to be President nor to be a candidate for the presidency. I was one among many who argued with him vehemently and at length that he must accept the Democratic nomination if it was forced on him.

He was an exceedingly reluctant candidate; if ever a nominee was genuinely drafted, he was. He had a good record as governor of Illinois, but he knew the job was only half done, and he badly wanted another term. As a national figure, he was only beginning to be known, and he would be running against the embodiment of all the football heroes, a man whose popularity as a presidential candidate could have been exceeded only by Babe Ruth.

At the Chicago convention in 1952 I was sitting in the press gallery when mimeographed copies of Stevenson's acceptance speech were passed around, a few minutes before he appeared on the platform. The head of *Time*'s Washington bureau skimmed through the speech, turned to me, and said, "Did you write this?" I had never seen a word of it before, of course, but I was proud of being suspected of being the author. Nothing like the language of this speech had been heard since the days of Woodrow Wilson.

My eye fell on one sentence, however, that horrified me: "Let this cup pass from me." Adlai was comparing his reluctance to take the nomination with Christ's agony in the garden of Gethsemane! I thought the comparison almost blasphemously bathetic, and I felt sure that Adlai had forgotten (or didn't know?) the source of the quotation. Later, when I called his attention to it, he too was horrified. But apparently none of the millions who heard or read the speech took the phrase amiss or saw anything in it out of the way, and since then it has passed into the accepted canon of political oratory.

I have an intermittently acute ear for what I call "besetting phrases," and Adlai was beset by one that appeared constantly in his speeches and to which I objected in vain: "if you please." All this phrase can do is, in some contexts, lend a faintly ironic underlining, but not in the way Adlai used it. It served no purpose whatever and merely sounded lawyerly and rather prissy. I told him that if the phrase set my teeth on edge, the chances were it would have the same effect on some other people; but I could never persuade him to drop it, and it kept popping up like a tiny King Charles's head.

No campaigning politician can possibly write all his speeches himself, but I am sure that Adlai came fairly close to the limits of the possible. His assistants might supply most of the material for a speech, but the actual phrasing was very largely his. From experience and through almost incessant practice he became an expert and accomplished speech writer. He had neither the voice nor the presence of a great orator, but he could turn a felicitous phrase with the best of them. I thought his speeches always read better than they sounded.

It was said and widely believed that his tart sense of humor and his frequent witticisms alienated many of his hearers and cost him votes. I don't see how this could be proved one way or the other, but I don't agree: I think he was in the good old American tradition of Lincoln, Mark Twain, Will Rogers, and Al Capp, and that his audiences recognized and welcomed this vein. And he shared the *tone* of these great humorists: the funny things he said were often penetrating, but they were always kindly.

One instance of this was a speech of his that was never reported in the press; it was given at the Gridiron Club in Washington, where the remarks of speakers are always "off the record." In Chicago a few days before, he had asked me to write the speech for him. I demurred, but typed out some pages on the sleeper to New York. When he sent me a copy of the speech he had given, I was pleased to see that he had used some sentences and even parts of paragraphs I had written — but I was first chagrined and then delighted when I saw how he had improved them, removing the sting but sharpening the humor, transforming a merely mordant phrase into something gay and funny. That was one of the many occasions on which it was borne in on me how nearsighted his roommates were, and what a progress Adlai had made since our college days.

It was said that he listened to too many people, and this criticism left me baffled and uneasy, for I was one of the many who wanted him to listen to *me*. He did listen, but I can't say that I ever really influenced him. At the start of his 1956 campaign he asked me to come to a conference at his farm at Libertyville. It was an all-day meeting to discuss the strategy of the campaign: I think the only simon-pure political amateurs present were John Hersey and myself. At some point in the long day I was sitting next to Adlai on a sofa: he nudged me and asked me what I thought — so far I hadn't opened my mouth. I said, "I think you should declare war on Ohio." He laughed; the others stared; and the solemn conclave went on.

The only time I felt that I may have swayed him (or, more likely, when my advice coincided with the experts') was at the Democratic Convention in 1952, when he had to pick a nominee for Vice-President. Adlai complained to me that he simply didn't know enough about the available cast of characters to choose one with any certainty. That morning I had heard some press pundits canvassing the possibilities; they had mentioned favorably the name of Senator John Sparkman — who was not even a name to me. So I said to Adlai, "What about Sparkman?" His eye lit up; he nodded. When Sparkman was nominated, I was terribly uneasy and thought: "My God! What have I done?"

Some years later, when Adlai was no longer a presidential possibility, I told him about an amendment (I called it "the Cincinnatus Amendment") that I would like to see added to the Constitution, making it a felony for any man to offer himself for President. Adlai agreed enthusiastically; I think he and I were the only two people in the country who thought such an amendment would be a good idea. At the time he was full of disgust and indignation at the reported amount Joe Kennedy had spent in New Jersey on behalf of his son, who had been running hard for the presidential nomination for two years.

One result of Adlai's campaigns was to make him well known and popular. It is difficult, perhaps impossible, for a private person to imagine what it is like to be a public figure. T. S. Eliot found it hateful to be recognized and addressed by strangers in the street, but most public men obviously like these encounters and value them highly. Adlai certainly did.

One evening in the fall of 1960 I went with him to Newark, New Jersey, where he made a speech supporting Kennedy. It was in the closing days of the campaign, which as usual had gone on too long, and the crowd that jammed the hall was bored and bad-mannered; they had really come to see Frank Sinatra, and when that popular demigod appeared, pandemonium took over. Police hauled Adlai and me through the yelling crowds and stuffed us into our official car. Adlai had the driver turn on the top light so that he could be seen and recognized, and open the window on his side so that he could shake some of the hands that were immediately thrust at him.

Another instance was in England. Adlai had wanted to get away from it all for a few quiet days and see a part of the countryside he didn't know. So the two of us had driven down to Somerset and were spending the night in the cathedral town of Wells. After a minimum of sightseeing (my limit) I wanted to go to a pub, and Adlai didn't, so we parted — he for another, longer look at the cathedral. When he found me at the pub an hour or so later, he was in high spirits. He said he had stumbled on a Boy Scout jamboree, where he was immediately spotted, and a lot of the boys had wanted his autograph.

Very few of our meetings were as private and leisurely as this one. Usually we met in Chicago or London or New York, at dinners or cocktail parties or political "skull sessions," or for a constantly interrupted "private" meeting in his or somebody else's office. Sometimes the only hour he could spare was breakfast, and after a few experiences of that, punctuated as it always was by aides and telephone calls and strangers who just wanted to shake his hand and have a few words, I drew the line at breakfast meetings. I was usually agog with something I wanted to tell him, but almost invariably on these hurried occasions he was abstracted or preoccupied by some imminent and worrying piece of business.

It was said that he was indecisive, and that he agonized so long over making up his mind that he would have proved to be a weak President. No one will ever know whether or not this would have been the case, but I should like to have seen him put to the test. I cannot honestly say that my confidence in him was never shaken, but I do not believe he was indecisive — or, if he was, that his kind of indecision would necessarily have been a weakness.

I knew from my own experience as an executive that quick decisions often result in blunders; and I had read how slow Lincoln, for one, had been to make up his mind, and how he was vilified for it at the time, and later canonized. I think Stevenson might have been a better President than either Kennedy or Johnson. He would certainly have advanced the American idea more effectively than Eisenhower.

No man can undergo the experience required to become a professional at any job without cost to himself; as he becomes more seasoned, he must also, in some ways, grow more obdurate and calloused. Whether you call him a politician or a statesman, Adlai was a professional in a career where a man learns, among other things, not to speak his whole mind. Even to his friends? I think not even to his friends. He can relax with them, but never altogether.

Even in this regard Adlai Stevenson was a striking contrast to other professional politicians, and the contrast was all in his favor. Among politicians he seemed an intellectual — though not among intellectuals — and better educated and better bred than the common run. He was a rarity in our anti-aristocratic society: a superior man who was generally acknowledged to be superior.

By the same token, his very existence as a public figure
irked those Americans who used to laugh at Mrs. Roosevelt's voice and manner. He was an egghead; he was "too
tenderly put together." But I have heard him giving orders
to a senator in a tone that might have been used to an
office boy; and though politics taught him to be politic in
public, in private he sometimes unleashed his contempt for
the Old Guard politicians. He had a much lower opinion
of Truman than the popular one; he despised him not because he was a vulgarian but because Truman had tried to
knife him in the back and then had tearfully apologized.
And Truman knew Adlai's opinion of him. Coming out of
a meeting with Stevenson before the 1956 Democratic Convention, Truman cried, "Goddammit, Adlai makes me feel
like the messenger of a ward heeler!"

I think Stevenson really hated Richard Nixon, and I
know he regretted that it wasn't Nixon who was his opponent for the presidency in '56. Adlai's feelings toward Jack
Kennedy were cool (they may have warmed up after 1960,
but I doubt it); furthermore, he regarded him as the son
of a nefarious politician who had unethically if not ille-
gally poured out millions of dollars to get his son elected.

Adlai would have been a natural choice for Secretary of
State in Kennedy's administration, and I'm sure would
have liked to have the job; but he was under no illusions
about Kennedy or about Kennedy's attitude toward him.
He knew that Kennedy would in effect be his own Secretary of State, and that Kennedy was not likely to forgive
his lack of support at the convention.

After Kennedy's election and while he was doling out
appointments, Adlai told me emphatically that the one job
he would not accept was the ambassadorship to the United
Nations. Why, then, did he take it? Because it was the best
he could get if he wanted to remain in public life. "What
shall I do? for my lord taketh away from me the steward-
ship: I cannot dig; to beg I am ashamed."

I hoped he would become ambassador to Britain, where he would not only very probably have been the most popular American ambassador in history but might have had a sounding board for at least the whole of Europe — which was still naïve enough to regard his voice as more truly than any government agency's the Voice of America.

He settled for what he could get and no doubt tried to see the bright side of what he got: the chance that he might shape as well as transmit U.S. foreign policy. What a hope! Did he in fact approve of the American policy he had to justify after the Bay of Pigs and in Santo Domingo and in Vietnam? The official story is that he did approve, officially, of all these American strong-arm actions, but some of his friends will never be convinced that he was happy to do it. A few were sure that he was about to resign or was thinking of resigning, because he could no longer square his conscience with his official duties. A letter from him, posthumously published, flatly contradicts this view. Nevertheless, doubts remain.

It may be that Lyndon Johnson had the "vein of tenderness and alert consideration for others" that Alistair Cooke was sure he had — also "a first-class mind, perhaps the best in the White House in our time," as Dean Acheson believed; but in the character sketch of Senator Lyndon Johnson that Adlai gave me, neither of these qualities was mentioned, though their near-opposites were strongly implied.

Is it possible that Adlai's considered opinion of LBJ could have been transmuted, after Johnson became President, into admiration and trust? In politics, they tell us, only the possible is of any concern, and I suppose it was possible for the U.S. ambassador to the United Nations to serve his President with a whole heart. Possible, or necessary.

The last two times I spoke with Adlai, we arranged to meet but didn't. Both times were in London, where as usual he had more to do than he could manage. On the telephone we made hopeful arrangements, but the night before our first date, he was summoned to Washington for an urgent conference. The second time, we canvassed various possibilities, including a game of tennis and having breakfast together, and at last agreed that he would come for a drink two days later. I said, "We won't be beastly to you, Adlai."

But I was skeptical about his being able to keep the appointment, and sure enough, the morning of the day he was to come to my house, a secretary from the embassy telephoned to make his apologies and offer his regrets. And that afternoon my wife came to my study to tell me what she had just heard on the radio: that he had dropped dead on the street.

How much easier it is to reconcile ourselves to the fact of someone else's death than to the idea of our own! After the first shock (or reminder?), we are soon able to see that on the whole he had had a full life, perhaps it was the best way out, et cetera, et cetera. I cannot reconcile myself so easily to Adlai's death, for I do not believe that he was really a defeated or embittered man. I do not think his country used him as well as it could have, but I think we can ill spare him. There has never been enough of his kind of American, and now that minority is fewer by one.

ₒₒ⟦ RAIMUND von HOFMANNSTHAL

⌒⟨ I THINK RAIMUND AND I first met in 1940, the year after his marriage to the beautiful Lady Elizabeth Paget. I don't clearly remember the time, place (surely it must have been New York?), or circumstances of our meeting, but my first impression of him is still vivid: it was like coming out of a winter night into a cozy, prettily furnished room with a welcoming fire and the certain prospect of a good drink and good talk. He was a warm and civilized contrast to the crass Joe Cools of the *Time* office of those days: affectionate, kind, and enthusiastic where they were calculating, bleak, and watchful.

It may have been some time in the winter of that year that Raimund and I became fellow conspirators plotting a palace revolution at *Time* — surely one of the oddest revolutions that ever fizzled out. If Raimund was not the actual instigator of this enterprise, I think he must have been its leading spirit, for our first meeting was held in his rooms at the Gladstone Hotel (long since demolished) on East Fifty-second Street, where he and Liz and their infant daughter, Arabella, were then living.

⟦223

And who else was in on this plot? There was Russell Davenport, always known as Mitch, a brooding, deaf zealot who later became managing editor of *Fortune* and left that job to follow the glory train with Wendell Willkie; Robert Fitzgerald, a young poet from Harvard, later its Boylston Professor of Rhetoric and Homer's latest and quite possibly best translator; Raimund; and I. There must have been one or two more, but I cannot for the life of me remember who they were.

None of us knew the others at all well. How, then, did we pick this particular list, and who picked it? Here again the visibility is poor: too many shimmering years intervene. Presumably Raimund and I together chose our fellow conspirators, and in each case I suppose because there was something about him we liked or because we thought him a cut above the majority of *Time*-servers. The point of the plot I do remember: very slowly and with great care we intended to gather together the elite (in *our* definition) of *Time*'s staff; one by one our membership would grow; little by little we would capture the key positions on *Time;* last of all we would admit the lost sheep, the brand snatched from the burning, Henry Luce himself. It was a very young idea, but it had something generous about it, and that something, I am certain, was Raimund's doing.

At this first meeting, because we didn't know one another well, we decided that the first thing to do was to tell each other who we were. (Again, I think this was largely Raimund's idea.) To that end each man was allotted two and a half minutes in which to tell the story of his life. As the host, Raimund was to speak last. Even after all these years, I remember three things about that autobiographical evening. First, how surprisingly interesting it was to learn each other's diversely American background and beginnings. Second, how difficult it was (for me, at least) to spin out my life story to fill the allotted two and a half minutes. Third, how overpoweringly absorbing Raimund's account was, and how shatteringly he broke the agreed time limit: he must have talked for more than an hour.

No one objected; no one could have objected — it was enthralling. Our American life stories, compared with Raimund's, seemed thoroughly small and dry, not in the same league. His tale was of war and the breaking of nations, the music and poetry, the thunder and lightning of life and death; a pouring waterfall of grand opera against our little driblets of Chautauqua.

After such a recital anything more would have been anticlimax. We agreed on another meeting; we must have decided on the names of the next one or two members we would admit. But I can recall only one further session — I think at the Players' Club on Gramercy Park. The neophyte (one of *Time*'s obligatory words) we then initiated was Charles Wertenbaker, who was rather nervous and defensive: he didn't quite know what sort of club he was being taken into or what exactly was required of him, and his apologia was rambling, started too far back, and took in too much; as I remember it, he began with Thomas Jefferson and Monticello. So the palace revolution petered out; Luce was never admitted to our company; I don't think he ever knew about our "plot."

When Raimund and Liz returned to London in 1943, he was already well embarked on the amorphous but invaluable job in which he served *Time* for more than thirty years, as ambassador, scout, mender of fences, social mentor and guide, interpreter, defender of the faith — faith in Luce, and he really had it. Raimund could introduce you, or get you introduced, to almost anybody you wanted to meet. His friendships were widely spread, his acquaintance enormous. It was through Raimund that I met such stars of the London establishment as Sybil Colefax, Ronald Storrs, Diana Cooper, and Victor Cazalet.

Just after the war I visited London again, and on my way back to New York Raimund and Liz were my shipmates in the *Mauretania* — not the old ocean greyhound of my youth, but her slower and roomier successor, and the last of her name. We shared a table in the dining saloon, and Raimund did the ordering for all of us. He ignored the menu and made his wishes known to the chief steward: a succulent succession of every sort of delicacy, with the central dish always steak; Liz and he had years of wartime, near-meatless rations to make up for.

Raimund's job at *Time* was indefinable; it could only be described. He started off on the experimental *March of Time*, then became an editorial consultant to *Time*'s London office, and after the war (in which he first served as a GI, and ended in the OSS) he and Walter Graebner launched the advertising for *Time*'s international editions. I believe he was quite good at these jobs, but they were the least of his many functions. His principal charge was the cultural care and feeding of Harry Luce: to try to explain Europe to this keen-witted but provincial Presbyterian, to whom patriotism, God, and "free enterprise" were interchangeable aspects of the all-embracing American religion. It was an impossible assignment, but Raimund wrestled with it as indomitably as Jacob with the angel.

In his early days on *Time* Raimund tried to fulfill his function as interpreter of Europe by writing long, painfully written memoranda for Luce's impatient and cursory perusal. It may have been one of these memos that first brought Raimund and me together. He was apologetic, much more than he need have been, about the quality of his writing, but the written word was not his habitual element; in writing, some of his intrinsic warmth and concern came through, but not clearly nor forcefully enough. Later, in London, he evolved a much more effective and more suitable means of communication: dinner parties.

Raimund's affiliation with the English language, like his adoption of the British heritage, was deeply felt, imperfectly successful. He had by birthright the glorious European *r-r-r*, which the British can imitate only by conscious exaggeration, and he could never quite come to terms with that thorny old English *th*. When he was worked up about something, as he frequently was, and tried to get it all out, his whole manner was eloquent of struggle. It was almost like watching a man wrestling with a stammer, straining every nerve against the throttling, serpentine syllables that bound him; and the happy issue of that warm work was like a triumphant irruption into air and freedom, the late-discovered words bursting into being at top speed and with pent-up force, carried to fountain height by a rush of happy laughter.

Luce had few real friends — his position, his wealth, and his nature shut him off from intimacy with others — but there were a few, and Raimund was one of them. He admired Luce and also was genuinely fond of him. And it was a cause of sadness to him that most people did not share his feeling. He knew that I too liked Luce, a good deal this side idolatry, but that there had been a coolness between us since my departure from *Time;* Luce never really forgave anyone who left his company, for whatever reason, and the implacability tended to become mutual. It grieved Raimund that two people of whom he was fond were not equally fond of each other. Once, when Luce was in London for a few days and I was living there, Raimund tried to bring us together. He said to Luce, "Harry, would you like to see Tom?" Luce frowned, pursed his lips, thought a moment, and said "No!" Raimund told me this with a rueful smile, and added, to cheer us both up, "At least he *sought* about it!"

When Raimund gave up cigarettes he developed the most frightful withdrawal symptoms, centering on an agonizing sciatica. The doctors tried various painkilling drugs, but nothing worked. Then he went to Ischia, to the mud baths there, and that did it. It was like a miracle, he told me. He and Liz went back every year, just to make sure the miracle would last — and because he liked the treatment. Each time he felt "r-r-r-rejuvenated!"

I saw a good deal of Raimund when I first came to live in London, in 1953. He introduced me to many people and places he thought I should know or would like. Then our paths diverged, and our meetings, no longer casual and frequent, had to be thought about and arranged. I can date one such meeting by a memorable television program: Max Ophuls' film of Clermont-Ferrand, a documentary record of French behavior during the German occupation. It was a long film that went on all evening. Raimund and I had both seen bits of it, but when the program was repeated we decided to have dinner together and see the whole thing from start to finish. The trouble was that it had been so long since we had seen each other, there was so much to talk about, and we drank so much that we watched the film only in patches and ended by not watching it at all.

During the last few months of his life we tried several times to meet but never did. On the eve of his going into the hospital for the operation from which he never recovered, we had our final conversation by telephone. My wife and I were about to visit his beloved Vienna, and I asked him whether the Sacher was still the place to stay. "It's no longer the best," he said sadly — and then (and I could tell he was smiling), "but it's still the nicest."

Appreciation, sympathy, praise, simply welled out of him; he was bursting to bring you good news, to tell you the best about yourself. Yes, he was an enthusiast, an intense admirer of certain people (generally but not always aristocratic, in the true sense) and of certain things (cities, empires, civilizations) and hence a passionate believer in them — even when, as was sometimes the case, they were no longer altogether there, or not quite as he saw them. Raimund was never at home in America, although he was (technically) an American citizen; he was deep-rootedly Viennese but transplanted happily to London. He would have been even more at home there, I think, in Edwardian days. He was a devotee of the British Empire who continued to expatiate on the glories and beauties of its setting sun long after the sun had set.

He loved and cherished all that enhances life, and was therefore himself a constant life-enhancer. When he was not laughing, you felt that he was waiting hopefully for the next opportunity, not so much because he found life amusing as because he felt it was *wonnnnderful*. When he did not succeed in laughing, he was sad, sometimes to the point of tears; but in the quarrel between affirmation and denial there was never any question of which side he was on: he was a man whose very being cried *Yes!*

∞⟦ BOOTLEGGERS

⌐⌐ M. LOIGNON

For some reason, his house has a doormat on which appear a number and street other than his own; perhaps it is a sign to the cognoscenti. Sometimes M. Loignon lets you in himself; sometimes it is his wife, a thin, tall, scraggy woman like a bright-eyed crow, voluble and metallic. M. Loignon himself is short and rotund; he even tends to revolve when he walks, each leg correcting the other just in time. He has a big Humpty-Dumpty head, a forehead constantly wrinkled over the anxieties of his business, and behind his pince-nez one eye is turned in so far that it never observes anything but the pores of his own nose. He is a man who suffers much, and proclaims it. Every scene with him is an emotional battle.

If he recognizes you and lets you in, he greets you with an air of quiet but profound satisfaction that you have at last returned; and he ushers you into the parlor as if he were about to give you his daughter in marriage. When you ask what he has in stock, his manner shifts immediately: he becomes defensive, noncommittal, excessively businesslike, and he watches intently the effect of his announcements. With a sudden gesture of man to man, let's face the facts, he leads the way to his big cupboard. He groans as he searches for his key, rolling his good eye at you and hissing imprecations on the weather. With a wave of triumph, he throws open the cupboard doors, and stands amazed at the richness of the display.

He pretends that all his stock comes straight off a liner, though he will mention confidentially, if pressed, that for nearly everything except champagne he has a "domestic" grade. With enormous cunning he elicits from you the price you paid him on your last visit, and you will usually find that the price has now risen fifty cents. You do not transact business with him; you negotiate. And the whole affair is finally wound up, on his part, with the air of a statesman who is familiar with compromise. But it is only an air. His prices are outrageous.

◁ Mr. Flit

Mr. Flit may not exist at all; no one, apparently, has ever seen him. He is a disembodied voice over the telephone, quiet, deferential, concise. When you call him up, though it may be for the first or the hundredth time, his voice never betrays any surprise, hesitation, or suspicion. These conversations could not possibly be briefer: his part in them consists invariably of four words. You ask for Mr. Flit: he says, "Yes, sir"; you tell him what you want: he says, "All right."

It is well understood by Mr. Flit's clientele that he is an unusual bootlegger, a man to be treated with consideration, a type to be encouraged. He is prompt, efficient, obliging, and ghostly, and has never yet, so far as is known, poisoned anybody.

Mr. Flit is a dealer in applejack, which he purveys in

gallon lots. When you are tipped off to Mr. Flit by one of his clients, you are warned never to offend him by too direct speech. When you want a gallon of applejack, you must say, "Mr. Flit, I'd like *one*, please." This formula, which should never be allowed to vary, keeps your relations with Mr. Flit on that dignified and impersonal plane which he regards as indispensable to the proper conduct of his business . . . Within half an hour after this colloquy, you will find a neatly wrapped parcel on your doorstep. Perhaps the bell will be discreetly rung. But no matter how quickly you hasten to the door, Mr. Flit himself will have vanished. He never waits to be paid; he never sends bills; with quiet confidence he leaves all that to your conscience. Is it possible that he could be the driver of that rather shabby coupé which is just disappearing around the corner? It is only too possible, but you are unwilling to believe it. There is so little polite mystery in the year 1928.

⌒◅ ELIAS TOPER

Elias' is a hard place to find, unless you have a good nose for country roads. But if you meet anybody on the way, he can always direct you, for everybody knows Elias in those parts. He is the sheriff and also, it is said, a Prohibition enforcement agent. His house, which was once a hotel, is a long, low building, with a pillared porch running along the front. In summertime, you will usually find him sitting on the porch, picking his teeth and staring gloomily off into space. In winter, he will be in the front parlor, with his feet on the stove, looking out the window.

Elias is a tall, big-boned old man, with a dirty-white moustache, drooping mouth, and puzzled, bloodshot eyes. He turns a vague gaze at you as you approach.

"Do you remember me, Mr. Toper?"

Elias squints a little harder with his bloodshot old eyes, and his mouth sags lower. "Naw. Can't say's I do."

This would seem to be a deadlock, but not really. In a minute he heaves himself up out of his chair, and says, "Come inside, boys."

While the jugs are being filled, Elias presents you with a drink and has one himself, then another. If he is feeling sentimental, he may show you the billiard room emeritus, with an old-fashioned bar across one end, now piled high with dusty junk. Or he may take you out to look at his hens. They are not doing so well this year.

"I dunno," he says heavily, "what's into them damn chickens. Nothin' don't seem to do 'em any good."

They are big hens, Black Giants, but many of them are emaciated, and some of their bodies are almost bare of feathers. Looking at them, and then at Elias, as he stands there among them, you can't help wondering if the trouble with both is what they put into their stomachs.

ᴧ O'HARA

O'Hara used to run a saloon before Prohibition came in, and after Prohibition he kept on running it. It has moved now, and has become just another speakeasy, but a few years ago it had a grand location — on a corner of Park Avenue, in the midst of the most expensive section. The little two-story, red-brick saloon was so completely out-classed by its towering white-stone neighbors that it was practically invisible. No one stopped you at the door when you went in, but night and day a man stood behind a curtain at the window, watching the street. If any suspicious character entered, the barkeeper immediately stopped serving drinks, and the atmosphere for a few minutes became electric. The barkeeper was a tall Dutchman, with pale hair, a perfectly white face, a long nose, and two weasel eyes. He was a picture of suspicion, and he never smiled. O'Hara was a great contrast to him. He must have had his worries, too, but he rarely showed them. He was affable and free-and-easy, and mingled with his guests like a natural host. He had a good memory for faces, if not for names, and after you had been in two or three times, he treated you like an old friend. It was not just a professional pose with him, either; he enjoyed meeting people, and in that queer locality he met many types. He would discuss politics, philosophy, or racehorses with equal picturesqueness. Very few things really annoyed him, but there was one young fellow who was always asking him questions about his past life. This irritated O'Hara, and he was once heard to complain to a friend, "If he didn't ask me so many goddam questions, I wouldn't have to tell him so many goddam lies."

⸻⟦ JAMES AGEE

⟆(IF YOU'VE PLAYED TENNIS all your life, you can get a pretty fair idea of a man's character after half a dozen sets of singles with him. By the same token, you can get to know a man by working alongside him. Perhaps you don't know him as well as if you had often sat up all night drinking together, or as if you were both survivors in the same open boat after a disaster at sea. All the same, if you work with a man you will read him — not like a book, perhaps, but at least like its chapter headings.

It was by working with Agee on *Time* that I got to know him. We had a few friends in common; I remember seeing him at a Greenwich Village party; and once I paid him a visit when he was in the hospital after an operation — for appendicitis, I think. But most of our meetings took place at the office and were strictly business: he was a *Time* writer (mainly of cinema reviews) and I was his editor.

There was no one at all like Agee on the *Time* staff, although there were some others who were also out of the ordinary and who also behaved as if they had a special license. Agee's officemate, Whittaker Chambers, was one of these. Physically and temperamentally they could not have been more unlike, and politically they were at right angles, but their preference for working at night led first to a mutually tolerant acquaintance and then to a warm friendship.

Many years later, recalling those days, and with Agee and Chambers (and one or two others) in mind, I tried to characterize these difficult individuals — difficult, that is to say, from a managing editor's point of view:

> I learned to value the steady man, the slogger, the writer who got his copy in on time and did what he said he would. If it had not been for him and his kind, we should never have got to press. I often thanked God for him. But my real Te Deums were reserved for the uncertain performance of his unsteady brother. There were never more than three or four (out of fifty-odd) of this breed on the staff, and I suppose that was about as many as we could safely carry. In many cases, they were "hard to work with" — touchy, suspicious, arrogant, unpredictable. Their working habits were spectacularly individual. When they worked, they often worked all night, then disappeared for indeterminate periods. They were not only subject to temperamental tantrums but prey to fits of despair; and they had absolutely no feeling about going to press, one way or the other. They sometimes missed the target completely, or failed to pull the trigger. But when they did make a hit, it was often a bull's-eye. They were regarded by the rest of the staff with mingled contempt and awe. I loved and cherished them . . . They were the sea-green incorruptibles who acknowledged no authority but some inner light of their own. These rarities were in journalism but never altogether of it. They gave their editors more trouble than anybody, but they made the whole undertaking worthwhile.

Two examples of Agee's journalism: on his own hook, after a week of working late nights, he stayed up all night and completely rewrote a cover story, a long review of Olivier's film *Hamlet*, because he thought I was disappointed in his original version. And I was, a little: it was well above *Time*'s standard but not quite up to Agee's. Nevertheless, a respectable piece of work, and he was so late getting it in that there was no time to make more than minor changes. All I could do about his revised version was thank him and try to explain that there simply wasn't time now to get the story retyped, let alone set. But what an effort to have made! And who else would have done it?

The other piece of journalism was a kind of editorial he wrote, at my suggestion, on the atomic bomb, just after we had dropped it on Hiroshima and Nagasaki. "When the bomb split open the universe and revealed the prospect of the infinitely extraordinary, it also revealed the oldest, simplest, commonest, most neglected and most important of facts: that each man is eternally and above all else responsible for his own soul, and, in the terrible words of the Psalmist, that no man may deliver his brother, nor make agreement unto God for him." When people tell me about "*Time* style" or assert that *Time* was always written in some form of pidgin English, I remember Agee — and this piece in particular.

Though my recollections of him are few and my overriding memory of him is one of admiration and deep respect, he does not play the hero's part in all the scenes I remember: not all are good, and some are ambiguous. When he came to see me about a leave of absence, I persuaded him to cut loose and resign, telling him that if he had to come back to *Time* he could always be sure of getting his job again. I hoped he would go off to some quiet spot and write whatever he felt he had to write. Instead, he did a couple of pieces for *Life*, and then went to Hollywood to work with John Huston, of all halfway people.

I knew or suspected that he had a violent temper; all the same, it was a shock when I picked up my office telephone

one night and by some accident of crossed wires overheard
Agee, his voice thick with drink and anger, cursing the
telephone operator as if he hated and despised her. And I
learned with an equal shock, this time of relief, that his
knocking down a girl at a *Time* party was an accident: I
was afraid that it had been an act of drunken rage.

And there were questions to which I never knew an adequate answer: Why did he leave so much of his own work
unfinished, partly finished, or not even begun? Why, after
quitting *Time* — and none too soon — did he waste his sub-
stance on Hollywood movies? Why didn't he get his teeth
fixed, and smoke and drink less; did he *want* his life cut
short?

But all such questions and doubts are of no account in
the light of what he saw, what he was, and what he tried
to do. He saw something sacred in the hopeless poor. He
was "human"; that is to say, contradictory and unworthy
of himself. By the seriousness of his intention, a seriousness
that pervades his writing as veins and arteries branch
through a body, he makes us feel like the liars we are.

Perhaps he was torn apart by all the different things he
was or might have been: an intellectual, a poet, a cinéaste,
a revolutionary, God's fool. A wild yearning violence beat
in his blood, certainly, and just as certainly the steadier
pulse of a saint. He wanted to destroy with his own hands
everything in the world, including himself, that was
shoddy, false, or despicable; and to worship God, who
made all things.

♣ JOYCE CARY

⌇✦ LIKE MANY BRITISH WRITERS, he went to the States to pick up a few dollars on the lecture circuit. It was in New York that I first met him. I had read two or three of his novels and was one of a small but growing group of American admirers. He was of medium height, spare and brisk, with a mobile, quizzical, hawklike face. And like a drifting hawk, he was always on the hunt, questing, watching, looking for signs of life on the ground below.

One of his short stories I reprinted in the Education page of *Time*, on the rather flimsy excuse that it was about children. From Cary's New York agent I bought another unpublished story, not knowing what on earth I was going to do with it, as *Time* had no place for avowed fiction and wasn't supposed to print any. A year or so later, when Cary's growing reputation warranted a cover story in *Time*, I printed his short story on a page by itself, as "an example of his work."

Cary hadn't had a novel published till he was over forty, and he was almost inured to the disregard of his countrymen. I think it was in large part the attention he began to attract in the United States that tardily brought him some of the recognition he should earlier have had in England.

Though he never had the smallest chip on his shoulder, he must have known his own worth, and nothing affected his enthusiasm for his work.

He was not one of those writers who have to be surrounded by just the right conditions. He could write anywhere, at any time. He thought continually about what he was writing or planning to write, and if he had half an hour to wait for a train at Grand Central Station, he would scribble off a chapter on his knee. One of my friends who had looked forward to meeting him complained that his conversation was not very interesting, and that was true enough; but he was always intently *interested*; a watcher, a listener, not a talker.

As a young man he had intended to be a painter. When he decided to become a writer instead, he chucked art school and went to observe the First Balkan War, as he believed that a writer should know war at first hand and he thought this would be his last chance to see any fighting!

When I visited him at his house in North Oxford, where, since his wife's death, he had lived alone, and which seemed to me featureless, drab, and bleak, I felt more strongly the cheerful fervor that lit and warmed him from within. *Alertness* and *energy* are two words that come to mind when I think of him. Though I never saw him do this, I'm told that he often used to leap up and catch the top of the door frame and swing himself — partly for exercise but also from high spirits.

Every Thursday two small girls, daughters of a friend of his, would come and make tea for him, and he would reward them by telling them a story. It was a continued story, in which each of them was a queen who had magical powers and commanded enormous armies. He made it up as he went along, and never wrote any of it down.

On one of my visits I found him walking with a slight limp. He had recently been in a plane, he said, whose take-off run had been checked suddenly, and the jar had wrenched his leg. But it was worse than that. The limp grew more pronounced, and the doctors eventually told him that he had what used to be known as creeping paralysis. It was a fatal disease, and there was no known cure. They suggested various experiments — injections of snake venom, electric massage. He cheerfully agreed to all their suggestions.

I went to see him at the hospital at Stoke Mandeville. He was thinner but as lively as ever. In the two weeks he had been in the hospital, he told me, he had written four stories — "three of them quite good!" When there was nothing more the doctors could do, he went home. Everyone knew, and he knew, that he was dying, but he continued to carry on his normal life as well as he could, yielding little by little to the inroads of the disease.

Even after he had to take to his bed, he still went on working. He invented a kind of bed-desk, with slings from the ceiling for his arms, and wrote and read as long as his hands had strength enough to turn the pages of a book or use a pencil. He was asked to give a series of lectures at Cambridge. He replied that he wouldn't be able to give them in person, but he wrote them anyway, to be read by another voice after his death. He had been pleased by my enthusiasm over his short stories (the best, I said, since Chekhov) and had agreed to collect them in a book. On one of my last visits he apologized for postponing this job and explained that he was very keen on finishing a novel first.

Funerals are seldom cheerful affairs, but his was. The church, St. Giles's, was crowded with his friends and family — you could see the Cary nose, the Cary cheekbones, the Cary head, all around you. A family affair, the service was straightforward Church of England, with no frills, and the hymns were good old thumpers that everyone knew and sang with a will.

∘∘[ALBERT EINSTEIN

⌒⊰ THE INSTITUTE FOR ADVANCED STUDY in
Princeton, that world-renowned center for scholars, the
American equivalent of All Souls at Oxford, might have
been merely a school for dentistry. Or so I've been told.
When the Bamberger family of Newark (they owned department stores) wanted to establish an educational institute, they went to Abraham Flexner for advice. They
mentioned dentists; he said, "Why not something more exciting?" And — he was a man of winning ways — he won.
Flexner was appointed director of the institute, and one
of his first acts was to invite Albert Einstein to come and
be a permanent fellow. Einstein by that time was a refugee
from Nazi Germany, a middle-aged man who had been
surpassed, or by-passed, by other men in his own field; but
he was still, in the popular estimation, the greatest mathematician in the world.
Einstein accepted the institute's invitation, but only
after a protracted haggle about money. This is what happened: Flexner told him to name his own figure; the figure Einstein named was so shockingly low, in American

terms, that Flexner insisted on tripling it. Einstein, shocked in his turn, refused to take so much, and the argument began. Eventually they reached a compromise: Einstein's salary was to be shared with a list of poor relations and needy friends, to each of whom Flexner agreed to send a monthly check. I never heard a story about Einstein, funny or serious, that didn't redound to his credit or make him more likable.

With Einstein as bellwether, the institute soon attracted other famous mathematicians. Many of them were Jews, like Flexner and Einstein. The small, complacent, parochial community of Princeton began to wrinkle its anti-Semitic nose. When the institute bought a tract of land on the outskirts of the town and put up some modest buildings, this area was promptly dubbed "the New Jerusalem." A Philadelphia lawyer, an influential alumnus of the university, wrote a letter to *The Princeton Alumni Weekly* in which he protested strongly against admitting into the Princeton community such a man as Einstein, who, being a Jew, was probably a Communist as well. Mrs. Einstein came to see the house that had been tentatively taken for them, and was alarmed to find signs stuck here and there in the shrubbery. One of them read: EINSTEIN, BEWARE! She had no means of knowing that small boys had done this; perhaps it would not have lessened her alarm if she had known it. She and her husband had lately escaped from a part of the world where such signs meant more, not less, than they said.

She took another house or, rather, half a house, in a different part of town. And once the Einsteins had moved in, her fears must have faded away. Princeton as a whole paid no attention to them, and they were treated like anybody else. The family who lived in the other half of the Einsteins' house were the Raymond Leslie Buells. Buell, who always signed his name in full, was an earnest, humorless analyst whose field was "social science": he talked and looked more like a computer than a human being. The walls between the two sections of the house were thin, and when Einstein played his violin in the evening, which he liked to do, Buell would pound on the wall and shout, "Less noise!"

As soon as they could, the Einsteins moved to a small house farther down Mercer Street, in a spot that used to be called Frog Hollow. It was an undistinguished little house, marked off from its neighbors by a wistaria vine that clung to the miniature porch. Here the Einsteins lived for the rest of their lives. My house was on a side street a couple of hundred yards away, and Einstein soon became a familiar figure to my family and to everyone in the neighborhood. I never saw him with a hat on: a hat would have seemed absurdly unnecessary on top of that coronalike explosion of hair. He had an absent-minded way of walking and of crossing the street. My wife, who had learned her driving with a Model T and never felt perfectly easy with later cars, on one occasion nearly ran him down.

Miss Juliana Conover, a lively old maid who was always on the lookout for new chess players, surmised that Einstein might be a likely prospect, and went one day to find out. Her ring was answered by Mrs. Einstein, whose English was far from perfect. She completely misunderstood Miss Conover's question.

"Jezz?" said Mrs. Einstein indignantly. "Not in zis house!" And she shut the door.

A younger lady had better luck. Adelaide was a little girl of about eight who went to Miss Fine's School, where she was getting very poor marks in arithmetic. Adelaide had heard her elders talking about Einstein, and she put two and two together. One day she went to see him.

"Einstein," she said, "can you do arithmetic?"

"Ja — *simple* arithmetic."

That was good enough for Adelaide. For a while her marks soared to such suspicious heights that her parents and teachers investigated, and her confederate was unmasked.

Other stories got around about Einstein and mathematics. There was one that told of his having his portrait painted by William Rothenstein. Einstein asked if he might bring a friend to the sittings. The friend turned out to be a little gray man who sat in a corner and said nothing. Einstein would start talking in German and gradually get more and more excited; when he finished, he would look enquiringly at the little man in the corner, who merely shook his head. Einstein would then relapse into dejected silence, but soon the same performance would be repeated. Finally Rothenstein asked Einstein who his friend was.

"Oh, he's my mathematician," said Einstein. "He corrects me when I make a mistake."

And there were rumors that Einstein was "brushing up on his mathematics" by taking undergraduate courses at the university. It was said that he had been sitting in the front row of "Lizzie" Gillespie's class in differential calculus. More authentic — and more to the real point of Einstein, I felt — was the quotation from him inscribed over the fireplace in Fine Hall, the university mathematics building, that said (in German): "God is clever but not dishonest." For it gradually became understood that Einstein had something besides mathematical genius: he was in his singular way a kind of holy man.

There is no more reason to suppose that holiness and mathematical talent go hand in hand than to suppose that they are mutually incompatible. Nevertheless, the general reverence for Einstein the man, in which I shared, made it a greater shock when I discovered what young mathematicians thought of him as a mathematician.

An old school friend of mine, Morgan Ward, who had made a name for himself in a branch of pure mathematics and was now a professor at the California Institute of Technology, came to Princeton for a few days. He asked me to join him for an evening with his young Princeton colleagues, and I did. The shop talk was of course far above my head, but the gossip wasn't. It was a free-and-easy gathering, and they all seemed to know each other well. They spoke fiercely of Eddington (or was it Jeans? I could never distinguish between the two). It seemed that Eddington (or Jeans) had been invited to Harvard's tercentenary celebrations, which were soon to begin. These young men regarded both Eddington and Jeans (*that* I am clear about) with loathing and contempt as vulgar and harmful popularizers. They thought it a crime that any such misrepresentative of science should be received or in any way honored by a respectable academy. They proposed various expedients to prevent Jeans (or Eddington) from showing up at Harvard. One suggestion was to form a posse to meet the visitor's ship, seize him, and disembowel him on the dock. That might give the public some idea of how Eddington, Jeans & Co. were regarded by serious mathematicians and physicists.

Perhaps Einstein's name wouldn't even have come up if I hadn't had the temerity to mention it myself. It was received with a chorus of kindly laughter. Einstein, I was informed, had done some interesting and even useful work as a young man, some forty years ago. Now he was an old fuddy-duddy who didn't even know what was going on in his own field.

These young men (they are not so young now) were in the forefront of physics and mathematics; they must have known what they were talking about. Since then I have heard other mathematicians discussing their colleagues, and I gather that in these high altitudes a man's mind withers early, though the man himself is seldom aware of it. So I must suppose they were right, not only about Eddington and Jeans but about Einstein too. Nevertheless, the world at large hasn't begun to believe them: it still reveres Einstein as one of the titans of creative thought. There aren't many men who elicit both our reverence and our affection. Wouldn't it be odd, but wouldn't it be like us, if, when we think we have discovered such a man, we value him for the wrong reasons?

₀₀❙ VOVO

⌒⊰ A RINGMASTER OF GENIUS — or of great tal-
ent. That's what he was: a ringmaster who at last got bored
with the circus. His name was Vladimir Perfilieff. To his
innumerable acquaintances he was known as the Captain.
His four thousand friends called him Vovo. The four thousand was his own figure; he said he kept a card index of
them, with their addresses and telephone numbers.

Vovo was a Russian refugee. He had been a captain in
a Cossack regiment and had fought for the Whites. During
the final collapse of the White resistance, Vovo had been
the bearer of dispatches from Wrangel to Denikin (or perhaps it was the other way around), had then found himself within striking distance of Vladivostok, and had escaped by ship.

The ship was going to America, and another of its passengers was a Princeton professor, Francis MacDonald, returning from a holiday in the Far East. Though neither of
them could speak the other's language, Mr. MacDonald
made friends with Vovo and invited him to come to Princeton. Vovo was a young man in his twenties, trained to be
a soldier, but he thought he would like to be a painter.

⟦248

Fine, said Mr. MacDonald; come and paint in Princeton.

So he did. Mr. MacDonald had very little money beyond his professor's salary, and he made it clear that Vovo would have to launch himself on the world within a reasonable and limited time. Meanwhile he would provide Vovo with board and lodging. Vovo was strong as a bull and clever as a fox. He worked hard at learning English and at painting, and also looked around for jobs that would bring in some money.

One of the first he found was cutting the grass at Dr. Spaeth's house on Edgehill Street. The bank above the sidewalk was badly worn where the Spaeth children had made a short cut, and Vovo decided to make a good impression on his employer by resodding it. After he had finished his mowing he went in search of suitable sod, found a lovely patch, carefully cut the strips he needed, and plastered them over the bare spots on the bank. Next morning the Greens Committee of the Springdale Golf Club were summoned to a special meeting: some vandal had scalped half the turf from the ninth green.

Vovo soon made himself popular in Princeton, in less spectacular ways. People liked his looks: he was not exactly handsome, but a masculine magnetism emanated from him. He was dark and heavyset, with a plump face that had nothing soft about it, and an abrupt patch of moustache that went well with his deep Russian voice. He had small talent for painting, but socially he was a master craftsman. He was completely sure of himself in any company, his manners were faultless — when required; he could be brutal to louts or bullies — and he was adept at turning the laugh on any target he chose. He was a virtuoso of the deadpan wheeze, and used his shattered English both as a defense and as a weapon. He gave the likable impression of unbounded energy coupled with tremendous good humor.

His English was a delight. It was in the style of Balieff,

the master of ceremonies of the Chauve-Souris, who would appear before the curtain, stare sadly at the audience, and finally announce that in the next number they would "sink — sat — sonks." Vovo's accent was almost as pronounced as that, his masklike expression just as effective, and his vocabulary really amazing. Everyone agreed that he could have spoken much better English if he'd cared to, but that he was too clever to do it. Even his stock remarks, uttered in his deep guttural, managed to sound fresh. Two of his favorites were "Speakink of insects, how's your aunt?" and "Let's have anozzer in gase of a tie."

As his popularity grew, he got numerous commissions for portraits (many of which, after Vovo's personal magic had faded, ended up in the attic). He gave a show in Princeton that was a moderate success, enough to warrant his moving to Philadelphia, where he took a large studio on Sansom Street and became the focus of the city's Russian colony.

That was where I first met him. Julie, the girl to whom I had just become engaged, took me there. Like all of Vovo's friends, she was proud to be able to introduce him. I was impressed by the grandeur and gloom of his studio and even more by Vovo himself. He was not as tall as I was, but he could have made mincemeat of me. By the grave, appraising way he looked at me, he may have been thinking the same thing.

He gave me some thick sweet wine (it was during Prohibition, when nobody dreamed of questioning the name or nature of anything your host handed you) and kept filling my glass. I soon began to feel a little sick, and this, with my shyness, made me silent. Julie, who was never shy, chattered away as usual, using the word *love* — meaning *like* — in the exaggerated way girls do. Vovo proceeded to read her a lecture. I got the impression that it was at least partly for my benefit.

"Loave!" he said, wrinkling his nose until his small clipped moustache almost disappeared up his nostrils. "You *loave* zis, and you *loave* zat. I vill never use ze vord" — pause, and then, an octave lower — "onteel I am *dyink.* Zen I vill zay, 'Life, I loave you!' "

In later years, however, he himself fell into the looser habits of those around him. He would appear at a dance in Princeton and cut in on Julie.

"Julie, darlink, I loave you. My drain leafs Drenton at three-twenty A.M. Can Tawm drife me in?" (Tom always did.)

In Vovo's heyday he must have been welcomed at hundreds of parties and scores of rich houses, where he was sure to be the center of attraction. It was Vovo who introduced my friend Schuyler Jackson to the Townsend family in Cooperstown; and when Schuyler married one of the Townsend girls, and I was best man, it was Vovo who was the unofficial master of ceremonies.

The wedding took place shortly after Christmas of a snowy winter, and the festivities centered on Brookwood, the Townsends' big house on the shore of the lake. For the first night no formal party had been arranged — an excuse the older people had seized to go to bed early — and most of us spent the evening in a large, cheerful living room at Brookwood, sprawling on the chintz-covered sofas and armchairs or sitting on the floor in front of the fire. It was an unorganized occasion, but Vovo soon took charge and organized it.

He led us in song and sang solos himself. (Our favorite was "Ochi Chorniye"; when I once tried to get Vovo to translate the words for me, he would give me nothing more than "Ve moost have Gypsy vomen and champagne!") And he did his best to get rid of Schuyler's Uncle Freddy, who stayed on after all the other members of his generation had gone to bed. Uncle Freddy was a Presby-

terian parson, earnest, simple, humorless, stubborn. He
liked young people and made the mistake of supposing
that this feeling must be mutual. Uncle Freddy wasn't
quite casting a pall, but he was making us self-conscious,
and we all wished he would go away. Nothing was further
from his thoughts. He was having a fine time; his spectacles gleamed with innocent merriment, and so did his
terrible Presbyterian smile and the top of his bald head.

In spite of Vovo's hints, which grew broader and
broader, verging on insult, Uncle Freddy continued to
beam, and sat like a walrus on a rock. Vovo changed his
attack to open mockery and tried to make a fool of him.
It was the first time I ever knew Vovo to fail at this cruel
sport. Uncle Freddy said he would like to sing a song.

"*Tsilents* for Uncle Freddy!" shouted Vovo, leering from
ear to ear and casting a glance of malicious delight around
the room. Uncle Freddy heaved himself to his feet, cleared
his throat, and, in a clear tenor, burst into "The poets sing
of an English king . . ."

The song was well known to me and I suppose to most
men in the room; it was very dirty. Vovo was beside himself with joy; at the first line he guffawed. Uncle Freddy
sang imperturbably on. It quickly became apparent that
his bowdlerized version, all ten verses of it, was not ob-
scene but, like Uncle Freddy himself, innocent, boring,
and interminable. At the end he got an ovation and, for
once seizing the opportune moment, waved a cheery good
night and left us.

Another evening, after one of the parties, half a dozen
of us went into an all-night diner in Cooperstown for some
coffee and scrambled eggs. At the sight of Vovo, dressed in
the fur cap, belted smock, and high boots of a Cossack officer, and the sound of his outlandish accent, the night
owls at the counter began to grin and nudge each other.
That was a mistake.

Vovo appeared to ignore them, but within ten minutes

he had taken command of the diner. His infallible eye singled out the most likely butt among these small-town sophisticates, and before he knew what had hit him this wise guy had become a clown: his pals, egged on by Vovo, were pointing at him and whooping with unkind mirth. Not yet satisfied, Vovo sent the victim out into the snowy night to fetch us a sleigh: the lodge where we were billeted was a mile or so from the town.

When we got there Vovo announced that he would give us a "Cawsack cocktell." He lined us up, took an enormous kitchen spoon, which he packed with snow and then saturated with whiskey, and rammed this shovelful of ice and fire into our gaping mouths. Soon the ranks broke and we went leaping and yelling into the snowdrifts. Vovo beamed at us indulgently, saying that real Cossacks would have stood steady for six rounds at least.

Julie was also at the wedding, and Vovo taught the two of us a different sort of drink. The Christmas decorations in the Townsends' house were still up, and hot punch was on a sideboard. Vovo said, "I veel shaw you a Rooshian tost." He handed us each a glass of punch, led us under a sprig of mistletoe hanging from a doorway, and told us to face each other, linking arms.

"Now dhreenk!" We did.

"Now kees!" We did.

"Now dhreenk!" This was delightful, and would obviously continue as long as our punch lasted. I took mine in small sips. At this point my college roommate, Hart, paused to stare at us. Vovo made short work of him.

"Hart, stawp lookink so conspeecuous!"

One spring Vovo and Schuyler Jackson went off together on a transcontinental tour, and both let their beards grow — Schuyler because he was getting bald and hoped that hair on his face would encourage the top of his head; Vovo in a spirit of competition. They drove in a stripped-down Model T Ford, a kind of home-made station wagon.

Schuyler did the driving, and Vovo sat beside him with an open Blue Book on his lap. On account of their beards and the open book, they were sometimes mistaken for Mormon missionaries. Schuyler's purpose in the journey was to discover unknown and unpublished writers; Vovo went along to see the country and paint. He added many new friends to his card index file, but his painting dwindled to very small potatoes.

At this point in his career I ran into Vovo only occasionally, and he still seemed as self-sufficient and as sought after as ever. Once we met at Princeton Junction, and as we waited for the train, Vovo, in his deep voice, gave me a severe talking-to about marriage: it was folly, he said, and worse than that, to marry a foreigner; one should always choose a girl of one's own nation. I was impressed, as always, but also a little surprised: surely Vovo hadn't forgotten that I was still hoping to marry the same girl I had been in love with for years? And she was not only of my nation but of my town. It wasn't till much later that I guessed Vovo may have been talking to himself, perhaps because some American girl had just turned him down.

After Julie and I were married, Vovo once brought an old friend and his wife to tea at our house in Princeton. Neither of the Tatischevs spoke English with half Vovo's scope or confidence, but they did their gentle best. Tatischev tried to tell us what Vovo was like when they had been cadets together in St. Petersburg: there was some incident in which Vovo had "rumpled" Tatischev's ears. Vovo boomed a denial: he had "neffer totched" Tatischev's ears — but what ears! Look for yourselves! (As a matter of fact there was nothing extraordinary or ludicrous about them.) And he went on to describe what a figure of fun Tatischev had been as a cadet. Tatischev was no match for him, but he wouldn't give up; after Vovo's final sneezing roar of laughter, he murmured, "Yess, you totched."

Like many of his fellow expatriates, Vovo had nothing but scorn for the riffraff who had taken over his country. We all knew this; nevertheless, one of his American friends once sang the praises of a Soviet film to him. Vovo gave him a hard stare and said, "Ferry vell, ve shall go to zee it." The film was being shown at an arty little theater on Fourteenth Street, where the audience was mainly made up of the intelligentsia, bohemians, and left-wingers. At every hint of Red propaganda on the screen, Vovo hissed loudly, answered by angry applause from the Communist sympathizers. Whenever this opposition showed signs of dying down, Vovo would say something that would make them jump, yell, and shake their fists.

When the lights went up Vovo remained in his seat, stretching a provocative leg out into the aisle. He got several nasty looks, but everyone took care not to stumble over him. One little man, when he was safely past, shook his fist and screamed, "You wait, we get you yet!" and then darted up the aisle.

A big Red with a girl on his arm who kept trying to pull him away came up to Vovo and said, "So you're a Cossack, hanh? A Nazi! Very nice, hanh?"

"I don't like your remarks. You are talking bersonal. I don't bermid bersonal remarks."

"A Cossack, hanh? Nice, very nice, hanh?"

"You vant to fight?"

"Sure I want to fight."

With sinister old-world dignity Vovo asked for the Red's address, wrote it down, and meticulously gave his own. Then he added, "I am zorry you are drying to drag zis lovely lady into a row. If it vere not for her bresence, I vould have teached you a lesson." He then gave a fillip to the Red's nose and contemptuously turned away. The Red kicked him smartly in the seat of the pants. This time it looked like a fight, but bystanders separated them. As Vovo and his friend drove off in a taxi, they saw the Red and his girl walking on opposite sides of the street. So Vovo had won, in a way.

He was still riding high when I next saw him, a year or so later, in New York. He had a house, he told me with proud satisfaction, just off Fifth Avenue. And what was he doing? He was holding classes: in astronomy, cooking, fencing with the saber, and drawing from the life. It all sounded multifarious, amusing, even gainful. Why, then, did I think I detected a stuttering false note in this trumpet voluntary? Had he given up his own painting because he was not good enough? Was he now spreading himself so thin because he didn't know what else to do — or because he had to have the money? We arranged to have lunch, and I was to meet him at his house on the appointed day at exactly ten minutes past one.

When I rang the doorbell, his man Joe let me in. Joe was of a fearsome ugliness and powerful build; he was devoted to the Captain, and looked quite capable of adding murder to his other chores. He was not very intelligent, but otherwise his looks belied him: he was kind-hearted and faithful. Vovo once told me that he used to try to get Joe to take an evening off and go to the movies, but Joe always refused to go, and finally told Vovo why: (1) he'd be spending the Captain's money; (2) it might put ideas into his head; (3) it would make him think.

Joe beckoned me to follow him down the narrow hall, led me into a back room, consulted his watch, and presently knocked on a pair of double doors. At Vovo's shout he threw the doors open, and I confronted a naked woman posing on a dais; beyond her a semicircle of girls (fully clothed), each behind an easel. Tableau!

"Ladies," said Vovo, with a sweep of his arm, "Mr. Matches!" And he exploded into his guttural, sneezing laugh.

And once at my office I found a sign that Vovo had been there. One of my sardonic officemates had pinned up over his desk an ad that had recently run in the paper, with the caption "A man in bed — an idle machine." Under this was written, in Vovo's scratchy hand, "If so, sorry for you." But this time he had missed the point or failed to cap it; it gave me the uneasy feeling that Vovo might be slipping.

And he was. Vovo was tremendously strong and liked to show it. One of his feats, which he sometimes performed at Russian nightclubs where he was favorably known, was to play a circus strongman. If no orchestra was available, he would supply the introductory music himself, giving a very fair imitation of a brass band by humming loudly through his nose. Then he would come striding in, both arms extended straight out from his shoulders, with a man hanging from each arm. It was a genuine show of strength, but he made it seem even more spectacular than it was.

So that when, one evening, instead of striding on stage with two men suspended from his mighty biceps, Vovo staggered in, dropped one, and nearly fell himself, his failure seemed catastrophic. Other evidence of decline soon followed. The house just off Fifth Avenue, that good address, was no longer his; he was always "visiting" or "on a trip." Joe vanished. Some of Vovo's peripheral friends — and it turned out that the biggest crowd was on the periphery — began to avoid him; others, he himself avoided.

On the rare occasions when I saw him, I couldn't help noticing how his social technique had coarsened. His sneezing snigger was more frequent now, but the sly tricks and funny stories for which it used to lead the applause were beginning to be too well remembered. To his remaining friends, Vovo was becoming a problem. He tried taking up a new career: expeditions.

First he went with a party to the Caribbean led by Dr.

Will Beebe. Nothing seemed to come of that, as far as Vovo was concerned. In fact, nothing seemed to come of any of his trips, except that he became a member of the Explorers Club, which figured frequently in his conversation. Then he visited Tibet and brought back a gruesome film, very flickering and grainy, of vultures pecking at corpses exposed on platforms on a bleak upland. I remember how wooden and hard the corpses looked, and how they jumped under the desultory hammer blows of the vultures' beaks.

His last three expeditions were organized and led by himself, and were supposed to be moneymaking affairs, or at least to supply him with material for lecture tours. The first two were to the Mato Grosso, in Brazil; the third to northern Canada, to the mouth of the Mackenzie River. The first was very nearly a success; the last was close to a disaster.

Vovo's first expedition to the Mato Grosso, a huge, hot wilderness in the farthest interior of Brazil, was intended to be a safari: Vovo, as white hunter and expert guide, would lead a party of rich sportsmen into this unspoiled tropical steppe, teeming with game; they would not only shoot all the wild animals they wanted but fill in some of the blank spaces on the map. That was the general idea. The climate turned out to be hotter and more uncomfortable than expected, and the game scarcer. In the course of their journeys, however, Vovo encountered a man who made the whole expedition worthwhile.

This man, whom he brought back with him to New York, was a fellow Russian who had lived for some time in the jungles of Brazil, hunting jaguars for their skins, using only a pack of dogs and a spear. Vovo, who by now was keenly aware of the cash value of publicity, aimed to make Siemel the drawing card for a bigger and better expedition to the Mato Grosso. Siemel was written up by a Hearst feature syndicate, and a ghost-written book about him appeared, called *Tiger Man*. In Brazil, jaguars were called tigers.

I don't think it was the book but Siemel himself who told me the reason he had gone to Brazil: to hunt not jaguars but a German. The German had run off with Siemel's wife, and when he found him, Siemel said, he intended to shoot him in the belly so that he would have a lingering and painful death. Siemel was a cold personality. When he described his technique of hunting jaguars, he made it sound bloodcurdlingly simple, at the same time giving the impression that it was just a way of earning a living and didn't excite him much.

When his dogs picked up the trail of a jaguar and pressed it close, the big cat would sometimes take to a tree (that was the cowardly type and would have to be chivvied to the ground) or turn and charge. When it charged, the dogs would scatter, if they knew what was good for them, and the beast would come for Siemel. He would be waiting, down on one knee, with the butt of his spear braced against the ground and the point up. As the jaguar leaped, Siemel aimed the spear at its throat and let the jaguar impale itself. (He would get down on one knee to show you, and point out that if you got the point of the spear well and truly home, the jaguar's claws would fail to reach you by a good six inches.)

While the expedition was getting ready, its headquarters were a suite of rooms in the Seymour Hotel in New York. Vovo told me that any time I wanted a bed, I could find one there: the door was never locked, and there was always room for one more. He warned me, though, to move carefully and with the utmost quiet if I came in late, as Siemel woke at the slightest noise and would hurl himself at an intruder with the ferocity of a tiger.

One night when I had missed my last train home I availed myself of this invitation. Remembering Vovo's warning, I inched the door open as cautiously as I could; but once inside the dark and unfamiliar room I began to bump into things, and made enough noise to rouse the dead. Siemel neither stirred nor woke, and was much surprised to see me in the morning. The expedition finally got under way, but it turned out to be no more of a success, financially, than the others.

Vovo made one last journey into the wilds, which finished his career as an explorer and very nearly finished him and his companions. This time his goal was the mouth of the Mackenzie River, which empties into the Arctic Ocean, in northernmost Canada. On this dour excursion he took with him three or four youngsters, hardly more than boys; their families paid their expenses, under the impression that this was to be in the nature of a bracing summer holiday, rather like a month on a dude ranch.

The country was as new to Vovo, who undertook to guide them, as it was to the boys. By the time they reached the mouth of the Mackenzie, they were short of food. Instead of retracing their steps, they decided to try a short cut over the mountains into Alaska. They got lost. They nearly starved to death. When at last, more by good luck than good management, they stumbled on a settlement, their morale was low and Vovo's authority was in shreds. That was the end of his career as a promoter and leader of expeditions.

I never regarded Vovo as a close friend; my liking for him and my admiration of him both had their definite limits, so that when he disappeared from view for long stretches of time I bore his absence with equanimity, almost with relief. During these periods I imagined him as leading a debonair existence among the gay and opulent worldlings who were his real intimates.

In his heyday he may have done this, more or less, but no longer. Rumors about Vovo began to reach me, at first in the form of anxious questions (Had I seen him lately? Did I know what he was doing?), then as hearsay with the ominous ring of fact: he was down on his luck; he was drinking; no one saw him any more. Vovo had become unmistakably a problem, an increasingly shabbier problem. His means of support were less and less visible, his popularity was dubious, his behavior and whereabouts were uncertain, his friends scarcer. But there was one who still stuck by him and who did as much for him as she could. She was a worldly and kind old lady, a native of prewar Vienna, named Lise des Renaudes.

Mme. des Renaudes lived in New York but owned a small factory in Kentucky that turned out quilted silk wrappers, eiderdowns, bed jackets, and such things for the tonier New York women's shops. She needed designs for this quilted stuff and gave Vovo as much work as he would take. This wasn't as much as he should have taken, and he didn't always perform according to his promises; but when she could find him and could get him to work, she was full of hope of his reform and even of his eventual revival as an artist.

In a year or so he shook off even this last helping hand and dropped out of sight. It was rumored that he had gone to California, was living alone at Laguna Beach, and had begun to paint again. His monstrous regiment of friends had dwindled to a corporal's guard: they clubbed together and sent him a small monthly check, hoping it would at least keep him alive.

His last letter, written on both sides of an envelope, was to one of these friends:

Dear Jack:
Excuse the envelope. I got to the Post Office and discovered, that I forget the papier. There is nothing to report about my life, except that to my amazement I am still

alive. I been to the Hospital, got examined got more insulin and might have to go next Thursday to making stay there for a few days. Nothing in Town — all the people walk around like hungry wolves.

I played chess with my Dr. friend here and we made about even so at least my brain still works. I try to sell one of my paintings in N.Y. If I succeed I will hotch-hick to you and embrace you and eat your fish. I let you know in time so you can by some and keep it on the Ice. Love to you dear man, friend and human being.

Yours thankful Vovo

Presumably the illness he suffered from was diabetes. Either from poverty or carelessness, he frequently ran out of the necessary insulin. Two months after he wrote this letter a California friend went to see him and found him "in a far worse condition than I had ever seen him. Coming into the light from his darkened room he was blinded, in an old pajama suit he tottered on his feet and shook as though with palsy." The friend brought him some fruit and mineral water, which was all he could be persuaded to take, and got Vovo to agree to go with him to the hospital three days later. When the friend came to fetch him, early in the morning, Vovo was dead; the doctor said he had died two days before. He was forty-eight.

Had he remembered, at the end, to make his declaration of love to life? Or had he forgotten, or was he too deathly weak, or had he changed his mind? All the same, he had said it once, and perhaps that was enough.

⁂ W. MACNEILE DIXON

⤳ I SAW HIM ONLY TWICE, a few weeks apart, in wartime London. He was almost old enough to be my grandfather, yet we took to each other on sight and got along like two old cronies. He must have been about eighty, perhaps older; a tall, lean, fine-looking old man with a white moustache.

I had read only one of his books, and he was barely a name to me. I was of course a complete stranger to him, and he had never heard of *Time*, *Life*, or *Fortune*, whose representative I was. It was part of my mission to London to find Professor Dixon (nobody in New York had been able to tell me where he was to be found) and persuade him to write an article for *Fortune*.

It was the telephone operator at the office who ran him to earth: he had retired from his university chair in Glasgow and was living in a "restricted area" in the south of England. He was coming to London in a few days and would see me. We met at his club, the Athenaeum, where he gave me a Spartan lunch, and afterward we went upstairs to the library, where it was quiet, and talked in pas-

⟦263

sionate whispers about the difficulties of writing. He told me how hard it was for him to make sentences say what he wanted them to say: they were always going off at a tangent. When he wrote, he said, "the air is *blue* around me!"

Our hissing conversation might have sounded like a fierce argument, but we agreed profoundly on everything. At our second meeting I popped the question of the *Fortune* article; he said yes, of course he would write it (and did), and we got quickly back to our muttons: the condition of a writer, the human condition. At the end we were exchanging confidences, some horrified, some puzzled, about our children.

I never saw him again, but I heard of him. *Fortune* sent a photographer to take his picture, a formal "cabinet photograph" in color. Professor Dixon regarded this as sensational journalism and an outrageous invasion of privacy to boot; he demanded the return of his manuscript and said he would send back his check. *Fortune* apologized (I hope) and called off the photographer.

◦⊦ EDNA GELLHORN

⌐⊣ THIS ONE I'M SURE OF. If there are any angels at all, she's one. More than twenty years ago, when she was still alive, I wrote about her in a book that nobody read. (I called her Omi, which was the name her family and friends had given her.) So this is plagiarism, if you want to be litigious about it.

Omi lived in St. Louis. She was a lady who described herself as "quite grown up" — and she didn't regard people as really grown up until they were seventy. While she was being a doctor's wife and the mother of four inquiring and obstreperous children, she was also trying to make St. Louis a better town. Not the best of all possible towns, since she was a woman and a realist, not a booster; but a community of civilized people, a place she could be proud of. The city's affairs involved her with the state's as well, and her housecleaning spread all over Missouri. She went after ends that seemed to her both practical and modest but that didn't always look attainable to others (until Omi and her cohorts attained them): purer milk, wrapped bread, free clinics, better schools, smoke abatement, wom-

an's suffrage, the League of Women Voters, equal opportunity and rights for blacks, improved marriage and divorce
laws, better child-labor laws. All kinds of things. Inevitably, of course, she got into politics. She never held any
public office herself, but her prestige in liberal-minded St.
Louis was immense. Her civic firepower was estimated as
"the rough equivalent of six Marine battalions." In 1931
the Women's Advertising Club of St. Louis named her as
one of the ten outstanding women in the city; seven years
later a St. Louis newspaper poll found her one of the five
outstanding women in the whole country.

Unless you lived in St. Louis yourself, you could know
Omi a long time without getting more than an inkling of
all this. She wasn't the embattled clubwoman or the cru-
sading social worker type at all. True, she had a "Bryn
Mawr" voice, clear and unstrident and quite un-Midwest-
ern; she carried herself with natural and unconscious pride
and was plainly unafraid of anything or any person. But
she was not in the least aggressive. In fact, she was hopelessly attractive, to everybody. It wasn't so much that she
was pretty and sometimes beautiful (she was that) or that
her blue eyes were often as appealing as a little girl's. The
essential and peculiar thing about her was a quality that
I can neither describe nor analyze, but it was something
quite different from charm and good looks, and much
more. When you were with Omi, you felt better about the
human race.

Even her foibles were endearing. Never a day passed
that she didn't buy a present for somebody; she dashed off
letters and postcards by the daily dozen to friends and family all over the world, and her telegrams (she was always
sending birthday telegrams and cables) read just like her
letters, for the simple reason that she never tried to save
words. She didn't always sign her letters, but that was not
because she was forgetful but because she liked to vary the

ending; her letters often broke off in a dangling affectionate participle. She avoided wearing a hat whenever possible.
Instead, she tied a narrow gray ribbon around the coiled
braid of her hair and when she got indoors took off her hat
by untying the ribbon. Her combs were worn precariously
and often fell out. She wept at movies, even bad ones.

She had no sense of direction, and she never failed to
lose her way in any strange town. When that happened, a
group of wishful helpers collected around her, for there
was something about her, like a fire on a cold day, that attracted human beings of all kinds. If she herself felt chil-
liness or tension in the air, she talked — a kind of neutral
babble that seemed irrelevant but wasn't. Her daughter
called this "nattering," but it was more like a rescue party.
When it was a question of her own convenience or comfort,
the truth was not in her.

She was certainly not a bit formidable, unless in a deep
sense — the sense in which faith, hope, and charity are
formidable. Once I went on a trip with her and her daughter through some of the Western states. On the plane from
St. Louis to Seattle we got tired of looking at the scenery,
and talked.

"I want to talk about the American woman," said Omi's
daughter.

Omi looked alert. She had spent her life working with
American women and had a high opinion of them.

"I have seen a lot of American women. It is my impression that the girls are little better than Arab females, and I
would not be surprised to see them putting their hands
under the gents' feet and saying, 'Order, master, and I will
obey.' Doing the same to the children."

Omi sighed, lightly.

"If they are out on social occasions, it seems to me they
defer very sweetly to their husbands; I'd go so far as to say
they are building up the men's confidence. By the way,

why does everyone need so much confidence in this country? If I had to work as hard as most of the women I see, and notably the young women, I'd go into a decline."

"Yes," said Omi, in a neutral voice.

"The only really bad, stupid thing I can see that the American woman does is to shop. It looks like a mania, like being addicted to roulette or opium. In the higher brackets and the older age groups, it seems to me, many women drink too much: I mean, it shows. But, then, their men drink too much, so maybe they are keeping up; if everyone is going to slur their words, it's less tedious and less embarrassing to be in the same condition. But on the whole, I don't know what foreigners are talking about: the American Woman they describe must be a half of one percent of the population."

"Oh, my child," said Omi.

"What do you mean, Oh, my child?"

"I was thinking about generalizations," Omi said. "And how difficult they are."

In San Francisco we went out on the town one night. A newspaper friend took us after dinner to a bar on the waterfront known as Pier 23. It was an old-fashioned kind of saloon, with framed photographs on the walls. The proprietor was a small man named Havelock Jerome, who never sang unless he was drunk, and he was so awful it was funny, or anyhow people liked it and tried to get him drunk so that he would sing. Mr. Jerome himself appeared and was introduced to us. He was nowhere near drunk and said modestly that he had no voice. But the sight of Omi brought out all the grandiloquence of his nature. He bowed, kissed her on the cheek, and said, "May I reiterate that I love you?"

Omi's sharpest comments were invariably unspoken — either wrapped up in a kindly fuss of irrelevant, embarrassed, but determined small talk, or stated in her calm, cheerful, but completely withdrawn presence as she wrote a letter or read a book or played a hand of patience — much as Duse could express to an audience, by her silent profile, the fact that incest had been committed. Though always frustrated, once in a while I tried to lure Omi into saying something derogatory. No, she wouldn't even *join* me in it.

In my considered view, the vanilla milkshake, one of the glories of America in my youth, had gone to hell since my last visit. You still got a whole shakerful — enough for two glasses and sometimes a bit more — but now the concoction was so stiff with ice cream that you had to mumble and mouth your way through it like a caterpillar; you couldn't drink it. Also, it was sickly sweet; too much vanilla. Eventually I learned to persuade the soda jerk: "Go easy on the vanilla. And just half the amount of ice cream you usually put in."

Once Omi and I were having a milkshake together.

"Don't you find that a little too sweet, Omi?"

"Well, not for them."

The human beings who shine with a light that seems to come from some extrahuman source almost always seem to be *ex ecclesia*. Omi would never call herself a Christian, and tried hard all her life not to pray, but there were times when her prayerful feelings were almost too much for her. The prayers she didn't say were never requests for something, but were barely smothered alleluias of praise, happiness, and thanks. I was with her once on an Alpine mountainside when we came on a great meadow of wild flowers.

"Oh, *thank* you!" cried Omi — and then, crimped by her Ethical Culture conscience, she added weakly — "Flowers!"

How does Omi fit into the picture of waste, ugliness, carelessness of the past, and disregard of the future that mars America now as it did when she was alive? She doesn't fit at all. But she lived in the noisy midst of it; she too must be reckoned a part of the American scene. How do we explain *that?* One of my friends believes that the United States contains a quiet majority of people who are on her side, even if they aren't up to her level; he would say that she was no rarity but a characteristic representative of our country.

I wish he were right; I hope he may be. But the wishful hope reminds me of a line of Georgian poetry that appealed to us in undergraduate days: "O World, be nobler, for her sake!" Even at the time, the sentiment had too much sugar in it; it was rhetoric, not a statement of truth. If Omi and her kind are really representative of America, why doesn't the world see and acknowledge it?

The friendly part, the dwindlingly friendly part, of the world does acknowledge it or something like it. Though deprecating our American manners and behavior and our infuriatingly well-meaning, disastrous ignorance, our friends defend us — or think they do, or mean to — by adding that there is something terribly touching, kind, and generous about Americans. All very well as far as it goes, but it misses the gist of the best we have; it misses the gist of Omi. How can I explain what it misses?

Once, after a painful conversation with Omi (all she had said might have been broadcast from the housetops, and its gentle generalities wouldn't have made anyone look up), I said to her, "Omi, you're a hard woman!" I meant more than that; I meant, "You're the hardest woman I ever met." America isn't only well-meaning, ignorant, mannerless, and infuriating; the best part of it is also hard. It is *capable* of being hard. I mean the word in a good sense: hard against softness, hard against sentimentality, hard against nonsense. Like Omi.

A PANEL
OF PRIESTS

A PANEL OF PRIESTS

HAVING BEEN BORN and brought up among the clergy, and constantly admonished by my parents to show them respect and keep silence before them, I observed them and their ways with a child's pitiless attention. Though I had no words then to describe their behavior, many of them seemed to me childish, petulant, and silly. The exceptional ones, two of whom are presented here, stood out like Gullivers among the Lilliputians — or should I say the Yahoos? They gave off an unmistakable whiff that instantly differentiated them from us and from their fellows, a whiff of what might be called the odor of happy sanctity.

⟦ THE REV. JAMES
CONOVER

⟁ His younger brother, tom, was widely spoken of as a saint, but no one ever called "Chipes" that. He was known as "a character."

Both brothers were small, active men with small, pointed beards, and both were clergymen. Chipes, after taking orders, went back to his old school, St. Paul's, as a master. He was no teacher, but he had an instinct for harbor: he married the rector's daughter and wrote the authorized life of his father-in-law. The thing he seemed keenest on was his own reputation as an athlete. He played baseball in the days when no player wore a glove; he was a redoubtable long-distance runner; and later he made a name for himself as a passionate and expert small-boat sailor.

His wife was a handsome woman, taller than he, of queenly manner and aristocratic mien. Both were devoted egoists, but she had great charm; his grating lack of it was so pronounced that it passed for backbone. They had nothing to say to one another, disagreed on nearly everything, and were cooped up together for a long married life. She revenged herself for this misalliance by running up bills and living beyond their means. He developed asthma.

When Chipes finally left St. Paul's, his children were nearly grown. He was given two country parishes to look after outside Newport and a Victorian frame house, belonging to his wife's family, to live in. He served his two parishes as if they were military posts. The nearer, St. Columba's, was only a few hundred yards from his house. After finishing the service there, he would drive his horse and buggy across the island to St. Mary's, taking the garbage from the house to feed the chickens he kept near his second church. He wore sailing clothes under his clericals, and as soon as the service at St. Mary's was over he would drive back to Third Beach, where his boat was moored, strip off his parson's uniform, and go for a sail.

When he was entertaining strangers at lunch or dinner, he bored them glassy-eyed with a recital of his athletic triumphs. If his little granddaughters were present, one would look at the other across the table and silently form with her lips the word BOASTING!

As his wife's extravagance and his asthma grew worse, he found it difficult to breathe when he was lying down, and took to sleeping in a chair. The attic became his bedroom. There, sitting in a rocking chair and swathed in blankets, with a hat on his head against the drafts, he spent his nights.

He had always been a stickler for fresh air, and in earlier days, when he sometimes went on an overnight railway journey, the stale air in the Pullman bothered him greatly. He always took an upper berth because it was cheaper, but in order not to be stifled he would arrange the curtains so that his sleeping, bearded head was buttoned into the aisle.

THE REV. ROBERT WILLIAMS

⊶⸨ HE CAME LATE into the Church; he had been in some form of business, and didn't like it or wasn't very good at it. Before that, he had been at the University of Virginia, where in those days it didn't seem to matter whether you took a degree or not. There was a slight tinge of Virginian accent in his slow, bromidic remarks. He looked you firmly and meaningly in the eye, hung on to your hand with a long, hard grip, and broke off with a loud, hollow laugh and a slap on your back.

Bob Williams, as everyone called him, came to Princeton as assistant to the rector of Trinity Church. When the rector eventually went to a bigger parish, Bob Williams had been around so long that the vestry asked him to stay on as rector. He was never easy in the job. You could see that it worried him, and that he had thought a lot about the difference between being an assistant and a rector.

His style of preaching changed entirely. It was as if he had read a book about how to do it or had taken a refresher course. His sermons, which had been of the restful, droning variety, now became rather alarming in a vague way and quite impossible to sleep through. He adopted new tricks and mannerisms: after a long and challenging pause, he would start again in a low, grave voice, then suddenly shout a word (which was very likely to be BUT or AND), then whisper the verb or possibly the object; that part was always inaudible. The tone of his sermons was grim, not to say threatening; and though, thanks to his whisper-shout delivery, the meaning was confused, he did say some memorably tactless things. One Easter Sunday he told the congregation that some of the people who were here a year ago were not here today, and that some of those who were here today would not be here a year from now.

He had been a confirmed bachelor, but late in life he married a middle-aged widow, a lively, friendly person whom everybody liked and who did a good deal to cheer him up and make him more popular. He continued to be a worrier, but his worry seemed to spend itself in more practical ways. He tried to develop the parish paper, which was merely a bulletin, into something more dynamic, and once a month he wrote a Rector's Letter for it. He had a good deal of trouble with this letter, and at one point thought it might be easier if he dictated it to his secretary. Neither of them was much good at spelling, and once when she asked him how to spell a word, he told her to look it up in the dictionary. It then turned out that neither of them knew what letter the word began with.

His own shortcomings sometimes so preyed on Bob Williams' mind that he became quite depressed. He was in this state one evening as he left the Nassau Club with a friend. The friend, hoping to lift his heart, said, "Bob, you're the only man in this town who's a real Christian."

Bob Williams said sadly, "One of the stupidest."

THE REV. ALAN
WHITTEMORE, O.H.C.

WEST PARK IS A WHISTLESTOP on the west side of the Hudson River, about an hour and a half by train from New York — the actual terminus is Weehawken. Nearby, overlooking the river itself, stands the monastery of the Holy Cross, an Episcopalian order of monks who teach and preach. Kent School, in Connecticut, was one of their foundations. The Holy Cross is a small order, as such things go, and had its beginnings only a couple of generations ago. The monks are mostly simple men, though many of them have been to college as well as to a seminary.

My first visit to West Park was from curiosity. I had heard that anyone could spend the night there free, or stay longer if he liked. The job I had then frequently took me through that part of the state, and I was tired of putting up at provincial hotels. The prospect of saving my company the cost of a night's lodging didn't interest me one way or the other. When the lay brother who let me in showed me to my "cell," I was agreeably surprised to see a radiator and a cot with sheets and blankets on it. The washroom across the hall was also heated, and more up-to-date than some I had known at school. A printed card thumbtacked to my door informed me that I was expected to make my bed and sweep out my room in the morning; also, that I was not to talk to anyone during the hours of the Great Silence — about the first half of the day. The lay brother asked me whether I would go to early or late Mass. I chose late, and he said in that case he wouldn't call me till seven.

When he did call me, I flubbed the proper response. I think he said, "Let us bless the Lord," and I was supposed to reply "Thanks be to God" but instead called out, "Thank you." Once I was up, I found the order of the day not hard to follow: all I had to do was watch where the traffic was going and pay attention to the hand signals. After doing up my cell and finding the chapel where late Mass was said, I followed my leaders into the refectory for breakfast. When nothing more seemed to be required of me, I went back to my cell.

Late in the morning there was a knock on my door, and in came a medium-sized, smiling, soft-spoken monk in his early forties. He introduced himself as the father superior, Alan Whittemore. I thought him very easy, natural, and likable. On some of the monks, the long white habits seemed a poor fit. One in particular, a tall, ruggedly handsome man with a ravaged face, looked like a refugee from a cavalry regiment, self-condemned to the penance of his white robe. But Father Whittemore wore his monk's habit as though he were completely at home in it: he even looked *well dressed*. We had an agreeable chat, mostly about mutual friends, of whom it turned out we had several, and then he went back to his duties.

At lunch, with the whole household gathered in the refectory, I saw him in the seat of authority. Lunch was eaten in silence while one of the monks, standing at a lectern, read aloud (that day I think from a book by the late Archbishop Temple). After about twenty minutes,

Father Whittemore abruptly knocked on the table: the reader stopped in midsentence, and conversation broke out all over. Five minutes or so later, Father Whittemore knocked again, the talk immediately ceased, and we all rose from the table, filing out in order and reciting antiphonally verses from the Psalm: "The eyes of all wait upon thee, O Lord: and thou givest them their meat in due season."

The real life of West Park, ceaselessly active, took place behind the scenes, where no laymen were admitted. On later visits I sometimes faintly heard the hum of this communal dynamo. And there were frequent comings and goings, monks setting off on a journey or returning from one. I witnessed one of these departures. I was offered a lift to Poughkeepsie, where one of the monks was taking a train that was also convenient for me. On the drive from the monastery the monk who was leaving and the one who drove us chatted away to me and each other on various mundane topics. When we arrived at the station, the traveler got out of the car, crossed himself, and knelt on the pavement while the other monk blessed him and his journey — both of them quite oblivious of the passersby.

The order had a mission in Liberia, where most of the fathers served a tour of duty, or hoped to. Father Whittemore had had five years there, and spoke of it with love and longing. He wanted very much to go again, but as father superior he couldn't send himself, so he had to wait and hope that his successor would order him to go. (His successor didn't.) Another monk, who had been in Liberia with him, was equally enthusiastic about the place. He also told me that the natives gave nicknames to all the Holy Cross fathers, as slyly perceptive as the names schoolboys pin on their masters. Father Whittemore, he said, was known as the Rascal.

Whenever I visited West Park I looked forward to an

hour or so with this dedicated Rascal. The more I saw of him, the better I liked him. One day he said that his friends called him by a nickname, and he'd like me to do the same. The Rascal? No: Pudge. I couldn't bring myself to address a father superior, no matter how much I liked him, by any such moniker.

What did we talk about? I remember one or two things he said, perhaps because they surprised and encouraged me. He told me that he never began a service that he didn't wish it were over, and that he shared with Archbishop Temple a rooted dislike of God the Father. He never said much about his own life, but now and then something would come out. At Williams, where he went to college, he had been a bit of a playboy, he told me, and also enjoyed the sensation of being in love, which he had had several times. He had thought he was happy, but he wasn't — not till he became a monk. Then he was really happy. "Now," he said, "I'm in love with everybody."

THE REV. SAMUEL WELLES

⸿ CANON WELLES was our favorite clergyman: he always made us laugh. There was nothing forced or applauding in our laughter, as there sometimes was with other grownups, who acted up for us. Canon Welles never acted up, and the laughter he roused in us was sheer delight. When he was being very serious, as in church, he looked anxious, but most of the time he had a gentle, wondering expression. Sometimes his dark eyebrows climbed so high, they seemed to go halfway up his bald forehead. I always smiled or felt like smiling whenever I saw him.

He was an old friend of my father's, and the two of them worked together most of their lives. In the earliest days of their ministry they had gone out to Nebraska with some other young clergy and lived together in an associate mission. There the future Canon Welles met his future wife. She and her mother were the mainstays of the little mission church near Omaha that young Mr. Welles took over.

At their first meeting the two ladies sat in the front row and observed their new pastor with hope and curiosity.

Both of them shared the same peculiarity: they could not bear to hear about anything in the least gruesome, and when by mischance they did, it sent them into fits of uncontrollable laughter. Not that they were amused; far from it.

Mr. Welles's sermon that day was on "darkest Africa." He had not, so far, said anything actually gruesome, but the subject was full of dangerous possibilities, and the younger woman several times stole an anxious glance at her mother. At one danger point she laid a reassuring hand on her mother's knee — and this had a fatal effect on herself: she burst into loud screams of laughter. That set her mother off. As the two of them whooped and rocked in helpless paroxysms, the astonished Mr. Welles paused in his sermon and said to them gently, "My dear ladies, I assure you that this is no laughing matter." But they were too far gone, and they laughed and laughed, in paralyzed embarrassment, till the tears ran down their cheeks.

Years later, after this laughing young woman had married Mr. Welles and borne him five children, he became the missioner of my father's diocese. His missions included all the prisons, asylums, orphanages, and homes for the aged in that part of the state. He himself was always poor and, I think, never wanted to be anything else. But when his second son* won a Rhodes Scholarship, Canon Welles celebrated the occasion by turning on all the electric lights in his house, from cellar to attic, and letting them burn all night.

There was once a burglar in the house where we lived in Cincinnati. Canon Welles was staying with us then; he

---

* And his namesake, though his family usually called him by his middle name, Gardner, to distinguish him from his father. He was on *Time* with Whittaker Chambers and became his firm friend. Mine too.

heard a suspicious noise in the night and cleverly called out, "Is that you, Lizzie?" — frightening the intruder, who started to run and crashed down the back stairs. Canon Welles, in wild pursuit and without his spectacles, fell down the stairs after him. The burglar got away, empty-handed, and presumably at least as badly bruised as Canon Welles. We loved this story, which we always heard with whoops of laughter, but it gave us shivers as well.

Almost anything would make Canon Welles laugh, gently, helplessly, as if he were literally being tickled. The rest of the time he looked surprised and questioning, as if he were waiting for the answer that everyone but himself must know. When my father scored off him, which he liked to do and did frequently, Canon Welles's face would collapse into his almost silent crumple of laughter, as if he were delightedly and gratefully accepting the response to his eternal question.

My father called him Sam, which just suited him. We always thought of him as "Sam-Welles," but of course never said it to his face. When we were taken to our first musical comedy, *The Wizard of Oz*, and saw the Scarecrow, who was almost as kind and funny as the Scarecrow in the book, he reminded me very much of Canon Welles. People were always laughing at him, too, but he didn't mind; in fact, he seemed to like it. He must have known that the reason they were laughing was that he made them feel happy.

L'ENVOI

₀₈⟦ PATTY

⟍⟋⟨ HER GIVEN NAME was Cleopatra, but not because she was royal; she had no pedigree. She was a Jack Russell terrier, a breed not officially recognized by the dogs' college of heralds. Patty and her three brothers were all given Pharaonic names by my wife because of the incestuous inbreeding that brought them into being. Patty's sire was also her mother's.

And Patty did have "Egyptian ears," a feature that became noticeable while she was still a puppy. They were well-shaped ears but undeniably outsize, and when I said they made Patty look like a Basenji, my wife did not deny it, but she did take it to heart. She tried to alter the case by making Patty's ears less conspicuous. She got some chewing gum, a thing she abominates, chewed large wads of it, and stuck them on the tips of Patty's ears to weigh them down. Every time these counterweights were removed, however, Patty's ears perked up again, like a pair of exaggerated ventilators on a boat deck. And at last my wife gave up this hopeless struggle. After all, as she said, they were pretty ears, even if they were too big.

⟦287

Patty was the runt of her litter, as her mother had been before her and her father before that, and, like them, the brightest and the most aggressive. Patty was much prettier than her mother, Maggie: with her markings of brown and black and her alert, sharp-nosed little face, she was almost as good-looking as Bert, her father. She grew fast, and though she stayed small, her puppyhood was brief. Soon she was chivvying her mother, chasing and being chased, playing endless snarling games. The two snapped at each other's lips and noses, a kind of wrestling with bared fangs; they tumbled over and over, one breaking away and the other in hot pursuit, round and round, on and on — until at last the game ended as suddenly as it had begun. Occasionally Patty would try to lure Bert into this rough-and-tumble, but he always gruffly refused.

Patty was lively, indefatigably lively, and insatiably curious. She was finicky about her food, and liked meat so little that she would eat her supper only to keep one of the others from getting it. She had a passion for salted almonds and for Digestive biscuits. When I went to the kitchen to get my elevenses, Patty, as like as not, would be curled up in front of the Aga with the three Siamese cats. The moment I appeared, she would leap to her feet and rush me hopefully, demanding her share. Some sorts of cheese, especially Brie and Chaumes, she liked very much, and when they appeared at lunch she would hurl herself against my knee, barking. And there was a period of a week or so when my wife was anxious about Patty's diet, and I was told to boil an extra egg in the morning, for Patty to eat later in the day.

All three dogs had the normal canine passion for bones, and the attendant jealousies and possessiveness. And yet they had an endless and constantly renewed supply: twice a week the butcher sent our meat, and the woman who brought it, and who loved dogs, always had a bone for each of them. None of these bones was ever buried outdoors; it wasn't necessary, and there would hardly have been time before the next lot arrived. All over the house there was a scatteration of bones — bones of all sizes, shapes, and degrees of being gnawed. If you stepped on some unfamiliar object in the dark, that would be a bone; if you wanted to lie down on the chaise longue in the library, you first had to remove a bone from it; there was usually a bone on the sofa. There was at least one bone in the middle of the floor of any room you like to mention, and also on the half-landing.

The three dogs were almost always together. Indoors, if my wife, Pam, was safely committed to some household task, they might be napping in a room by themselves. Out of doors, except when they were in full cry after a squirrel or a rabbit, they stuck close to Pam. Whenever I was looking for her, if I got sight of one of them I could be sure she was very nearby.

The barking crescendo of this trio, sprinting to confront the suspect rascal who had dared to ring the doorbell, was a fearsome sound. If the intruder turned out to be an old familiar friend, the dogs immediately stopped their yammering and trotted away, or switched their outraged yells into cries of delighted welcome. Their uproar was simply too much for some people. One of the three postmen who serve our rural route would sit in his car till I came out to see what the noise was about. "Frankly," he said, "I'm afraid of dogs." I said, "I don't blame you; so am I." And the man who brought the Sunday papers would open the back door, drop them in, and run.

When the dogs were roaming the house or their home grounds, I used to tease them by echoing and exaggerating their belligerence. They knew the sound of Pam's car, as they knew everything about her, by heart; but my car to them was like anybody else's. When they heard it coming they sounded the alarm, and by the time I was on the front steps they would be yelling bloody murder from inside. I would pull my hat over my face, get down on my hands and knees, and slowly open the front door, growling. The dogs' clamor would almost instantly die away and they would jump up at me, licking my face.

Patty was the loudest of this Pretorian guard, but not the bravest. I once went too far and actually frightened her. As she scurried toward me, shrilling menaces, I tried to imitate the lurching progress of an abominable snowman, and must have seemed to her convincing, for she stopped in her tracks, turned sideways, pretending to be interested in something in a different direction (but her little tail was down), then, as the snowman still terribly advanced, turned and fled for her life.

Like all the Jack Russells I know, Patty was easily embarrassed or put to shame. She did not have her father's innate terror of thunder, which he obviously regarded as the accusatory voice of an angry and unappeasable God; but like her father she was wide open to reproof, whether or not she had done anything reprehensible. At the slightest note of chiding (especially, of course, from Pam) her stubby little tail dropped and clung between her legs, her head drooped, her alert ears crumpled. She had too much imagination for her comfort and lived with too many fears. But these were usually dormant, and for most of her lively day she dashed busily from one promising situation to another — or, when none existed, stirred one up.

On November 4, a Monday, Pam went to Cambridge after lunch to see an old lady who was lonely and ill. I took the dogs for a walk in Clare water meadows. It was muddy, but not enough to make walking unpleasant. The river was full, and under the bridge at the old mill, where the water pours down over the weir, it was so loud that Patty was nervous about crossing. Though she scampered about the meadows with the others, poking her sharp nose into every interesting clump of possibilities, most of the time her stubby little tail was flat down. I think she always felt apprehensive when she was away from home. I kept calling to her, "Patty, get your tail up!" Once in a while I could coax her into lifting it; then some whiff of fear would bring it down again.

We finished our walk about three o'clock, piled muddily into my car, and headed home. As we turned into the gate there was the usual uproar, led by Bert but joined hysterically by the other two. I stopped the car, opened the door, and cried "Out!" Bert shot out, followed (I thought) by Maggie; one dog stayed in the car. I started up again and had not gone ten feet when I felt the softest possible little bump — WHAT WAS IT? Had I heard a faintly protesting small cry? I stopped the car, tore open the door, got out, looked back.

It was true. And it was Patty. O God, make it not true. She lay on her side in the road, her back arched unnaturally, as if she were straining against something. Was she quite quiet, or did she give a little shudder and then lie still? I couldn't tell; I didn't know. All I knew was that *I wanted it not to have happened.* I couldn't touch her. I ran to the Old Lodge, ten yards down the drive, and banged the knocker. Nobody answered. I banged again. Phillips came to the door. I wanted Flo, who had a special way with animals. When Flo came, I said, "O Flo, Patty!" She ran out into the road and bent over the little dog.

"I'm afraid she's gone."

"Would you lift her for me?"

She lifted the limp little body. I opened the trunk of the car, and Flo put Patty in. Then the two dogs and I drove up to the house.

It was just after three o'clock. Pam wouldn't be back from Cambridge, at the earliest, for at least three hours.

(Actually, it turned out to be four.) I couldn't telephone her there. I would have to wait till she came home.

The two little dogs were very quiet. They looked at me inquiringly. I could only look at them and weep. I had to do something. I took them up to the pasture where the sheep were grazing. Pam had said there were some dead poplar branches near the wood that needed cutting up. I found the branches and set to work. But I could think of nothing but Patty, and as I thought I groaned and wept. How would I tell Pam? "I have bad news. Dreadful news. Patty's dead; I killed her."

Patty was one of our family; she was almost like a little daughter. Have animals got souls? If they haven't, I said to myself, then neither have I. And where is that little spirit now? Why shouldn't I pray for light perpetual to shine upon her? I did pray it.

Bert and Maggie are waiting for the sound of Pam's car. Perhaps they expect that she will produce Patty, alive and well. I'm sure they don't regard me as Patty's murderer, although I am.

All the sadness and horror of life come flooding over me. I weep and weep and cannot stop weeping. This is unmanly; it befits neither my age nor station. But I cannot help it.

There must be *something* I can do. Suddenly I think: the vet! Of course. I telephone to that kind man. (All vets are kind, I think.) He tells me to bring Patty to him. So the dogs and I get in that accursed car again, with Patty's little body in the trunk, and drive to Haverhill.

And there I have to face the dreadful necessity of touching Patty, whom I have killed. When I open the trunk, the other two want to jump in and sniff her. I lift the limp little body, her head dangling against my arm, and carry her in to the surgery. The vet and his nurse take her from me and lay her on the table. Yes, he assures me, she is quite dead and must have died instantly. (Is he being merciful to me? How I hope he is telling me the literal truth!) A fracture at the base of the skull. What shall he do with her? I don't know which dreadful alternative Pam would prefer: to bury her on the grounds of Cavendish or let the vet dispose of her. We agree to leave her there until Pam decides.

So the two little dogs and I drive home again and go on waiting for Pam. It is dark before she gets back. The minute I see her, I blurt out my rehearsed speech. To my astonishment she doesn't blame me but is sorry for me. She says, "These things happen." Yes. Offenses will come, but woe unto him through whom they come. Pam says, "She had a happy life." Yes, but I cut it short; she had less than two years.

The question of what to do with Patty's body is finally decided by Pam: she is to be buried here, where she spent her short and happy life — but in an unmarked grave and in a spot we won't know. So next morning I drive again to the vet's. The nurse hands me a small, neatly wrapped box. I take it home and go to find Charlie, the old soldier who gardens for us. He and the other gardener, George Fenn, are standing in the back yard, and George says, "Too bad about the little dog." I hold out the box and manage to say "We don't want to know where you bury her."

It is twelve days now since she died, but I am typing these words through a blur of tears. I didn't even know I loved Patty until it was too late — too late to do anything but mourn. Why don't I feel the same way, or more, about the human children, millions of them, who are killed or who die young? But I didn't know them and love them, and I didn't see them die.

Five days after Patty's death Phillips came round, peddling cloth poppies for Remembrance Day, and Pam got her to join us for a cup of tea. When Pam was out of the room I said, nodding at the two dogs, "They miss her." And my eyes swam. Phillips, as watchful and as tactful as any duchess, replied evenly, "Two days without rain; it amounts to a drought."

When I think of Patty now, I see her standing alertly, her pretty little head up and her ears cocked forward, her right foreleg drawn up like Colleoni's horse — and then inexorably the other picture follows: Patty lying on her side in the road, her back arched in a final shudder, her eyes glazing, her lips parted in the grin of death.

Never again shall I feel the importunate thump against my knee as she hurls herself on me, demanding her rights; never again feel her cold muzzle sniffing the lobe of my ear; never again hear the scrabble of her paws over the floor and her threatening yelps magicked into cries of welcome. I have blotted all this out of existence; on account of me these things will never happen again.

Unending patience, unswerving trust — these are virtues we extol and sometimes pretend to possess, but we never really attain them: they are to be found only in dogs. That is part of the message Patty has brought me, a message without words but heavy with meaning. And the message? It's entirely about love — that's all I can tell you just now.